A
Writer's
Companion

Fourth Edition

A
Writer's
Companion

R i c h a r d   M a r i u s

HARVARD UNIVERSITY

Boston   Burr Ridge, IL   Dubuque, IA   Madison, WI
New York   San Franciso   St. Louis
Bangkok   Bogotá   Caracas   Lisbon   London   Madrid   Mexico City
Milan   New Delhi   Seoul   Singapore   Sydney   Taipei   Toronto

McGraw-Hill College

*A Division of The **McGraw·Hill** Companies*

A Writer's Companion

This book is printed on acid-free paper.

10 11 12 13 14 15 DOC/DOC 0 9 8 7 6 5

ISBN 0-07-304015-0

Editorial director: *Phillip A. Butcher*
Sponsoring editor: *Tim Julet*
Editorial assistant: *Alan Joyce*
Marketing manager: *Lesley Denton*
Project manager: *Kimberly Schau*
Production supervisor: *Lori Koetters*
Freelance design coordinator: *JoAnne Schopler*
Cover Designer: *James Shaw*
Compositor: *Carlisle Communications, Ltd.*
Typeface: *10/12 Times Roman*
Printer: *R. R. Donnelley & Sons Company*

Library of Congress Cataloging-in-Publication Data

Marius, Richard.
    A writer's companion / Richard Marius.—4th ed.
      p. cm.
    Includes bibliographical references and index.
    ISBN 0-07-304015-0 (alk. paper)
    1. English language—Rhetoric.   2. Exposition (Rhetoric)
    3. Report writing.   I. Title.
    PE1429.M27   1999
    808'.042–dc21   98-7379

http://www.mhhe.com

About the Author

Richard Marius directed the Expository Writing Program at Harvard University for sixteen years, teaching students and creating the philosophy for the only course required of all Harvard undergraduates. That philosophy is embodied in this book. He is the author of several novels, biographies, and textbooks on writing, including the *McGraw-Hill College Handbook,* which he wrote with Harvey Wiener. In the fall of 1998 Harvard University Press will publish his new book, *Martin Luther: The Christian Between God and Death;* and his novel, *An Affair of Honor,* will be published in 1999. His play, *The Coming of Rain,* had a five-month run at the Alabama Shakespeare Festival in Montgomery during the spring and summer of 1978. His articles have appeared in publications as diverse as the medieval journal *Traditio* and the nonmedieval journal *Esquire.* He reviews books for many periodicals, including *The New York Times,* and for ten years he wrote a regular book review column for *Harvard Magazine.* He was one of the editors of *The Yale Edition of the Complete Works of St. Thomas More*, and with Keith Frome, he has edited the *Columbia Anthology of Civil War Poetry.* He now teaches English and Religious Studies at Harvard, and was awarded the Harvard Foundation Medal in 1993 for his contributions to minorities at Harvard.

For
Willis C. Tucker
and in memory of
John Lain
Beloved Professors
The University of Tennessee
School of Journalism

Contents

CHAPTER
F O U R

CHAPTER
F I V E

CHAPTER
S I X

CHAPTER
S E V E N

Appendix Two

Appendix Three

Preface

Scarcely a week goes by that someone does not say to me, "I've always wanted to write." Usually I detect a sad and wistful tone. It is as if the speaker has decided that he or she will never write, that the world of writing is a glittering shore passed in the night and now seen from afar on a ship bound to an uninteresting destination. Most people who say such things to me are older, successful in their work, and full of experiences and thoughts that they should share with others. Sometimes I become so interested in their ideas that I batter them with pleas to get on paper the stories they have to tell.

I also have pushed my own students in the same literary direction, and after 36 years in the college classroom, I am proud of the many books and articles my students have written and of the notes of appreciation I have received from them both privately and in the acknowledgment pages of their works.

My lifelong conviction as a writer has been that good writing requires good thinking. Style is important, but it is not enough. The solid writing needed by democratic society is based on evidence, on reasoned presentation, and on the best and most fair-minded idea of the truth that the writer can achieve. This is not to say that writing should be bland or marked by indecision. One can study all sides of an issue and come down on the right side with rhetorical guns blazing. But the stronger the opinions, the stronger the evidence should be for them, and in putting forward strong opinions, writers should be sure they have looked at every side of the issue and know what they are talking about.

My original plan for this book was to set down in a conversational way the things I have tried to teach my students through the years. In writing the first edition, I tried to talk to the page the way I talk to my classes and to the students who brave the clutter of my office to talk to me there.

In this respect I have tried to duplicate the advice and the kindness and the generosity that marked my relations with the men to whom this book is dedicated, Willis Tucker and the late John Lain, who taught me in journalism school at the University of Tennessee when the world was young. And I never have had far from my mind the open-mindedness and the aversion to formality and rules that marked the teaching style of the late Sydney Ahlstrom, who taught me in graduate school at Yale. If there is a heaven, I hope that these three and I can put our feet up on a cloud somewhere and talk for ten thousand years about all the languages of the universe.

The response to the earlier three editions of the book lets me think that readers have taken it in the spirit that it was written. I continue to receive more correspondence about *A Writer's Companion* than about anything else I have published. Now and then somebody calls me up or sends me a note on e-mail to say, "I love your book." I love it, too. It has been a joy to write. As best I can tell, the only continent where it has not found readers is Antarctica. I am especially pleased with those schools who use the book as a guide for first-year students to the kind of thinking that is required in college courses.

As I did in the third edition, I have revised this one in response to comments from those who use the book, from the advice of friends, and from my own experience in teaching. I have made several revisions aiming at greater clarity and usefulness without making the book so heavy that it must come slipcased with a wheelbarrow. I have compressed some sections and expanded others, and in keeping with the avalanche of computer use in America, I have now given some attention to the Internet. But I refuse to have my own web page. Some things are too much.

Above all I am interested in answering this question: "How do we use the best American English to write good essays?" This question implies several others: What is the best American English? What is an essay? What makes an essay good? Why should we care about any of this? I hope to answer all these questions as we go along together.

The philosophy of the book remains simple: We learn to write by reading and then by writing and by thinking about what we are doing. I have never found any use in grammar drills. We learn the rules as we write and begin to want to write better and discover ourselves enjoying our writing despite all the hard work that writing requires. Teaching students to write by teaching them grammar first is as fruitless as teaching them how to play baseball by studying the official baseball rule book. We learn to play baseball by starting with a few basic rules and by playing the game. We pick up the rest of the rules as we go along. In far too many American schools, students get years of instruction in grammar and almost no opportunity to write real essays. That's like telling children they can't play baseball until they've studied the rules for twelve years, but when they get to college they are going to play the game and discover that they love it. No wonder so many of my students come to me telling me they hate to write. I have my students write drafts; I comment on their drafts and help them improve them; and so we get to our common goal—a good final draft.

A fundamental conviction motivating this book is that writers must think logically about their own premises and about evidence if they are to write well about anything. I don't care much for sappy personal writing where writers tell me what they feel about things rather than what they know. We seem awash nowadays in the literature of confession where writers gush over their emotions about some of their most intimate experiences. I suppose some little demon down inside most of them is that some enterprising producer will make a movie of their lives and they will become celebrities because of all they have suffered and how much they have felt.

Our literary tradition includes some great autobiographical works. But the best autobiography is a recounting of events, the telling of a story where the details carry us along without the continual moist intrusion of the writer's emotions into events. But this is the age of therapy, and too many autobiographical writers use the story of their lives to vent their feelings and to heal themselves rather than to tell a story of interest to others. I recall a few years ago canoeing with a friend down the Ardeche River in France, admiring its splendid canyon and shooting its thrilling rapids. To our astonishment, after emerging upright out of the foam and roar of our last and most difficult burst of white water, we heard from above a great clamor of cheering and applause for our successful run. (Most of the other canoes in the river that day flipped at the last in that run of rapids.) When we looked up, we discovered that we were in a nudist colony and that we were being cheered by a great crowd of naked men and women. We felt honored by their attention and good will, but I could not help remarking to my friend that most people in this world look better clothed than naked. Only a few have a natural talent for nudity. I feel that way about the kind of autobiography that tries to reveal all, for it usually aims at making the writer either the hero or the victim of his or her story, and it becomes self-indulgent and self-serving.

To take part in a democratic society, to have a true liberal education that, as the word *liberal* implies, makes us free, we need to know experiences beyond our own. Despite all the difficulties in trying to be objective, we need to cultivate dispassionate investigation and to make our decisions on our reasoned knowledge rather than on the blind passions of the moment, no matter how noble these passions seem to be at the time.

Societies stand or fall on their ability to know the world and come to terms with it. We must learn facts, consider our assumptions about those facts, and wrestle them into meanings that can be apprehended by the human community around us. We have to ask questions, look for contradictions, find the puzzles, and admit it when we cannot answer all our questions or make all the evidence fit into the explanations we would like to give for it. The most honest kind of writing about serious matters never claims to possess all knowledge or to answer all the interesting questions.

I have designed this book primarily for writers of academic essays written in college. It might also be useful for writers of interpretative articles in journals of various kinds, including newspapers. I have included some advice for those writing autobiographical essays, for I know that many teachers assign such writing in their classes. If you are going to do it, you should try to do it well.

As the examples in the book show, I have tried to show how good writers—those widely read and appreciated by the community of educated men and women—achieve their effects. I have quoted many modern American writers and a few from Great Britain.

As always I owe debts to many friends and friendly readers. Barry Maid, University of Arkansas–Little Rock; Michael Hennessy, Southwest Texas State University; Kathryn C. Mincey, Morehead State University; Marguerite Helmers, University of Wisconsin–Oshkosh; and Amy Joyce Pawl, Washington University, reviewed the first draft of the manuscript for this edition and made thoughtful suggestions, most of which I have incorporated into this book.

Over the years my colleagues in the Expository Writing Program at Harvard made me think every day about what we do and why we do it. Above all I am grateful to the superb intelligence, boundless energy, loyalty, and writerly good sense of Linda Simon whom I had the good luck to hire to run the Harvard Writing Center for many years. She now continues in her good work at Skidmore College. I must also mention Stephen Donatelli, Gordon Harvey, Jerry Doolittle, Bob Ginna, Bill Rice, Nancy Kline Piore, Sue Lonoff, Lowry Pei, and Larry Weinstein for intelligent and vigorous discussions about the teaching of writing, for often disagreeing with me, and for giving their loyal and unselfish service to a university that was never as good to them as they were to it.

My dear friends Rod Kessler at Salem State here in Massachusetts and Nancy Anderson of Auburn University in Montgomery, Alabama, share with me their experience of using the book in the classroom, and we have talked and laughed away many an evening together. Paul Doherty at Boston College has been a big help in previous editions of this work.

Others from the past remain in beloved memory—my late and dear mother, a dauntless newspaper woman in the second and third decades of this century when the profession was not thought ladylike, a woman who read her children the King James version of the Bible every day and left its soaring cadences indelibly planted in our hearts; Bill Bayne, editor of the *Lenoir City News,* who suffered my early prose and even paid me for it when I attended college classes and worked for him in the afternoon; the late John Lain who with the vigorously alive Willis Tucker made himself the enemy of my adjectives when I wrote for him at the University of Tennessee School of Journalism.

I had the very good fortune to fail Latin as a freshman at Lenoir City High School in Tennessee in 1948. Sent off in disgrace to live with an aunt that summer in Philadelphia, I took Latin from Myron V. Harrison at Simon Gratz High School and discovered suddenly that I loved it. Myron Harrison, age 96, and his wife Bea remain beloved friends.

My wife Lanier Smythe, and my sons Richard, Fred, and John sustain me by their love and their good talk and their laughter. Fred's wife Sue and their daughter Ellen are part of the family now, the three of them 6.9 miles by bicycle from my front door. My brother John and my friends Ralph and Connie Norman, Milton and Margaret Klein, David and Jean Layzer, John and Judy Fox, Rod Kessler and Sarah Abrams, and Linda Simon and Thilo Ullmann endure through the decades.

Richard Marius

First Principles

W riting is hard work, and no book can make it easy. It is a mysterious and complicated business, bringing together muscles and brain, memory and desire, and a rhythm of motions and subconscious impulses much as we do when we dance or sing or talk or play baseball or ride a bicycle. It is a solitary occupation intended for a community of readers, most of whom we will never see. We write to inform them, to persuade them, and, yes, to entertain them. For our readers, we are the words they read. We are not there to tell them what the words mean, to smile in approval, to frown in disapproval, to gesture, to explain when they do not understand. Our words, silent on the page, must create in our readers enough interest to keep them reading. When they lay our work aside out of boredom or disbelief or irritation, we fail.

No wonder most good writers approach writing with just a twinge of terror in their bones. Writers put themselves out for judgment, and that judgment can be harsh. But to be read and appreciated is one of the great joys of life, a triumph heightened by our sense of danger when we dare to put words on paper. Some writers say they don't care what anyone thinks of their work. They lie. We all care. My favorite baseball writer, Roger Angell, of *The New Yorker,* had this to say about the late William Shawn, editor of that magazine for more than three decades:

> Journalists like to think of themselves as tough birds, old pros. It's a business, this writing game, and when you finish this piece, it's time to go on and knock off the next one. But Shawn, who was as tough as manganese-molybdenum in some ways, knew better. He had somehow perceived that writers are desperately in need of praise for their work—wild for it. The hard creative process, even when it's only

getting things down on paper for a magazine, isn't just another line of work but also represents the writer's semineurotic need to rearrange the world and set it out in more orderly and appetizing forms. It's something a child would do, and children can never get enough praise, particularly if it comes in the form and person of an adult who will give them full attention: attention beyond measure. Praise makes them grow and go on, and those who bestow it are remembered vividly, even after they are gone.[1]

Writing is performance—like playing a piano, competing in the Olympics, acting on stage. When the crowd cheers, the performer is in ecstasy. When someone says, "I liked that letter you wrote to the editor," the writer glows.

Like all the arts, writing requires discipline. If you don't *want* to write enough to spend hours writing and rewriting, you can never write well. Like playing a piano or fielding a baseball or dancing ballet, writers must master the fundamentals of their art. You must observe how others do what you want to do, and you must try to imitate them—while always leaving room for your own unique creative gifts to show up in your work.

Many different parts of the writing process go on at the same time. While the hand moves, the brain selects from many opinions, memory informs, and some vague sense of what is appropriate crowds into our heads. In this book I consider the elements of writing separately just as a piano teacher may consider touch, rhythm, and notes separately, knowing that in performance they will all come together at every instant. The elements all come together when you write, and if you write enough, you begin to handle all these elements at the same time.

My advice throughout is descriptive, not prescriptive. That is, I have examined many readable and published writers to see how they achieve their effects, and I have sought to pass on what I have learned to you. Our writing is useful and necessary even if we don't publish it. Reports, notes, journals, and letters help keep our lives ordered, and some of the most entertaining writing we do may be in notes sent to friends, perhaps on the Internet, that violate all the conventional rules of both grammar and style. But I presume that most writers would love to publish and thereby be read by a larger audience, and I have based my principles on what I observe in published writers whose work I admire.

Writing has few rules, and most of them can be broken now and then. But writing does have principles, created by those who have written and read the English language over the centuries. You should test my principles by your own reading. When you start thinking about principles in writing, you see that writing and reading both take place within a community of expectations developed in an unfolding tradition. The French critic Roland Barthes has said that we can never write without taking into account what has been written. Saul Bellow has a fine phrase to describe writing—"Breaking bread with the dead." Readers approach any text with habits they have picked up from everything else they have read in their lives. These habits raise expectations, and when the expectations are not met, readers become uneasy. They may tolerate a long, swirling sentence here, a misspelled word or typo there, a breakdown in diction somewhere else, occasional blandness, or even some confusion. But frustrate them too often, and they will give up. The writer's job is to create an audience and keep it to the end.

Writing must *communicate*. That is, it makes a community. In some ancient societies, writing was considered a sacred act because it had so much authority in the community, and thus only priests were allowed to do it. In its various forms, writing is still the strongest cement of the social order. Both writing and speaking follow conventions about the meanings of words, the forms of sentences, the shapes of various kinds of discourse, the standards for evidence, and even what can be said and what cannot be said. Conventions are habits built up over centuries within communities, and writing has its conventions that are part courtesy, part necessity, part simply habits long established by custom.

Discourse Communities

We can never write to please everybody. All of us belong to several "discourse communities," groups with shared knowledge and interests within which we communicate—communities where our own discourse makes sense. The largest of these discourse communities consists of those who speak English, especially American English. Within that community we don't have to define words like *table* or *chair* or *dog*—unless we happen to be talking about some rare or special example of each of these objects.

Within that huge community of English speakers are multitudes of subgroups—computer addicts, baseball fans, students of Shakespeare, dog lovers, book collectors, movie buffs, and legions more. Each community has its special language. The definition of a *discourse community* is that its members easily share terms that may be meaningless to those outside that community.

For example, if I write that the Red Sox beat the Yankees in the last of the ninth last night on a suicide squeeze, a reader who does not belong to the discourse community of baseball will find the sentence opaque if not alarming. Did a Red Sox player kill himself so the team could win? But no serious fan has any problem here. For starters, no long-suffering Boston fan can imagine that any millionaire Red Sox player would make a personal sacrifice for the team. The sentence rather tells us that the teams were playing at Fenway Park in Boston, that the game was tied in the last of the ninth inning, that the Sox were batting with a runner on third with no more than one out, that the Boston manager ordered the batter to bunt, and that the runner on third started for home plate as soon as the pitcher committed himself to throwing the ball. If the batter had missed the bunt, the catcher could have easily tagged the runner out, but the batter made contact with the ball, hit it slowly along the ground in front of the plate, just out of the catcher's reach, and the runner scored, ending the game.

Can a nonfan understand even this expanded explanation? Perhaps not. But any baseball writer who set out to explain every term in every story would quickly be fired. Baseball writers address a discourse community that knows a lot about baseball and is familiar with the language used to describe the game. They use what readers know (here the rules and language of the game) to report something new (how the game came out last night).

What discourse community are you addressing when you write? That is, what do your readers already know that you do not have to tell them? These questions have no easy answers. But you must consider them with every sentence that you write. Sometimes the answers are obvious. For example, if you are writing an essay on Shakespeare's *Macbeth,* and everybody in your class has read the play, you do not have to summarize the plot. That would be like explaining the game of baseball to fans who already know the game well. You may assume that your audience, including your teacher and your fellow students, knows the plot already. You can therefore write about something that interests you in the play, calling attention to a theme or an interpretation that may not be obvious to the others.

Without communities, human society could not exist, but communities have their bad side. They are quick to exclude people who seem not to belong. Sometimes it may be a point of honor to be excluded from this or that community. Most of us don't want to belong to communities of bigots or fanatics. But our use of language may cause us to be excluded from valuable communities to which we want to belong—communities of educated readers whose attention and respect we would like to have as we write about a subject that excites us. I always hesitate to speak of "good" usage or "bad" usage. "Good" and "bad" imply a moral judgment of language. Having grown up on a farm in East Tennessee, I know you are not stupid or immoral if you say "ain't" or "between you and I" or "he don't." But these usages do not conform to the expectations of educated readers, and they are likely to judge you on your "mistakes" if you write such things. Foolish? Unfair? Perhaps. But groups are like that. Basketball fans would howl if they heard a would-be sports announcer call the playing surface a "field" rather than a "court" or a "floor." Such usage would tell them that he pretends to be a member of a group to which he does not really belong. Groups can be cruel. Readers can be cruel to writers who fail them.

The "Right" Word Versus the "Wrong" Word

Writers deal in words, and the "right" word is all important. Mark Twain is supposed to have said that the difference between the right word and the wrong word is the difference between lightning and the lightning bug. Some words are clearly "wrong" in writing for educated readers. You shouldn't write "between you and I" or "I seen him when he done it." But many other usages exist in a gray zone of uncertainty. No language is like the geometry of Euclid, a logical system based on unbreakable laws flowing in perfect harmony from primary assumptions. Too many books and too many teachers have tyrannized beginning writers with rules. Many of these teachers are modern Puritans, convinced that our corrupt world is about to topple and that only stern discipline and their infallible wisdom can save us. These Puritans typically lament the decline of language in others, holding themselves aloof in a superior world.

In his angry and unpleasant book *Paradigms Lost* (the title is a heavy-handed play on Milton's *Paradise Lost*), critic John Simon asks why language changes. His answer: "Language, for the most part, changes out of ignorance."[2] Simon's fierce pages burn with denunciations of the "permissiveness" that descriptive books like this one inculcate in the young. In a typical passage he assaults the National Council of Teachers of English (an organization to which I belonged for many years) as "a body so shot through with irresponsible radicalism, guilt-ridden liberalism, and asinine trendiness as to be, in my opinion, one of the major culprits—right up there with television—in the sabotaging of linguistic standards."[3] Frenzied rhetoric like this makes Simon sound a little like a puppy yapping at the mail carrier.

For at least a couple of centuries, doomsayers like John Simon have been lamenting that good English was dying. In *Grammar and Good Taste,* Dennis E. Baron tells us of the frustration of the English grammarian Robert Lowth, who in 1762 wrote a book intended to provide a scientific understanding of good English. Lowth laid down rules for good writing—and then complained bitterly that Shakespeare, John Donne, John Milton, and the translators of the magnificent King James Version of the Bible had violated the rules.[4]

That is the fate of any quest for proper English usage carved in tablets of stone by the moving finger of God. Look around just a bit, and you will find some good writers who violate these commandments. Like the Puritans of old, our latter-day linguistic purists find evil everywhere, even in authors known to be great. Poor John Simon mentions several writers he considers exemplary—but then, like Lowth before him, cannot resist the temptation to point out their errors. He comes across as a man who must get sick every time he reads a book. No wonder he sounds so grouchy!

"Language is art, not science. It has "standards," but they change with life." Classical Greek and Latin don't change much nowadays; the people who used them are dead. They changed a lot while the Greeks and Romans lived. Our language changes all the time.

"Editors' Standard"

In our society the most important umpires of language are editors who will decide what will be published and what not. Editors want to publish readable writing that others will buy. Editors who publish unreadable stuff get fired. Editors who can judge what the public will read keep publishing alive. Editors decide who will be our "professional writers," writers who get paid for writing and who make editors look good.

The flexible standard for this book is the work of professional writers published by editors. I call it "editors' standard," and I have tried to describe what works most of the time. Nothing works all the time. Every writer occasionally breaks the "rules," and every writer sometimes fails. If your audience likes your work when you break the rules, you win. If you break too many rules, no editor will publish your work. The real "rules" of language are the expectations of readers, and editors make their living by trying to define those expectations.

Writers must respect readers. Like writing, reading is hard work. Words have histories and shadings of meaning. They have contexts. Times change. Readers of different generations read into words thoughts that differ from what the writer intended. In Anthony Trollope's delicious nineteenth-century novel *Barchester Towers*, the slimy hypocrite Obadiah Slope "made love" to the virtuous Eleanor Bold in a carriage. Trollope meant that Slope proposed marriage to her. Today we are likely to be startled by coming upon this phrase in such a context with such a proper couple.

Readers bring their own experiences to every text. The same reader may see one thing in a text in youth, another in the same text in middle age, and yet another in old age—and all the interpretations may make sense. All this complicates the writer's task. Readers bring their own experiences to any text they read, and they can easily be confused. Good writers work hard to make sense and to avoid confusion and to write with grace as well as clarity.

Writing Versus Speaking

Most modern writing has a conversational tone. It is not stuffy and formal. When read aloud, it sounds a lot like someone talking. But speaking is always easier than writing. Speakers can misuse words and still be understood because of their tone of voice, their gestures, and their expressions. They can repeat themselves until we get the point. Speaking is a democratic art; nearly everyone speaks well enough to be understood by others.

The movies, radio, and television have inundated us with speaking by all sorts of people who might find it difficult to write an essay. We hear their words, their tones, and their repetitions, and on TV talk shows we see their carefully informal and humble grins. Often the spoken words of celebrities and politicians do not mean much of anything. Confronted by a TV camera, they speak in sound bites. If they are asked questions, they try to sound bold and decisive and inoffensive, all at the same time. Even so, we can usually construct some meaning out of what they say through their words, their tones, and their body language.

Writing and reading are far more demanding. Readers construct meanings from texts. Texts do not have body language and intonations. They stand alone. Writing represents more extended and more complicated thoughts than those expressed in most conversations. The writer develops ideas in chains, each thought carefully linked to what has come before it and joined with equal care to what comes afterward. This linking of thoughts adds difficulty, for readers must remember what has come before, pay attention to what is there now, and anticipate what will come in the next paragraph or the next page. Reading puts a strain on short-term memory: We have to remember the beginning through-out the piece. We must be reminded continually where the writer has been and where he or she is taking us. Good writers use various devices to refresh the memories of their readers throughout any essay.

A few years ago I joined a 500-mile bike tour through the Pacific North-west. Some seventy bikers pedaled on country roads through spectacular scenery. We had maps, and every evening we heard a lecture on the country we would be traversing the next day. The organization in charge did not stop there. Its leaders painted bright yellow arrows on the pavement at every intersection. Sometimes, on long stretches of road where we did not turn, we were glad to see one of those bright arrows pointing us straight ahead, saying, in effect, "Yes, you're heading in the right direction."

The generous writer provides arrows all through his or her prose to keep readers on track. The limitations of our short-term memory and the purposes of reading require that written language be more precise and better organized than spoken language. Professional writers succeed in taking readers to a destina-tion, offering plenty of help along the way.

A CHECKLIST OF PRINCIPLES

Study the following principles as a means of checking your hopes and your per-formance in your own writing.

1. Conceive of Your Writing as a Story to Be Told.

Professional writers try to interest readers in their story—a tale about some-thing that has happened to them or the story of their thinking and the thinking of others on a subject. They set out to tell us that story as engagingly as possi-ble, asking themselves this question: How can I make readers turn the next page? Yes, of course good writers want to be correct—just as the pianist wants to hit all the right notes. But professional writers—like professional pianists—never assume that being correct is enough. They want life in the performance.

The shape of stories is formed by custom, and I think that shape can be ap-plied to essays. Let's take a look at the beginning of a familiar story. Here is a lean statement of the facts:

> Once upon a time, a little girl named Red Riding Hood lived on the edge of a great forest. On the other side of the forest lived her grandmother, and in the forest lived a big, bad wolf.

After that beginning, any five-year-old knows that somehow the forest, the grandmother, the little girl, and the wolf are going to come together in the story that follows. We feel tension. Will the big, bad wolf hurt Red Riding Hood? Here is a story that the listening child will relive step by step as his or her imag-ination is stirred by the telling. The story operates best when the teller gets quickly to the facts and relates them as concisely as possible.

Most beginning writers—and a great many college professors—have trouble with this concept. Should I write to make a reader *relive* a story, *relive* my thoughts? That's too much trouble. Why not summarize the facts and lay them out for readers to pick up if they need them? So we get papers like this in composition courses and in academic journals. Composition teachers generally groan within when they read a beginning like this:

> In the following paper, I am going to tell of a young woman named Red Riding Hood who got into trouble with a wolf in the forest. I shall first tell how she started through the forest to deliver some cakes to her grandmother. I shall then tell how she encountered the wolf, together with some details about the wolf's trickery and his ugly disposition. Finally I shall tell how Little Red Riding Hood and the grandmother came to a bad end in some versions of the story, and I shall tell how the wolf came to a bad end in some other versions.

This is the writing of someone who wants to give us all the facts but to offer us no life or drama with which to season the facts and make them more memorable, more interesting to a wider audience.

Then we have writers who think their intentions are more important than the story itself. They want us to know how sincere they are, inspired perhaps by public figures who suppose that no matter how dishonest and incompetent they are, they will be forgiven if they can make others think their intentions were good. Inexperienced writers often write like this to prove that they have feeling. They have been deceived by a confessional age.

> It is a sad fact that human beings encroaching upon the environment, especially the forest, have created unpleasant and aggressive attitudes in the animals who ordinarily might live there peacefully with their human colleagues in life. Wolves, for example, have been proven to be harmless and even gracious to human beings in the wild. But when their habitat is destroyed by improper lumbering activities, usually in the interests of corporations manufacturing unnecessary paper products, disastrous consequences ensue. We see how far ecological damage to the environment may go as we study the story of an unfortunate and innocent young woman when she encountered an equally unfortunate and innocent young wolf in a forest that had been unforgivably damaged by those out to make a profit rather than serve nature.

Or we may get the essay shaped by the conviction that a piece of writing must be the consequence of a deduction and that it must contribute to a great truth already certified by noble and established authority stretching back for centuries. This is the appeal to history and the past.

> From the dawn of time, forests have been the preserve of wild animals often dangerous to human beings, especially to children, and numerous indeed are the tales of bloody encounters between wild beasts and little girls and boys. Let us look at one example of this oft-repeated drama in history by examining an old folk tale in which a young woman, armed only with a basket of cakes, was set upon by a wolf in the forest with results that in most versions of the tale were extremely unpleasant for the little girl involved. First, let us survey the geography of the forest where the story takes place.

The original version of the story gets right to the point. It combines elements in tension with each other—a little girl, a forest, a wolf quickly identified as being big and bad, and a grandmother. To put them together in the beginning signals danger to the little girl. The beginning of the story is a sort of promise that all these elements will come together and that the tension we feel at the start will be resolved. Suppose we break that implied promise. Then we might get a version like this:

> Once upon a time, a little girl named Red Riding Hood lived on the edge of a great forest. On the other side of the forest lived her grandmother, and in the forest lived a big, bad wolf. Now one day Little Red Riding Hood's mother gave her a basket of cakes and said, "Little Red Riding Hood, take these cakes across the forest to your grandmother's house." So the little girl started through the woods. But suddenly she met a talent scout from the Dallas Cowboys, and he said, "Little Red Riding Hood, you don't want to waste your time out here in the woods. You want the bright lights, the big city. Come with me to Dallas and become a cheerleader for the Cowboys, and you will be on TV every Sunday afternoon." So Little Red Riding Hood threw down the basket of cakes, and her mother became her agent, and they both left the forest forever.

Any five-year-old hearing the tale told this way would cry out in misery, "But what about the wolf? What about the grandmother?" The beginning of any good story should introduce elements in tension that come together as the story goes along. As writer Rosellen Brown has said, "All fiction, to some extent, depends on the entry of disorder, or the threat of disorder, onto the scene."[5] If you do not do something with those elements that you introduce at the beginning of your story, your reader is left disappointed and usually confused and frustrated.

Much the same can be said of the essay. Something has to be explained, and we get a pretty good idea of what that "something" is at the beginning. Something is out of order. You have a problem. Both the story and the essay establish connections between elements in conflict. The story with the happy ending may resolve all the conflicts; a more realistic story will show the consequences of conflicts. The essay operates in a similar way. It may tell of success or failure in dealing with the tension, or it may simply argue that the problem presented by the introduction deserves attention.

Like the story, the essay proceeds in a linear way, although at times, like a railroad winding over hill and dale, it may seem to wander. When we get to the end of the story, we see that everything in it has had a purpose and that this purpose is to work out the tension presented at the beginning. A good opening makes us wait for something to happen. Then that "something" happens at the climax of the story or the essay. The climax is the moment of resolution, the moment we see how everything is tied together. Facts piled on top of each other do not make a story or an essay. They make only a mess on the page.

Therefore, when you begin to write, look for the story—the elements in tension with one another—the puzzle that needs to be explained, the threat that needs to be faced, the opportunity that cries out for action.

2. Observe Carefully.

How do you find the tensions that are worth writing about? Answering that question successfully makes the difference between the good writer and the person who does not write. Good writers are careful observers. They are infinitely curious. They ask questions all the time, especially of themselves, but also of the data they are exploring, either their own experience, texts they read in books and other sources, visual images, interviews, or life as they observe it. Because they ask questions, they see things—including connections—that others may overlook. For example, most journalists who conduct interviews will notice what their subject is wearing and often what the interviewee was doing when the journalist showed up.

Observation may require careful study. That is, you may have to spend a lot of time going over and over whatever it is you are observing before you begin to see it clearly. You may have to read a book or a short story two or three times before you begin to see something in it that you can write about. The same is true with other kinds of observation. A little later on in this book I shall talk about the "journalistic questions" and ways of heightening your powers of observation. For the moment, remember this: Close observation is one of the essential requirements of writing. The writer observes and then sets out to make sense of those observations.

3. Write Efficiently.

Here is one of the fundamentals of modern English style: Use as few words as possible to say what you want to say. This principle does not mean that you write to sound like a first-grade reader. It does not mean that you write only bland and simple thoughts. On the contrary, if you have complicated thoughts, you may have to use complicated language to express them. But you should avoid always the inflated language that pretends to say much more than it does. This inflated language springs to the mouths of politicians who pretend to principles they do not have or to other self-important people who seek to impress others by the complexity they can write into simple facts. When Vice President Al Gore was caught soliciting campaign contributions by telephone from the White House in 1997, he could not say, "I'm sorry I broke the law. I made a mistake." Instead he appeared before a press conference and said that he had been told there was "no controlling legal authority" to keep him from doing what he did.

Academics striving to seem profound can be as bad as politicians. This sentence came from an academic journal:

> Individuals with a strong home-defense orientation in living areas noted for multiple instances of criminal behavior in urban regions are most likely to practice the acquisition and continued possession of firearms.

The writer meant that in urban neighborhoods where crime is common, people buy guns to defend themselves.

Efficient prose may not even mean brevity. Sometimes a longer version of a thought is clearer—and therefore more efficient—than a shorter version. The shorter version may abbreviate ideas so much that readers have a hard time following them. Here is a sentence from an article in a recent scholarly journal. The article analyzes what various groups of white people believe about opportunities for blacks in our society.

> The category of persons who see black opportunity as average and not greatly improved appears to contain a subtype who seem to be saying that opportunity for blacks has always been equal, denying the existence of past inequality of opportunity.

I think this sentence can be translated as follows:

> Some people think opportunities for blacks are about equal to those for whites and that there has been no great increase in the prospects for blacks in recent times. Some of these people seem to think that blacks have always had equal opportunity and that inequality of opportunity never existed.

The issue here is in part honesty. Don't be mealymouthed. Don't pretend to more profundity than you have. Say what you mean. But the issue also concerns style. Writers should want to be read. Efficient prose allows your readers to read your work without having to back up time and again to read it again to see what it means.

4. Be Direct.

Professional writers begin most sentences with the subject and tell us quickly what the subject does or what happens to the subject. Note that they don't begin *all* their sentences with the subject; they do begin most of them that way. They do not write many long, looping dependent clauses between subjects and verbs. They usually put direct objects immediately after the verbs.

We read silently now. Only a couple of centuries ago it was common practice to read everything aloud, even if one read alone. Readers murmured to themselves. And if one reader read to a group—a common practice—the reader could modulate his or her voice and emphasize phrases to make the audience understand the long sentences that were then common in prose.

We also read more quickly than our forebears did. Even a slow reader absorbs about 250 words a minute. Hardly anyone can speak that fast, and scarcely anyone tries. But the patterns of speech still influence how we read. When we speak, we usually put the direct object immediately after the verb. We say, "I broke the window with a baseball." We don't say, "I with a baseball broke the window." So in our reading, we understand more quickly if subjects are close to verbs and verbs close to direct objects. Direct writing is more conversational; that is, it follows the speech patterns we use in conversation.

In his fine little book, *The Philosophy of Composition,* E. D. Hirsch, Jr., illustrates the increasing directness of English style by giving several translations of the same text from Giovanni Boccaccio, the great Italian storyteller of the fourteenth century. Hirsch demonstrates that as English translations come forward in time, they become shorter and more direct. Here is a version from the sixteenth century:

> Saladin, whose valiance was so great that not only the same from base estate advanced him to Sultan of Babylon, but also thereby he won diverse victories over the Saracen kings and Christians; who through his manifold wars and magnificent triumphs, having expended all his treasure, and for the execution of one exploit lacking a great sum of money, knew not where to have the same so readily as he had occasion to employ it. At length he called to remembrance a rich Jew named Melchizedech, that lent out money for interest in Alexandria.

An eighteenth-century version reads like this:

> Saladin was so brave and great a man, that he had raised himself from an inconsiderable person to be Sultan of Babylon, and he had gained many victories over both the Saracen and Christian princes. This monarch having in diverse wars and by many extraordinary expenses, run through all his treasure, some urgent occasion fell out that he wanted a large sum of money. Not knowing which way he might raise enough to answer his necessities, he at last called to mind a rich Jew of Alexandria named Melchizedech, who lent out money on interest.[6]

An even more recent and direct translation is the following:

> Saladin, who was so powerful that he rose from an ordinary man to the rank of Sultan of Babylon and won countless victories over Saracen and Christian rulers, found that he had exhausted all his wealth, both in war and in the exercise of his extraordinary munificence. Now, by some chance, he felt the need of money, and a lot of it, too, and not knowing where he could get it as quickly as he wished, he thought of a rich Jew called Melchizedek who was a moneylender in Alexandria.[7]

We can understand the first version only if we read it slowly, preferably aloud. It is littered with cumbersome dependent clauses and participial phrases that come between subjects and verbs. We can understand the second version fairly well by reading it silently, and we can follow the third even more readily.

You can improve your own writing by going over and over it again, seeing how few words you can use to say what you want to say. Computers make this process much easier than it once was. Revise for as much simplicity as you can achieve without sacrificing either the content or the style of your prose.

5. Engage Your Readers.

Good writers stimulate the imagination, the image-forming ability of the mind. The children of my generation listened to radio dramas and made pictures in their heads of what they heard. Ages before that, a bard singing the epic tales of the tribe by the fire at night summoned up pictures in the minds of the circle of silent listeners.

These pictures are painted by the experiences of readers and writers, experiences that come together as the sentences unfold. I want to shout right here,

"This point is important!" I'm talking about the most fundamental way we communicate. Good writers provide details. Readers understand because these details remind them of their own experience. Writers communicate by depending on what readers already know, what readers remember.

Let me explain. Our most vivid memories are of sense experience. Our five senses—sight, hearing, taste, smell, and touch—provide all we know of the world. Good writers develop a knack for calling on our sensory memory. Here is a superb descriptive paragraph about the great Mississippi River flood in 1927. Read it, and let's analyze its power.

> It was like facing an angry dark ocean. The wind was fierce enough that day it tore away roofs, smashed windows, and blew down the smoke-stack—130 feet high and 54 inches in diameter—at the giant A. G. Wineman & Sons lumber mill, destroyed half of the 110-foot-high smokestack of the Chicago Mill and Lumber Company, and drove great chocolate waves against the levee, where the surf broke, splashing waist-high against the men, knocking them off-balance before rolling down to the street. Out on the river, detritus swept past—whole trees, a roof, fence posts, upturned boats, the body of a mule. One man working on the levee recalled decades later, "I saw a whole tree just disappear, sucked under by the current, then saw it shoot up, it must have been a hundred yards away. Looked like a missile fired by a submarine."[8]

Now notice what writer John M. Barry does. He gives us a panorama of sensory details that call on our own experience. No, probably none of us remembers the 1927 Mississippi River flood. I had not yet been born. But we have seen "an angry dark ocean," either in reality or on TV or in the movies. We have experienced high winds—although probably not winds like those Barry describes. But we can imagine such winds by what he tells us of their effects. They "tore away roofs, smashed windows" and blew down smokestacks whose dimensions he gives us. We have seen roofs. We have probably been inside a house with a storm howling outside, but our windows did not break. We have all seen tall smokestacks (alas) against the skies of our cities and towns. Think of the power of wind to blow such things down! And in an especially vivid description, he speaks of "great chocolate waves" driven against the levee. We know the color of chocolate. We can quickly imagine a river such as the Mississippi, colored like chocolate because of all the mud it carries downstream with it. We can also feel a sense of the fear of being smashed by waves up to our waists, for if we have ever been in the ocean, we have probably been up to our waists, and we know how little control we have over our bodies when the surf is coming in on us. Again, if we have not done such a thing ourselves, we've seen enough representations in movies and on TV to help us understand what Barry is telling us. We get details of the wreckage carried along by the flood, and we can imagine all of them because we have seen something like them in our own experience. Finally we get the marvelous metaphor of a tree shooting up out of the flood "like a missile fired by a submarine." The man who provided that metaphor had never seen a "missile fired by a submarine" at the time of the flood, and in all probability he had never seen such a thing at all. But in his later life he had seen it on television.

Barry could have written, "The wind was high, and it blew the water over the levee, and the river ran with debris washed into the current by the flood." Instead he puts together a chain of sensory images that we can imagine because they activate fragments of our memories. He makes us break down and recombine our own memories and thus become engaged with the experience he describes.

When teachers say "Be concrete" or "Be specific," they mean you should use the solid, sensory words good writers use to call up some memory, some experience, something readers have seen and heard, felt and smelled and tasted. Our most vivid memories are of our senses—a rumble of thunder on a stormy night, the sharp blue sky of a clear wintry day, the taste of mustard, the smell of perfume, the feel of sandpaper. Use sensory words in your writing, and readers respond.

COMMONSENSE EXCEPTIONS

You do not have to convey sense experience in every sentence. Of course you may write abstractly if you are a specialist writing to an audience of specialists who already know a lot about your subject and have a great interest in it. You can be less vivid just because you know your readers want to learn from you something important to them that they do not know already. For this reason, articles in specialized journals may seem dull to outsiders. They are addressed to people already deeply interested in the subject and knowledgeable about it. Cancer researchers want to get quickly to the point in a technical article about cancer; they do not have time for vivid descriptions. But when they read other things, cancer specialists are like the rest of us. They want to be engaged by lively writing addressed to sense experience.

Even articles in specialized journals should use vivid examples now and then. Too many writers forget to keep the minds of readers alert and responsive. For years and years I was a member of a committee at my university that gave handsome prizes for both graduate and undergraduate essays written in three categories—the physical sciences, the humanities, and the social sciences. Our committee at various times included a biologist, an astronomer, a writer, a Shakespearean scholar, a philosopher, several historians, and sometimes a random chemist. Year after year we agreed that this or that paper in every category must have great possibilities because it had been given a top grade in the class where it had been written. But year after year we gave the prizes to papers we could understand and that by our consensus were written well. Sometimes we worried about our choices. What right did we have to reject a paper because none of us could bear to labor over an inscrutable style? But year after year we followed our tastes.

I am pleased that through the years a great many of my students have published books and articles and mention the aid that I have given them on their road to success. I hope that this book will help you along the same road. You should read it not as if its principles are sacred. They are, as I repeat time and again, flexible principles, not laws. If you read it carefully and think through its advice for yourself, you will come to your own sense of authority when you write. I hope you will write more efficiently and vividly and that you will gain the other rewards that writers win—not wealth certainly but the satisfaction of writing well and having an influence in the world of the written word. You may even get to the point where writing becomes an addiction. Let me know if that happens. I answer all my mail.

One final word of advice: Read. Read everything you can. Read day and night. Good writers in my experience are always avid readers. When they like a piece of writing, they seek to understand why. When they dislike something, they ponder their aversion. If you make reading a lifelong habit and try to imitate in some way the writing you like best, you will be on your way to writing well. And you will enjoy your reading more, too.

The Writing Process

N o writer I know gets it right the first time. No writer I know writes easily. We don't begin at the beginning, write steadily, and get up at the end—whenever that may be—with an unblemished manuscript ready to go off to the publishers. Most of us struggle to get ideas, labor with blood, toil, tears, and sweat to get them into some kind of order, wrestle them down onto the page, and then decide that we've made some wretched mistakes, that we have repeated ourselves, that we have written some sentences so incomprehensible that they make us ashamed, and that perhaps we should have been forest rangers or bankers or welders—anything other than what we are, writers with this addiction to our craft. I've never been surprised that a great many great writers are also alcoholics. No, I do *not* advise drinking as a means to creativity. Drinking has destroyed many a good pen. But I can understand the frustration that writing evokes. Writers are like baseball players; they fail so often that to get it right one-third of the time seems like the peak of success.

Writing is an effort to woo readers. Readers nowadays are in an almighty hurry. They will seldom struggle to understand difficult writing unless they are forced to do so. Samuel Johnson, the great eighteenth-century writer, said, "What is written without effort is in general read without pleasure." Today what is written without effort is seldom read at all.

Here is a fact: Writing takes time—lots and lots of time. Good writers don't dash off a piece in an hour or two. They observe. They take notes on what they observe. They think about what they want to say. They plan. They write first drafts. They revise, both structurally and on the level of the sentences. That is, they move sections of their work around, seeking a better natural flow of their prose. Or they go over and over their sentences, searching for the right word, eliminating words and phrases they don't need. Sometimes they delete whole sentences and even whole pages. Even small writing tasks may require an enormous investment in time. Even in this age of technology, computers can't do your work for you. You may use the computer to do the work that finally only you can do.

So it is with all worthwhile disciplines. A great athlete may run a marathon in a little over two hours. But to train for those two hours requires months of preparation. If you want to be a writer, you must be serious about the task, willing to dedicate all the time it takes to your work, revising it again and again.

Writer's Block

Most of us suffer writer's block now and then. We can't get started on an assignment, or once started, we lose sight of our destination. Our brains seem to go dead as if our batteries had all died. Many major writers have suffered paralyzing writer's block at one time or another in their careers. So if you suffer from writer's block, you are in good company.

For most of us writer's block is not a matter of sitting at a desk while words fail to come. Usually it is a consequence of impatience with the task. The words seem not to be there. We tell ourselves we will write for a while and then watch television. Then we decide to watch television and write for a while. Then we decide to watch television all evening long and write tomorrow morning. Many people, even established writers, put off writing as if it were like a visit to the dentist.

The best way to avoid writer's block is to sit down at your desk and stay there, fingers on the keyboard or wrapped around your pen or your pencil. Years ago B. F. Skinner, the great behavioral psychologist, rigged a clock to a light over his typewriter at his desk. When he sat down to write, he turned on the light, automatically starting the clock. He spent four hours a day writing. The clock told him when he had completed his task. Mechanical? Yes. But it worked. First he developed the habit of writing. The clock told him when he had kept the goal he set for himself. He was an astonishingly productive writer, turning out books and articles until he died in August 1991, almost ninety years old. I knew him fairly well, and I think his writing helped keep him so vibrantly alive.

Sit Down and Do It

So the first rule of writing is this: Sit down and do it. Stay put. Keep going. We all get discouraged—especially before the mountain-climbing task of writing the first sentence of the day. Yes, you will have trouble organizing your thoughts. Yes, the thought of making another cup of coffee is tempting, but don't do it until you have written *something*. And don't read the magazine lying on the couch, and don't make a telephone call, and don't turn on the radio or the TV. Keep going.

Don't write a page and start all over again. Writers love new beginnings, clean slates, unblemished pages. We think a new start will get it right—and that may be true. But give it a little time. Don't start and restart and restart without getting on into the body of your work to see what thoughts you may stir out of yourself. When we begin and reject, begin and reject, begin and reject, we deceive ourselves, looking for an excuse not to get on with it, to put it off until tomorrow. And when we put it off until tomorrow, the game is lost.

Many writers have one or two favorite places to work. I love to work in my cluttered study here on the second floor of my house or in my equally cluttered office in the main library of my university. When I walk into either place, something inside me says, "You are here to write." You must find your own place. The Southern writer Thomas Wolfe was large and tall; he wrote in longhand while standing up, using the top of his refrigerator as a desk. Ernest Hemingway often wrote standing up at a little portable typewriter. William Faulkner sat at his kitchen table in his rambling frame house on the edge of Oxford, Mississippi. He usually wrote a draft in longhand with a fine-pointed fountain pen, and when the entire manuscript was complete, he went over it, editing with a pen or a pencil. Then he typed it all out himself, making final revisions, with a small portable typewriter. Make a workplace for yourself that says to you when you sit down, "This is the writing place."

I've always tried to write whole drafts of a book or an article as soon as possible. As I have said to innumerable students over the years, once you get a work "in being" in the form of a pile of paper or, nowadays, on the hard disk of your computer, you can start revising. This is the fourth edition of *A Writer's Companion.* I have computer diskettes going back to the second edition. But in writing each edition I have typed through the whole book anew, putting it on the computer, then working through it a little every day, adding, subtracting, changing a word here and there, eliminating a sentence or a whole paragraph, finding new examples, rethinking my own thoughts. It is always a work in progress. Planning is important. You ought to have a reasonably clear idea of what you want to do in a piece of writing. But if you plan too much, planning sometimes takes the place of writing. Some of my best planning takes place after I have a lot of text written and then start seeing how to shape it finally into what I want. That is to say that I sometimes don't know exactly what I want until I see what I have written in a first draft.

But although I believe in getting a first draft together as quickly as possible, I do not always write the draft in the order that the piece will appear. Very often I think of the middle or the end before I'm clear on the beginning. I don't put off writing what comes to mind, even if it means that I write the middle before I write the beginning. Put off writing out an idea, and it may be lost. You may discover, as many writers do, that the beginning is the last part you write.

What We Do When We Revise

When you have your first draft before you, the real fun begins—revision. With my first draft, no matter how messy or even chaotic it is, I am confident that I have something to say. I can then set myself to the task of working through the draft, slashing and burning here, fine-tuning here, shifting sections around, paying attention to transitions—those bright yellow arrows along the road.

Revision requires that you read your own work again and again. Inexperienced writers find this task hard. Too many new writers deliver their first draft with the air of weary coal miners eager to shed their dirty clothes at the end of the day. In my days in ROTC in an age that is past, our sergeants used to hammer on us to fire our rifles once we were in combat. We were told that many soldiers in the thick of a fight refuse to fire their weapons lest they attract hostile attention. As an ROTC cadet (who never made it to the regular army or combat), I thought this caution seemed like good sense. But I have often reflected that a similar dread afflicts inexperienced writers who refuse to reread their work once it is done. They seem afraid they will find something wrong, and they want to get their work off their hands as quickly as possible.

It may be a comfort to know that professional writers suffer similar pangs. If anything, their unhappiness is greater because they make a living from writing, and their first drafts may persuade them that they need to find another job or else face starvation. But battle-hardened professional writers do not regard the first draft as final. Rather they expect it to be like a blob of clay that the skilled potter flings onto a spinning potter's wheel. Potential beauty resides in the blob; it can be brought out by the skilled and careful touch of the potter's hand.

All writers must reconcile themselves to slow improvement rather than instantaneous perfection. Now and then all writers have sudden revelations. A sentence or an idea leaps unexpectedly into the writer's mind like a gift from God. More often, however, the writer labors steadily on details that add up to a book or an article, just as bricks laid carefully together finally make a wall or a house. It's worth saying again that writing well is like preparing for a musical concert or an athletic contest; you work on every detail so that the final performance will make you one with your audience.

PREPARATION FOR WRITING

But let's take a step back. How do we get to the moment where we start putting words on paper. First, we have to have something to write about; we have to know something. You can't write anything unless you have something to say. Some beginning writers think that the world is waiting for their sweeping generalizations and their firm opinions about controversial subjects. It is not. Opinions are cheap. Everybody has them. They are worth something only when they come supported by knowledge. *Write about what you know.* That is a familiar piece of advice to writers. The backside of this aphorism is that you cannot write well about anything you don't know.

When you ponder a possible subject to write about, your first obligation is to read as much about that subject as you can. I love to write surrounded by my books. I often tell my students to write their first drafts of papers in the quiet reference room of our own main library. When they want to check a date, a spelling, a historical event, a quotation, or the plot of a book or a play, they can find it. But the most important use of your library is to find books and articles written about the subject you want to write about. Now that library catalogs are on-line and accessible by computer, you can easily tap into titles of books and articles written directly about your subject. The Internet has opened another vast resource for information, and I shall have more to say about this amazing new technology a little later on in this book.

Other sources of knowledge abound all around you. One of the best ways to gather information is to talk to people either by interviewing them formally or else by simply conversing with them. An immediate resource is the teacher in the class where you must write a paper. All teachers have office hours. Surprise! Teachers truly like to see their students when the students have something serious to discuss. Go in for a chat about your paper. And don't depend solely on the teacher in your class. Other teachers in your college or university have special knowledge about a large variety of subjects, and they are usually delighted to talk to a curious and interested student about them. They may even be flattered at your interest.

If you are writing about some historical events of the recent past, you can probably find somebody who has participated in them. Students writing about a subject pertaining to the Vietnam War, the Korean War, or World War II can find scores of men and women with vivid memories of those conflicts, and a conversation with two or three of them can open avenues of exploration that lead to fertile fields of inquiry.

The main point is this: When you are writing about a subject, saturate your mind with information about it. Only then can you write a paper that will interest both you and your readers.

Finding Fact Patterns

As you study a topic, you find data falling into what lawyers call "fact patterns." That is, the facts start indicating conclusions. For example, to prepare to write a paper on Hamlet's friend Horatio, you may read every speech Horatio gives in the play, and you should ponder the opinions expressed about him by other characters. You may recall that Horatio was the name of the legendary Roman soldier who stood valiantly at a bridge over the Tiber, defending Rome single-handedly from its enemies. The name Horatio is also, for anyone who knows the classics (as Shakespeare certainly did), a synonym for loyalty. These facts begin to add up to a conclusion: Horatio may be the only unambiguously unselfish and faithful person in *Hamlet.* When that thought strikes you, you have a standard by which to measure the morality of the other characters.

Keeping Notes

Keep notes on your readings and your observations—not merely factual notes but notes about your thoughts about the facts. I have always been a notebook keeper. I carry one or two notebooks in my shoulder bag on my daily bicycle commute between home and my university. I never travel without one. I am always scribbling ideas, trial sentences, random observations, questions. A notebook is portable, durable, and efficient since you are not likely to lose pages out of it, but you can use other devices. A friend of mine carries a small pack of 3 × 5 cards wrapped with a rubber band in his shirt pocket. The cards are hard on his shirts but good for his mind and memory. Some people now keep notes on their computers, resting their sources beside the keyboard and reading with their fingers on the keys. The advantages here are considerable, one being that you can use the search function of the computer to find words quickly in your own notes.

If you keep a notebook, don't be afraid to let it get messy. It's your private property, your fenced-in garden—or pigpen—where you can play with your thoughts. No one else will see it. Professional photographers throw away fifty shots for every one they keep. You can toss away ideas you decide not to use. But if they are there in your notebook, you may discover sometime in the future that they come back to you with new possibilities glittering around them. The habit of writing notes keeps your mind working, seeking, playing, and out of all this will come things you can use in your final drafts.

Learn to paraphrase and summarize information. The best reading is done with a pen or pencil in hand and a notebook open beside the book or magazine on your desk. Let's note the difference between *paraphrase* and *summary.* A summary condenses information. A paraphrase puts in different words the thoughts of a source. Summarize when you want a ready reference to the contents of a book or an article. A summary should be as brief as you can make it. You can waste time by trying to include every detail of your source in a summary. The late Barbara Tuchman, one of our most popular historians, gave her own view of taking notes:

> As to the mechanics of research, I take notes on four-by-six index cards, reminding myself about once an hour of a rule I read long ago in a research manual, "Never write on the back of anything." Since copying is a chore and a bore, use of the cards, the smaller the better, forces one to extract the strictly relevant, to distill from the very beginning, to pass the material through the grinder of one's own mind, so to speak.[1]

PARAPHRASES AND SUMMARIES   Paraphrase when the source text is difficult, perhaps written in early modern English or in a convoluted style or in a foreign language. Paraphrasing offers the opportunity to interpret the source as you read it, and you may use your interpretation in your later writing. Here is a description by the English traveler, Frances Milton Trollope, who visited the United States in 1827. She wrote one of the most humorously savage books ever written about our country, which she thought populated by ignorant barbarians. Here is her account of a religious revival in a Presbyterian Church that she observed in Cincinnati:

> The priest who stood in the middle was praying; the prayer was extravagantly vehement, and offensively familiar in expression; when this ended, a hymn was sung, and then another priest took the centre place, and preached. The sermon had considerable eloquence, but of a frightful kind. The preacher described, with ghastly minuteness, the last feeble fainting moments of human life, and then the gradual progress of decay after death, which he followed through every process up to the last loathsome stage of decomposition. Suddenly changing his tone, which had been that of sober accurate description, into the shrill voice of horror, he bent forward his head, as if to gaze on some object beneath the pulpit. And as Rebecca made known to Ivanhoe what she saw through the window, so the preacher made known to us what he saw in the pit that seemed to open before him. The device was certainly a happy one for giving effect to his description of hell. No image that fire, flame, brimstone, molten lead, or red-hot pincers could supply; with flesh, nerves, and sinews quivering under them, was omitted. The perspiration ran in streams from the face of the preacher; his eyes rolled, his lips were covered with foam, and every feature had the deep expression of horror it would have borne, had he, in truth, been gazing at the scene he described. The acting was excellent. At length he gave a languishing look to his supporters on each side, as if to express his feeble state, and then sat down, and wiped the drops of agony from his brow.[2]

A paraphrase of this extended comment would include both an account of what Mrs. Trollope wrote and any explanation that a modern reader might need.

> Mrs. Trollope out of her English curiosity for strange American things visited a "revival" meeting in Cincinnati and described with considerable distaste a sermon she heard there from a Presbyterian minister, whom she called a "priest"—the term used for clergymen in the Anglican church in her homeland. The preacher stepped up after a hymn and offered a prayer that Mrs. Trollope found vehement and irritating, doubtless because of the American habit of addressing God as an intimate friend. He then launched into a detailed account of death and the decay of the human body afterwards, and after that he described in great detail the torments of everlasting hell fire as though he were looking down into the pit of hell itself and observed all the horrors he described. Mrs. Trollope describes the minister's contortions and his final exhausted collapse at the end. To her it was all "acting," and she makes an ironic comment that the description of hell was as detailed as if the heroine of Sir Walter Scott's medieval romance, *Ivanhoe,* had been speaking to her beloved of things she saw through a window. To her the entire show was ridiculous, but her detailed account offers a valuable description of a part of frontier cultural history.

A paraphrase may be slightly longer than the source, but a summary is always shorter than the source. Here is a summary of Mrs. Trollope's account:

> Frances Trollope, visiting Cincinnati in 1827, described with withering scorn a raging sermon on death and hell preached by a Presbyterian minister who, she thought, was vulgar and hypocritical.

When you write either a paraphrase or a summary in your notes, write down the page number and title of your source. You can easily look it up again if you have later questions. But if you have taken the notes carefully, you will probably not have to do so. I have often found that as I summarize or paraphrase for a source, pen in hand, ideas pop into my head that I have not thought of before. I jot them down, and sometimes I use them in interpreting the texts I am writing about.

Get in the habit of commenting as you read and take notes. Make a list of questions about any subject you want to write about. Part of knowledge is the recognition of your ignorance about subjects and facts that make you curious. Unanswered questions drive you to seek more information, and if after a search you still cannot find an answer, you will have learned something important about the limits of knowledge about your topic.

Summaries and paraphrases save time for you and your readers. Now and then we all quote word for word from a source to capture a colorful phrase or an important meaning. But avoid long quotations if you can summarize or paraphrase accurately. Quote when the text is so rich that no summary would do it justice. In his biography *Truman,* David McCullough tells the story of President Harry Truman's fierce letter to music critic Paul Hume after Hume had panned a concert given by the President's daughter, Margaret, who fancied herself an opera singer. Truman wrote to Hume: "Some day I hope to meet you. When that happens you'll need a new nose, a lot of beefsteak for black eyes, and perhaps a supporter below!"[3] One cannot summarize such a comment and do it justice. McCullough quoted that line and the whole letter—and he did the right thing. But use a direct quotation only if it is necessary to express the information or the mood you find important.

AVOIDING PLAGIARISM   When you copy a source word for word, use quotation marks in your notes. When you summarize, make a note of the source for use later in your footnotes or endnotes. Always indicate in your own text when you are relying on information supplied in your sources. Plagiarism is the most serious offense a writer can commit. It represents dishonesty on the part of the writer, and in my own university any student guilty of plagiarism is forced to withdraw for a year. Such a penalty is mild compared to the penalties writers incur when they commit plagiarism in the world of published books and articles. Alex Haley, the author of the historical novel *Roots,* was forced to pay thousands of dollars in damages to writers from whom he plagiarized much of his story of slavery in America. The television series developed from the book became one of the great turning points in American consciousness about race. But Haley's reputation and his book never recovered from the proven charges of plagiarism against him.

The penalties of plagiarism are so severe that you must take care to avoid even the appearance of stealing ideas and language from others. To avoid confusion and plagiarism, some people write direct quotations, summaries, and paraphrases on one page and their own comments, thoughts, and questions on the facing page. I put a little arrow (→) next to my own thoughts to distinguish them from summaries and paraphrases of my sources. And in the text itself, I always put a footnote at any place where I am indebted to a source. (I shall discuss plagiarism again later in this book.)

FINDING A TOPIC

What will you write about? Good students told to write a paper for a course are sometimes terrified by this question. They often believe that they must write about something no one has ever written about before, and so they feel driven into a corner where the only way out is to fly off on some level of incomprehensible abstraction that neither they nor their readers can understand. Or they may go to the other extreme and write only the thoughts that they find in the work of others who have written about their topic.

I offer two broad answers to the question, "What will you write about?" Write about things that you know that your audience does not. Or write about the puzzles you find in your evidence. And, obviously, you can combine these two categories. In whatever you write, you should do more than merely convey information. You should provide some sense of why the information is important. So even a factual argument should have in it some element of tension, something out of balance that must be put right.

The Common Topics

Aristotle taught his students certain "common topics" that could be subjects for speaking or writing. Here they are. We can write about what kind of thing something is. That is, we can define a thing or describe its parts. We may compare something with something else, pointing out similarities and differences. We can discuss relations such as cause and effect, oppositions and contradictions. We can speak or write about circumstances—whether something is possible or not, whether something happened in the past, whether something is (or was) good or bad. Or we can provide our reasons for accepting a theory or a belief that we cannot prove beyond a shadow of a doubt. What is plausible for us to believe, even if we do not have all the evidence we wish we could have?

All these "common topics" may help us write. I always ask my students to define the abstract terms they use in writing about ideas. We often use terms such as *humanism, reason, socialism, science, democracy, mysticism, fascism, theory, renaissance, medieval,* and hundreds of others as if we all agree on what we mean by them. But we don't. One person's *reason* is another's *folly. Humanism* today often gets confused with *humanitarianism* or even *atheism. Science* as it is used in a university curriculum usually means a carefully organized methodology that involves ways of gathering and classifying evidence and also a means of shaping theories that explain that evidence and that can be tested, often in laboratories under carefully controlled conditions. But *science* as it is used in television commercials often means only that well-paid actors testify that using certain salves grew hair on their bald heads. Define your major words as you intend to use them in your essay. Sometimes it helps to quote an authoritative definition from a well-known authority on the subject. (But don't be content with dictionary definitions. We'll touch on their weakness later.)

You can expand the common topic of "what kind" into the common topic of comparison. One person's definition of *reason* may be compared to another definition used by someone else. For Shakespeare's King Henry V of England, *honor* seems to be a willingness to fight to the death without fear. The young king talks fervently about *honor* the way saints talk about faith. In the stirring battle scenes of the play, we see this abstraction applied to the world where people live and die, and by examining the circumstances of Henry's use of the word, we see what honor means to him. We can see its parts, seek its causes, compare it with the *dishonor* of other characters, speculate about whether Henry's definition is satisfactory, comment on the circumstances of his times and Shakespeare's that made such a definition popular then, ask whether his way of speaking about honor allows him to be a worthwhile character. Like most teachers, I am delighted when my students hand in papers in which they use these "common topics" to analyze an important word in a text. My students are delighted when they discover how many questions they can ask a text, using ancient Aristotle as a guide.

Making Yourself Creative

What is *creativity?* Here is a word with many definitions, but in writing, to be creative often means that the writer sees things that are not obvious to others and that the writer makes connections that others do not easily see until the writer has shown them. The creative person often sees patterns that others have missed. We come back to something I said at the start of this book: Observation, learning how to see, is one of the writer's greatest gifts.

It is a gift that can be cultivated. Creative people have to know a lot. This comment may seem unnecessary, but I have read too many papers written by students who think they can write something creative off the tops of their heads. Every one of the creative arts—painting, sculpture, music, poetry, fiction, nonfiction, and heaven knows what else—requires the artist to know intimately the field within which he or she seeks to create something. Writers depend on observation of character and events in daily life. But they also work hard in libraries to learn everything they can about the subject they are writing about in the time they have to devote to the task. Unless you spend your life writing frothy personal essays about your soul, you cannot begin to write well unless you know enough to have something to say. Inspiration is one of the great gifts for the writer. But inspiration usually comes after hours and hours, years and years of reading and rereading. No one can be a good writer without reading voraciously.

The Internet has opened a world of opportunity for academic writers, students and professors alike. Some of the Internet sites are splendid. The Library of Congress site is one of the best. (Try it at **lcweb2.loc.gov/ammem/**.) The *New York Times* offers a free Internet service at **www.nytimes.com**. Among other things you can access thousands of book reviews that have occurred in the *Times*. Professor Carl Smith of Northwestern University is curator of an astonishingly detailed and interesting site on the Great Chicago Fire that changed the city in the last century. At **http://www.chicagohs.org/fire** you can find hundreds of pages of essays, pictures, and newspaper accounts from the time.

You can also find barrels of worthless trash on the Internet. Any fanatic can set up a site and distribute everything from raw hatred of minorities to horoscopes that predict the future of those who tap in. The information you get from the net is no better than the site where it is posted. Sites whose addresses end in **.edu** and **.gov** are generally reliable. With a good search engine you can get hundreds of hits on almost any subject you choose to explore, and you can also find primary texts—novels, classical texts, historic documents—that a previous generation could have found only in a large library. The Internet has not replaced books, and it probably will not. My main advice is that wherever you get the sources for your writing, you have to work, read, study, and think before you can produce anything worthwhile.

Use your notebooks to work your way through your reading and your ideas. Trust yourself. Most people have interesting thoughts, but they often do nothing with them. A major difference between creative and noncreative people is that the creative take their idle musings seriously enough to make something of them.

Try to focus your thoughts on a limited problem, one you can define precisely. You cannot do an elaborate psychological analysis of Henry VIII in five pages. You cannot use the simple title "Luther" for a ten-page research paper. Limit your topic to a problem you can develop carefully in the space at your disposal, and become an expert in that issue while you are studying and writing about it. Yes, you have time to be an expert in a limited subject; believe that, and you can be a writer.

Write titles that describe your work. Good titles are essential to good writing, but I'm surprised at how seldom students think of them until the last minute. Try different versions of a title in your notebook.

Now, let's look in some detail at ways of making yourself creative as you fulfill a writing assignment.

1. Be a Close Reader—or a Closer Observer.

We use the "common topics" in life even when we know nothing about Aristotle. In looking at people, we ask, "What qualities give this person his or her identity?" In looking at a painting, we say, "How is this painting different from anything else I have ever seen?" In looking at a written text, this question becomes, "What exactly do the words say?" "Why is this paragraph essential to the whole?" "How dependable is this source?" "What bias did this writer have in putting down this account?" "What can I read between the lines of this source?"

A close reading is the first step toward understanding written texts. I used to give my students sources by both British and American participants in the battles of Lexington and Concord fought outside Boston on April 19, 1775, to open the Revolutionary War. I asked my students simply to tell me the story of the battles so they could offer some explanation for the way things turned out on that bloody day in American history.

Among the sources is an account Paul Revere wrote about his famous "midnight ride" that most Americans know from Henry Wadsworth's stirring poem, which Longfellow wrote to stir loyalty to the Union at the beginning of the Civil War in 1861. In the poem Revere asks a friend to place lanterns in the steeple of Old North Church overlooking the tidal basin of the Charles River, the lanterns to signal how the British army would be leaving Boston. Says Revere in the poem:

> One if by land and two if by sea
> And I on the opposite shore shall be
> Waiting to ride and spread the alarm
> Through every Middlesex village and farm.

Longfellow gives us a heartthrobbing account of Revere doing just that—standing by his restless horse, waiting impatiently to see the lanterns gleam out through the dark across the Charles to signal that British troops would be boated across the Charles, coming "by sea" to march along the country roads of Middlesex County to seize arms and gunpowder the Patriots have stored at Concord.

The first time I gave this assignment, one of my students saw that Revere had ordered the lanterns posted *before* he had himself rowed across the Charles to his waiting horse. Revere knew already how the British troops would slip out of Boston, but he feared the British might capture him as he was crossing the river. He had the lanterns posted to warn others who might then carry the message in his place. Who is the superior source, Longfellow or Revere? Obviously Revere. Once we see the differences in Longfellow's account from Revere's, we can ask another question: Why did Longfellow change the story? Answering that question is a paper in itself.

Always ask yourself how dependable your sources are. In my assignment on the battles of Lexington and Concord are two accounts giving the number of British troops in the expedition. Lieutenant John Barker marched with the British troops and was furious with his own officers because he thought their bungling led to the British disaster that day. He kept a diary. In its pages just after he was one of the lucky ones who marched about fifty miles that day and got back to Boston alive, Barker wrote a scathing account of the fighting. He said the British attacking force numbered about 600 men.

The following year on the anniversary of the battle, an American minister in Lexington, Jonas Clark, preached a triumphant sermon about the fighting. He said that some 1200 to 1500 British soldiers attacked the "patriots." Now who is a better source for the number of British troops engaged, one of their own officers at the time or a minister preaching a year afterward? My students too often had been taught that if something was written down in a book, it had to be true. So they wrote something like this: "The British attacking force consisted of from 600 to 1500 men." You have to trust yourself sometimes to choose among contradictory sources.

Here is an essential point. Students commonly believe that all possible truth has been written down and then squeezed out of the sources they study for their papers. In fact, a delight in any kind of scholarship is to discover that old texts yield new truths to those who study them diligently. Read carefully, and you may well discover that previous scholars have missed something. Read the texts again and again and again, trying to see everything you can in them, asking yourself questions. And you may become like the fictional detectives Sherlock Holmes or Hercule Poirot, who find clues that suddenly reveal a truth the casual observer has overlooked entirely.

Observing Your Own Experience

Defining, sorting out, examining causes and effects, and comparing events in your experience serve much the same purpose as examining a text carefully. I usually don't like the autobiographical writing I see students doing in college. I once heard a college teacher say that he thought one of the worst influences of television and the movies was to convince students that their own lives had not been interesting. Other young people had had great adventures, suffered great wrongs, or overcome great obstacles while all college students had done was to go to high school. Recently I read that a student writing her "personal essay" for her college application said she found herself wishing somebody in her family had died so she could write an affecting story of how she had overcome grief.

Any college teacher who assigns an autobiographical essay is familiar with this pattern. Too many students want to make themselves heroes or victims. They want to write about great turning points in their lives or to show how they were unfairly persecuted by those who do not understand them. The impression conveyed by such essays is often monotonously the same. Readers feel the bragging, the exaggeration, and the one-sidedness of them.

Some young people do go through terrible experiences, and some have remarkable adventures. But in any autobiographical essay, it's always best not to make yourself the hero of your own story. Most readers don't care for braggarts. It should go without saying that you should always tell the truth. I once had a teacher on my staff who loved autobiographical writing. One of his students wrote an interesting personal essay called "House of Cards." In it the student told of an uncle who used to build his young nephews an elaborate house made of playing cards. The uncle allowed his nephews the pleasure of removing a card that brought the whole house down in a heap. The student writer went from that anecdote to some reflections on the human love of destroying things. Later the teacher told me, "You know, the great thing is that he made the whole thing up. He didn't have an uncle, and he never did tear down a house of cards, but isn't it a great idea?" The teacher thought that some "larger truth" was more important than the "facts" in what purported to be an essay. He was not happy at all with my response.

Any writer claiming to write nonfiction must tell the truth. To do otherwise is simply to lie, and writers who lie deserve the unhappy consequences that come when they are found out. One reason journalists are so often scorned in modern America is that they have too often been caught circulating rumor instead of what they know to be true.

Alex Haley made a problem for himself in claiming that he had written *Roots* out of careful historical research. Gradually as the years passed, historians looking for the sources Haley claimed to have located concluded that they did not exist, and after his death, in a careful and distressing article in the *Village Voice* in 1993, Philip Nobile demolished what was left of his reputation, much to the consternation of people like myself who thought they knew Haley well and wanted very much to believe in him.

Students writing autobiographical essays may feel tempted to make things up to add to the drama of their own lives and therefore make themselves seem more important. But if you observe your own experiences carefully and think about them critically, you can write magical essays without telling lies and without making yourself either hero or victim. You can ask yourself, "What really happened?" And then you can ask, "What were my responses? And how should I have responded?" You can also ask yourself about the motives of people you have observed as you infer them from their acts.

Try hard to see the conflicting motives that stir all of us in all our major acts. I often think that the best "autobiography" is in reality a careful observation of others so that the mind and heart of the narrator are reflected not in meditations on his or her soul but in the way that he or she speaks of others.

2. Look for Patterns in the Evidence.

Many writers return to the same themes over and over again, perhaps using the same words to describe them. In writing about people you have known and about your own experience or theirs, you will find that certain of their habits and their acts work out into patterns that help define their personalities and their characters. Pay attention to the obvious. When you see the same words or themes or incidents again and again, ask what they mean. William Faulkner, the Mississippi writer and Nobel Prize winner, wrote about families in many of his books and stories. How were these families alike and how not, and how do his families differ from common conceptions about the family today? One answer is that in Faulkner's world, divorce was rare. What did that mean for the family?

In using the common topic of comparison, one may look at different writers to see how they deal with certain situations. In Faulkner one of the great social situations is drinking whiskey. Drinking becomes the occasion for much dialogue and much action. But in the writing of Toni Morrison, who also won the Nobel Prize, her black American characters share meals where they talk. What can we make of that difference?

Look for silences in the evidence. What did Franklin D. Roosevelt say about blacks, about Jews, and about women in his speeches? Almost nothing. Why? What did American political figures say about Hitler's hostility to Jews in the 1930s? Why did Luther seldom speak of hell when he spoke of his fears before God? Many Southerners to this day claim that the Civil War was about something called "states' rights" rather than slavery. But what issue other than slavery stirred talk about states' rights before the outbreak of war in 1861? I hear only a crashing silence on that issue. The silences are clues to the larger world view of the writer or whoever may be the subject of your inquiry.

3. Learn to Infer.

Inference is one of the surest ways to originality. We'll consider inference again when we talk about argument. But let's consider it here because we can scarcely avoid it in any kind of writing or thinking or indeed in conducting our daily lives.

When we infer we bring previous knowledge and experience to help us understand something new. Inference is basic to all reasoning. It is the skill of Sherlock Holmes on a murder case. It is also the skill of the medical researcher looking for a cure for breast cancer or AIDS. Without inference we merely report facts. But inference suggests what the facts mean. We see smoke and infer fire. We see a woman smile and infer that she is pleased; we see a child cry and infer that it is unhappy. We see two men shouting and shaking their fists at each other beside their cars in the street, and we infer that they are angry. Past experience tells us that people smile when they are pleased, cry when they are not, and sometimes shout at each other when they are angry.

We infer from statistics. Eighty-three percent of the men who die from lung cancer are cigarette smokers. We infer that cigarette smoking causes lung cancer.

We infer from texts. "The Lord is my shepherd," reads the Twenty-third Psalm. "I shall not want. He maketh me to lie down in green pastures; he leadeth me beside the still waters." We infer that the writer of these words lived amid sheep and shepherds and that the first people who heard his song understood him because they were children of a life among pastures and herds in the open air. We can also infer that since God here is masculine, men had a dominant place in the society that produced the Psalm.

The more we know about a subject, the more reliable our inferences. If a scholar has carefully read again and again the thousands of pages left to us by Sir Thomas More, I trust his or her inferences much more than I do the claims of someone whose only knowledge of More comes from the Hollywood movie "*A Man for All Seasons*" or from pictures of More drawn or painted in his lifetime.

Our inferences may be wrong. The woman we see smiling may be hiding anger. The child who is crying may have been told that tears will make a grandparent deliver a present. The two men shouting at each other in the street may be actors in a movie being filmed. The final uncertainty of inference makes some writers afraid to infer. Nobody likes to be wrong. Yet knowledge advances as we test inferences. And it is almost impossible to write an interesting essay without inference. Without inferring, you only report that one thing after another happens, and although happenings can add up to an exciting story, they do not make an essay where the writer must try to make sense of them.

Suppose a teacher asks you to write a 2000-word essay on Shakespeare's *Hamlet.* You will bore her into a trance if you summarize the plot. She's read the play a hundred times. She's seen it on the stage and in various movie versions. She knows what happens, and she has probably memorized many of the lines. If you tell her only what she already knows, your paper is doomed to be as forgettable as last year's TV sitcom.

Your assignment is to write an essay. We write essays to tell readers something they don't already know or else to make them see in a new way what they do know. We write to share our reasoning, our thinking. When they merely summarize the play, student writers make a subtle and lethal change in the assignment. They make it an exam. We read exams only to see if the writer of the exam knows what we know about something. And we read them only because our jobs force us to read them. Not many readers sit down in their easy chairs at night and say, "Well now, I think I'll relax and improve my mind by reading a few exams."

When you begin to infer, you start thinking. If you think, some readers— including your teachers—will be interested in what you have to say. For example, look at these words from Hamlet's famous soliloquy:

To be or not to be: that is the question:
Whether 'tis nobler in the mind to suffer
The slings and arrows of outrageous fortune,
Or to take arms against a sea of troubles,

And by opposing end them? To die: to sleep;
No more; and by a sleep to say we end
The heartache and the thousand natural shocks
That flesh is heir to; 'tis a consummation
Devoutly to be wish'd. To die, to sleep;
To sleep; perchance to dream; ay, there's the rub;
For in that sleep of death what dreams may come,
When we have shuffled off this mortal coil,
Must give us pause.

We have all heard these lines a thousand times. What do they mean? Why is Hamlet not sure that there is life after death? The church of his time taught that eternal life in heaven or in hell was the fate of every mortal. Anyone who denied these doctrines publicly was likely to be put to death by both Protestant and Catholic governments. European governments assumed that no one who denied life after death could be a good citizen. Why does Hamlet not profess that faith? We may infer that the faith in an afterlife was being eroded, that to people of Shakespeare's day death appeared more final, heaven and hell much less certain, than they had appeared in medieval thought. Maybe Hamlet's view was distinctly unchristian. One can go from that inference to an argument about the whole play—and the whole of Shakespeare's work.

A geologist observes a boulder resting on the naked granite of a mountain in New Hampshire and sees that the boulder is unlike the granite and unlike any other of the layers of rock exposed in the state. But the geologist observes that the boulder is exactly like a layer of rock in a part of Canada to the north. She may infer that the strange boulder has been carried to this place by the ice sheets that once covered New England, pushing huge boulders down from the north. Since no one in historical memory ever saw these huge layers of ice cover New England, the entire theory of an ice age rests on the inferences of geologists. A particular inference may stand until someone can come up with another that seems more valid.

Inference is a powerful tool. Be brave enough to infer when you write, and be aware of what you are doing when you use inference.

4. Ask the Journalistic Questions.

Writers ask questions and answer them. The writer who asks the best questions usually writes the best and most original piece.

Journalists are trained to answer these five questions in every story they write: Who? What? Where? When? Why? They are the natural questions of readers. We hear that a friend has had a wreck. What happened? Who was driving? Who was hurt? Who was responsible? When did it happen? When did the police get there? When did the ambulance come? Where did it happen? Where were the injured taken? Why did it happen?

By asking these five questions in multiple ways, you can scan any subject you want to write about and fill out a paper with answers. These questions can help you see a text more clearly and help you define topics for a paper. For example, when you read the short story "A Rose for Emily" by William Faulkner, you can ask the question: Who is Miss Emily Grierson? Answers might run like this:

> She is a woman grown from beautiful youth to ugly old age in a changing Mississippi town.
>
> She is the only daughter of an overprotective and tyrannical father.
>
> She is a member of a family that takes pride in its reputation.
>
> She is a woman with very little money.
>
> She is lonely.
>
> She is unloved.
>
> Her only living companion is a black man who is her servant.
>
> She is a monument of curiosity in the town.
>
> She is a secret murderer.

The list can go on and on. As you write down every variety you can imagine of the question "who?" you begin to see details and meanings that you might easily have overlooked in a first reading. The same process works for the four other questions. As you write the answers to these questions, you begin to see other questions you have not thought of before.

Asking these questions does not end your writing process. You must weave your answers into an essay. In doing that task, you may discover that some answers are unimportant or that they do not fit your purposes. But with the questions before you, you have some raw material to help your thinking.

5. Make Connections between What You Observe and Other Things You Know.

When you read any text, ask yourself how you can bring your larger experience to bear on what you read. If you write for an English class, think of ways to bring in information you learned in history, in philosophy, in physics, in economics, or other disciplines in your paper. Creative people have a mental scanner in their heads that plays across the entire range of their knowledge and experience when they study any subject.

The connective quality overlaps the ability to infer things. You may read Hemingway's *For Whom the Bell Tolls* and may then see the later Hollywood motion picture made from this romantic novel about the Spanish Civil War fought between 1936 and 1939. The Spanish Civil War pitted "Republicans" against "Nationalists." The "Nationalists" under General Francisco Franco were helped by the Nazis under Hitler's command in Germany and Fascists under Mussolini's authority in Italy. The "Republicans" were helped by the Soviet Union, and many of the Republicans were Communists. In the novel, published in 1940, the ideological divisions are clear. In the movie, produced in 1943, they are muddled. Looking at the movie alone, we find it hard to understand what the Civil War was about. Why the fuzziness? Some knowledge of the historical situations in 1940 and 1943 may help you write an interesting paper on this question. With any experience in Spain and in Mexico or other parts of Latin America, you might also notice that the actors in the motion picture are dressed like Mexicans rather than Spaniards and that the "Spaniards" speak English with strong Mexican accents. Such an insight might help you write an interesting paper on cultural criticism.

As I have noted, comparison is one of the "common topics." By comparing one thing with another, you may see them both more clearly. But not every comparison is illuminating. Any two things can be compared, but the comparison helps only if it is significant. You can compare a novel to a train in that each has a beginning that pulls after it a middle and an end. Or you can compare a college education to climbing a mountain in that in the beginning you prepare yourself and start out, in the middle you are tired and discouraged, and at the top you have a view for miles and miles and feel that the struggle has been worth it. But clever as such comparisons may be, they don't do much to help our understanding about anything.

I love reading papers written by those rare students who bring knowledge of other disciplines to papers they write for me—the woman who brings some knowledge of religious studies to her paper on *Hamlet* or the man who uses something learned in a Southern history class to illuminate an essay on William Faulkner. My students don't do this sort of thing enough. My colleagues in other disciplines make the same complaint. The student in a history course doesn't think a reference to literature belongs in a paper about history. The student in literature does not imagine that something learned in economics might help interpret Shakespeare. Therefore when teachers find a paper that reaches across the disciplines, we are likely to leap for joy and show the paper to every colleague we find in the hall.

To live each day we consciously or unconsciously interpret our present experience by comparing it with experiences from the past. The good writer brings that impulse into the assignment to write an essay. Remember that our experience includes everything we read, study, and research. "Experience" doesn't happen only to the body; it happens to the mind. You have experience in reading, in reflection, in conversation. Your experience in writing is as intimate as any experience you have. It is your ceaseless effort to make sense of things and to communicate your understanding to others.

6. Look for Contradictions.

Most interesting topics if probed far enough reveal contradictions and paradoxes. Some things don't add up. Every good reporter learns to interview people with an ear open to contradiction. In a good press conference, reporters ask questions to get the speaker to consider contradictions. "Mr. Vice President, you say you didn't know that these Buddhist nuns were contributing someone else's money to your campaign, but where did you think Buddhist nuns would get so much money to give you?"

Contradictions and inconsistencies may be efforts to deceive, especially among politicians. But they are not necessarily moral flaws. They are simply part of human character. Ralph Waldo Emerson said in his essay "Self-Reliance" "that foolish consistency is the hobgoblin of little minds, adored by little statesmen and philosophers and divines. With consistency a great soul has simply nothing to do." Emerson meant that the ability to be honest in the moment sometimes means that a person will contradict something he or she has said or done in the past. The aim of life, he thought, ought to be honesty rather than an effort to be consistent for consistency's sake alone. Good writers recognize inconsistencies and take them into account, recognizing that some are only part of the human comedy.

Inconsistencies abound in texts, and they may be just the place where careful study may fuel a good paper. In *Utopia* published in 1516, Thomas More had his mythical Utopians practice religious toleration. They had to believe that God exists, that He rewards and punishes human beings in an afterlife, and that He guides the world by His providence. Utopia is an imaginary island off the coast of the New World, and many readers through the centuries have assumed that in this little book More was writing of an ideal society. But when the Protestant Reformation burst on Europe and spread to England, More wrote hundreds and hundreds of fiery pages demanding that Protestants be burned at the stake. While he was Lord Chancellor of England, he supported the burning of several Protestants. What can we do with the contradiction between what More wrote in *Utopia* and what he wrote and did when the Protestants started making converts in England?

Keep your eyes open for disagreements among authorities—another sort of contradiction. Some years ago, a student of mine named Simon Frankel, now a lawyer in California, did a fine paper comparing essays written through the years about *The Age of Jackson,* a book by Arthur Schlesinger, Jr. My student showed that when the book came out, in 1945, scholars praised it. But after this first enthusiasm cooled, they took a second look and began to argue that the book was badly flawed. My student read ten reviews of the book written over twenty years and sketched his findings in an interesting and original paper. Many books about important subjects create arguments among scholars when they are published, and only slowly is a consensus developed. If you survey these arguments and interpret the reasoning behind them, you may make some important contradiction to knowledge yourself.

Never pretend that contradiction and inconsistency in your own evidence do not exist. Knowledge of any subject is partly clear, partly obscure, and partly perverse. We don't know what parts of it mean. Too many writers are like bad mechanics: When something doesn't fit, they look for a bigger hammer. If you try to pound your evidence into a scheme where everything fits perfectly, you are certain to distort the truth. Be bold enough to face contradictions squarely when you meet them. Be honest enough to admit defeat when you cannot reconcile them or explain them. We'll come back to this point when we think about making concessions in arguments.

7. Study Consequences.

We love to know how things turn out. Good papers often establish chains of cause and effect and sometimes try at the end to show some enduring consequences of an act, a book, a battle, a treaty, a court case, a critical appointment, a presidential election, or whatever. Sometimes you may wish to speculate about what might happen if a course of action were adopted. As you will see in the chapter on argument, the connection between cause and effect is often more difficult to work out than it may seem at first glance. The difficulties should not deter you from trying to sort out both cause and effect, for such speculations may enlighten us about the events we study.

In August 1945 the United States dropped two atomic bombs on Japan. The first, on August 6, fell on Hiroshima. Three days later the second fell on Nagasaki. Within a few days the Japanese announced that they would surrender unconditionally. For a half century debate has raged over whether the bombs were necessary to end the war. What were the consequences of the bombs? The war did end, and the United States did not have to invade the Japanese home islands with the immense loss of life on both sides that such an invasion would have caused. But would the war have ended without an invasion and without the atom bombs? Since the atom bombs were dropped, what were the consequences beyond World War II? Some have argued that the horror of the bombs demonstrated by their effects on Hiroshima and Nagasaki has been one of the major reasons atomic weapons have not been used in war since. Is this argument sound?

You can see by this example some of the complications of any question about cause and effect. In previous editions of this book I suggested that students might sometimes write papers asking the question "what if?" In preparing this edition I came across an article in *The New York Times* describing a movement among historians called "counterfactual history." In this group historians ponder questions like these: "What would have happened if Hitler's armies had repulsed the Normandy invasion in 1944?" "What would have happened had the Spanish Armada succeeded in conquering England in 1588?" "What would have happened if Lee had won at Gettysburg?"

We can never answer these "what if" questions to anybody's complete satisfaction. But asking them may help us see more clearly what *did* happen. One of the most famous "what if" essays ever written appears in Virginia Woolf's book *A Room of One's Own.* She poses the question, "What if William Shakespeare had had a sister as gifted as he and as ambitious to become a playwright?" The question allowed Woolf to make a vital critique of the disadvantages women in the Western tradition have faced when they set out to be writers. *The New York Times* article that I have mentioned cites Niall Ferguson of Oxford University in England, who says that the purpose of asking the "what if" question is "to recapture the chaotic nature of experience and see that there are no certain outcomes." "The approach," he says, "is anti-determinist and anti-Marxist."[4] In short, history did not have to be what it became. It is not predestined. Something else might have happened, and then our world might have become dramatically different from what it is.

The "what if" question is playful. But remember that the creative person often has a playful mind, the ability to ask questions that may at first seem nonsensical but then can open a serious inquiry. Never imagine that genius must be somber.

Use your notebook to play with ideas. Scribble notes to yourself that overcome your inhibitions, that ask unanswerable questions, that follow leads that you may think at first are unpromising. As you write, even in play, your mind generates ideas, and some of these may prove to be worth writing about.

WRITING DRAFTS

Finally the moment comes! You sit down and start writing. It's always a good idea at the start to list points you want to cover. A list is not as elaborate as a formal outline. In writing your first list, don't bother to set items down in the order of their importance or even in the order that you will write about them. Simply jot down your main points and trust your mind to organize them. You will probably make a list, mark it up, rearrange things, write it again, study it some more, and perhaps make yet another. You can organize each list more completely than the last. This preliminary process may save you hours of starting and stopping. It may also help to write out a one-paragraph summary of what you intend to do in the paper—or the book. Such a summary will clarify your mind as you start to work.

Stick to the Task

Once you start writing, stay at it. Don't get up until you have written for an hour. Write your thoughts quickly and steadily if you can. Let one sentence give you an idea to develop in the next. Organization, grammar, and even sentence clarity are not nearly as important as getting the first draft "in being." No matter how desperate you feel, keep going.

Keep your mind open to new ideas that pop into your head as you work. If you have made a summary, don't be a slave to it. Writers often do their research and start an essay with one topic in mind only to discover that another topic pushes the first one aside as they work. Ideas you had not thought of before you began writing may pile onto your paper, and five or six pages into your first draft you may realize that you are writing about something you did not imagine when you started.

If such a revelation comes, be grateful and accept it. But don't tear up or erase your draft and start all over again. Make yourself keep writing, developing new ideas as they come. If you suddenly start all over again, you may break the train of thought that has given you a new topic. Let your thoughts follow your new idea, sailing on that tack until the wind changes.

When you have said everything you have to say in this draft, print it out if you are working on a computer. Get up from your desk and go sit down somewhere else to read it, without correcting anything. Put it aside overnight if you can. Many psychological tests have shown that our minds organize and create while we sleep if we pack them full before bedtime. Study a draft just before sleep, and you may discover new ideas in the morning. This sort of discovery has happened to me all my writing life.

The Second Draft

Be willing to make radical changes in your second draft. If your organizing idea changed while you wrote your first draft, base your second draft on this new subject. Even if your major idea has not changed, you may want to move paragraphs around, cut some sentences, or write in some connections to make your paper read more smoothly. Inexperienced writers often suppose that revising a paper means only changing a word or two or adding a sentence here and there. This kind of editing is part of the writing process. But it is not the most important part. The most important part of rewriting is a willingness to turn a paper upside down, shake out of it the ideas that most interest you, and set them down in a readable form that will interest the reader, too.

For me at least the second draft usually involves radical revisions. Now and then you may hit the correct order in your first draft, but for me that kind of luck is rare. In the days before computers when most of us used typewriters, I knew writers who cut up drafts with scissors and pasted them together again in a different form. Word-processing programs have the "cut" and "paste" functions that look back to those days. I used to draw elaborate lines and symbols from one part of a draft to another. Computers allow us to keep a copy of our first draft intact while we make another copy to revise. But computers do not relieve us of the necessity of reading and rereading our work and thinking about it.

Cut to the Chase

Always be firm enough with yourself to cut out thoughts or anecdotes that have nothing to do with your thesis, even if they are interesting. Cutting is the supreme test of a writer. You may create a smashing paragraph or sentence only to discover later that it does not help you advance your thesis. You may develop six or seven examples to illustrate a point and discover that you need only one.

Now and then you may digress. If you digress too often or too far, how-ever, readers will not follow you unless your facts, your thoughts, and your style are so compelling that readers feel drawn along. Not many writers can pull such digressions off; most editors will cut out the digressions even when they are interesting. In our hurried and harried time, most readers get impatient with the rambling scenic route; they want the fastest way to their destination. To ap-peal to most of them, you have to cut things that do not apply to your argument.

The Third Draft

In your third draft you can sharpen sentences, add information here and there, cut some things, and attend to other details to heighten the force of your writ-ing. In the third draft writing becomes a lot of fun. By then you have decided what you want to say. You have a paper in being. You can now play a bit, find-ing just the right word, choosing just the right sentence form, compressing here, expanding there.

I find it helpful to do what I am doing right now with this revision—which for me represents a fourth major draft of this book. That is, I put a printed draft down beside my keyboard and type through the whole thing again as a final draft, letting all the words run through my mind and fingers one more time rather than merely deleting and inserting on the computer screen. Do what works for you.

FINAL COMMENTS ON THE WRITING PROCESS

I have outlined here my own writing process—the one that works for me. You must find the process that works for you. It may be different from mine. A friend of mine tells me that he writes a sentence, agonizes over it, walks around the room, thinks some more, writes the next sentence. He does not revise much. I think it unnecessarily painful to bleed out prose that way. But he bleeds out enough to write what he needs to write. Several friends—older people—tell me they cannot compose at a typewriter. They must first write with a pencil on a yellow pad. Most younger writers learn to compose at a keyboard, and they cannot imagine another way to write. I have composed at a keyboard since I was sixteen. But sometimes I go back to a fountain pen or a pencil and write on a yellow pad or in a notebook for pages at a time. I love to write on airplanes with a yellow pad, and I become extremely surly when my seat companions try to talk to me on long flights. I have written a lot of things in public parks, and once I wrote a successful speech for a government official while sitting on a bench before paintings of Thomas Cole in the National Museum of Art in Washington, D.C. Eventually I put things on the computer. But something about handwriting still grabs me now and then, and I grab a pencil or a pen.

The main thing is to keep at it. B. F. Skinner used to point out that if you write only fifty words a night, you will produce a good-sized book every two or three years. That's not bad production for any writer. William Faulkner outlined the plot of his novel *A Fable* on the wall inside his house near Oxford, Mississippi. You can see it there to this day. Once he got the outline on the wall, he sat down at his kitchen table and wrote, following the outline to the end. If writing an outline on a kitchen wall does the trick, do it. You can always repaint the wall.

Think of writing as a process on its way to a product—sometimes painfully. Don't imagine you must know everything you will say before you begin. Don't demean yourself and insult readers by letting your first draft be your final draft. Don't imagine that writing is easy or that you can do it without spending time on it. And don't let anything stand in the way of doing it. Let your house get messy. Leave your magazines unread and your mail unanswered. Put off getting up for a drink of water or a cup of tea. Don't drink alcohol when you write. Don't make a telephone call. Don't straighten up your desk. Sit down and write. And write and write and write.

Kinds of Writing

I find it useful to classify non-fiction writers as either reporters or essayists. Like most categories, these two overlap. But let's try to think of them as distinct for a moment.

A reporter collects information and presents it much as one does a news story in a daily or weekly paper. The reporter's point of view is in large measure limited to choosing the data, and we all know that choice is important and can be dishonest. But on the surface, at least, the reporter is not personally wrestling with an idea that he or she wants readers to accept in opposition to the ideas of others. Newspaper readers do not read the reporter's story to see what the reporter thinks. They read to see what has happened. When the reporter writes an interpretation, it is usually a quotation or summary of the opinion of an authority. For example:

> Secretary of the Interior Al Dillinger promised today that drilling for oil in Yellowstone National Park will not seriously damage the ecology of the region. "Except for a slight smell of oil in the air and the sound of the drilling machines, everything should go on just as it has," Secretary Dillinger told a press conference this afternoon. Dillinger admitted that drilling might put an end to periodic eruptions of the Old Faithful geyser in Yellowstone. But he said, "Frankly, after all these centuries I think people are tired of Old Faithful. I mean, what is it anyway? It's just hot water. You can get that in your bathtub, and it will be cleaner, too."

Here the reporter lets Secretary Dillinger's words speak for themselves. The reporter does not express an opinion.

But in an essay the writer is the interpreter, thinker, explainer, the authority. The essay inevitably has about it a whiff of argument. It may not present forensic argument against a sharply expressed point of view—although some essays do just that. But in one way or another the essay informs us that the writer has studied the issue or experienced it intimately enough to interpret it. The essay involves a line of reasoning beginning with commonly accepted assumptions and proceeding to consequences that are not self-evident.

What Part Does Our Experience Play?

Some people believe that a good essay must be about the writer's experience, that essays have to be autobiographical or that at least they should include some autobiographical anecdotes. Some teachers say that student writers should shape essays around some image out of the writer's life. Thus a woman battling anorexia might give a new insight into standards of feminine beauty represented in nudes painted by male artists. A young man's recollection of an abusive father might help him interpret some of the fiction of James Joyce. I see such essays coming out of college writing programs, and they make me uneasy. Many examples of such essays seem self-indulgent and narrow, and teachers who give assignments that call forth such essays seem often to think that young writers are too stupid to write well about anything other than something that has happened to them. As I pointed out in the last chapter in writing of one such essay called "House of Cards," the student author felt compelled to make up an anecdote, which he then presented as a true story. This is not a good avenue toward either good writing or good ethics.

In over thirty years of teaching in three schools—a small private college, a large Southern university, and a large private university—my best papers have come from students excited about books, ideas, paintings, architecture, science, history, and a host of other topics that did not require them to make explicit reference to their personal or even intimate experiences. Writers cannot free themselves from their own pasts. But part of becoming educated is to learn to stand off somewhat from ourselves, to bring a certain detachment to the subjects we write about. Certainly it is no part of the definition of the *essay* that it be autobiographical or "familiar" as some writers now call the autobiographical essay. The essence of the essay is that it involves a struggle to explain, to inform, and to suggest. Essays involve efforts to think seriously about important matters.

The Example of Michel de Montaigne

The word *essay* was coined by a Frenchman, Michel de Montaigne (1533–1592), to describe his written reflections on various subjects. His essays resembled public letters about his observations, his reading, and his ruminations. He rambled much more than essayists do now. His thoughts jumped from subject to subject. He was curious, as all good writers are, asking questions and seeking to answer them. His integrity and his wit have made disciples of his thought four centuries after his death.

Montaigne wrote with an independent mind, without accepting the prejudices of the crowd and without seeking the favor of the powerful. His writing is natural, unaffected, simple. "I speak to the paper," he wrote, "just as I speak to someone I meet for the first time."[1] He never talked down to readers. Nor did he pander to their prejudices. He never feared to be in the minority on an issue. He tried to see things as they were, and his observations are still surprising for their freshness. He proved that an honest observer always has something new to say.

He called his pieces *essays* from the French word *essai,* meaning an "attempt" or a "trial." For him an essay was just that—an attempt to think clearly. He was far too humble to claim that he had established truth beyond all doubt. "I freely give my opinions on all things," he wrote, "even those that may go beyond my competence and on which I by no means claim to be an authority. And so my thoughts about them are only to reveal the extent of my vision and not the limits of things themselves."[2] He supposed that he had made an "essay" toward truth—observing honestly, marshaling his evidence, reflecting on his experience, interpreting it as fairly as he could. When he could not answer a question, he admitted his ignorance. He never claimed to have found the truth about everything he considered, although his opinions were strong about some subjects.

He knew his conclusions would not satisfy everyone. Still he advanced them tolerantly, serenely, without insulting foes, without heating his prose with passion except on the rare occasions when he condemned the religious wars burning across France in his time. He was confident without being arrogant. He did not believe he had to save the world. He believed that reason, clearly and gently set down on paper, would win its own battles. He did not try to crush his foes. He remained somewhat detached, like a man calmly taking us across a varied landscape, expertly pointing out features we otherwise might have missed. He claimed not to be an authority, but he was. His opinions demonstrate wide reading and deep thinking.

Most good essays are akin to Montaigne's—civilized efforts to arrive at truth without rancor, without destroying those who disagree. Good essays appeal to the best in readers, to their sense of fair play, to their best emotions, to their wish to do the right thing, to their ability to think.

Now and then you may be tempted to write passionately for a noble cause. Resist the temptation. A few writers manage great passion for great causes, but success is rare in passionate writers because few of them control passion well. Angry passion easily becomes bombast and self-righteousness. Sentimentality often becomes cloying. Most readers dislike prose dipped in syrup. Superheated prose easily becomes embarrassing.

Martin Luther King As Example

One of the greatest essays of modern times is "Letter from the Birmingham Jail," written by the Reverend Martin Luther King, Jr., when he was arrested by a city government whose police chief had turned savage dogs loose on black citizens—including children—peacefully demonstrating for their rights as Americans. Young and old, men and women had been whipped, beaten, bitten, maimed, and killed, and King had every reason to be furious. But his essay does not project fury. Instead it rises to quiet eloquence and power just *because* it is calm and reasonable. King had such confidence in the righteousness of his cause and the fundamental fairness of his readers that he did not have to scream his convictions. The success of the Civil Rights movement in eliminating the worst abuses of segregation in the South is testimony to the triumph of King's vision.

In reading some student papers, I sometimes think that some young writers believe that if they say, "This is stupid" or "This is baloney," readers will immediately say, "Oh my! I thought I was right about this issue, but now I see that Tom Fireball says this opinion is stupid. So it must be stupid." In fact, unless you have tremendous fame and authority, readers will not take your passionate declarations seriously when you make them. Instead they will more likely roll their eyes and pick up something else. When you disagree with something or somebody in an essay, you have to work out the reasons for your disagreement and present these reasons in careful steps, maintaining the calm and the confidence of one who is unthreatened by dissent. Such careful responses can be crushing, memorable, and decisive—as Dr. King's "Letter from the Birmingham Jail" proves.

The best prose is tolerant and cool. If you are temperate and measured and reasoned, and if you think of your reader as a friend to persuade rather than a foe to slay, you will have a far better chance of carrying your point than if you dip your pen in fire and write to burn.

QUALITIES OF THE GOOD ESSAY

1. Most Essays Are Short Enough to Be Read at One Sitting.

Some books may be called *essays* since a serious nonfiction book involves a sustained argument meant to make us accept the writer's view. In the more common meaning of the word, an essay is a shorter nonfiction piece that can be read at one sitting. It is more than a sentence or a paragraph. The length depends on your purposes and your audience, but all of us should recall the sound advice of Polonius in *Hamlet*: "Brevity is the soul of wit." Perhaps the Spanish writer Baltasar Gracian said it even better: "Good things, if short, are twice as good."

For new writers, an assignment to write a 2500-word essay may seem monstrous. Experienced writers find the *short* essay far more difficult. They cannot fit all they know into the space available. They must decide what is most important in what they know and how to present it in the most striking way possible. Every word must count; every sentence must be just right. Every unnecessary word must be chopped out.

2. A Good Essay Gets to the Point Quickly.

Readers want to know right away why they should read your work. Nothing annoys a reader like delay: "What is this writer trying to say?" "Why am I reading this?" Remember "Little Red Riding Hood." In the first couple of sentences, we get to the tension that will be the subject of the story, and we read on. Let your readers know quickly where the tension in your essay lies, and get on with it. Don't keep them waiting. Some inexperienced writers love surprise endings. Avoid them. Your readers will not wait to the end to see what the surprise may be. By then they will not care.

3. Good Essays Have Good Titles.

A good title is part of your beginning. Use it to sharpen your purpose so your readers will know at once why you are writing. Many titles have a colon in the middle. "Your Humble Handmaid: Elizabethan Gifts of Needlework." That was the title of an article by Lisa M. Klein in a recent issue of *Renaissance Quarterly.* Professor Klein wrote about gifts of needlework given to Queen Elizabeth of England in the sixteenth century and about some of the more subtle meanings of exchanging gifts in that time.

Titles in popular magazines often use subtitles. A recent article in *Archaeology* has the title "Looking through Roman Glass." The subtitle reads, "An exhibition explores the impact of glass on Roman daily life."

Take the trouble to give your work a title. When I pick up a paper without a title, I am always almost certain that it will not be as well organized as the paper that comes in with a thoughtful title. Forcing yourself to find a title will be a means of organizing your thoughts better.

4. A Good Essay Stays with Its Subject.

A good essay explores a major theme, perhaps from several angles and perhaps with subthemes. It shows the writer thinking and linking thoughts together. It may develop some ideas only to reject them. Even so, it is finally about one subject. When you check over your final draft, make sure everything contributes to the matter at hand. Don't wander into interesting but inconsequential details. If, for example, you write about how the kings in Shakespeare's history plays claim the right to rule, don't wander off into a general plot summary of the plays that will dilute your main topic. If you are writing about Horatio's loyalty in *Hamlet,* don't wander off into a long discussion of the belief in ghosts in Shakespeare's England. If you want to write about Hamlet's ghost, write about ghosts. If you want to write about loyalty, a discussion of a general belief in ghosts is probably beside the point.

Digression in a rough draft may help you clarify a topic. You may be the kind of writer who wanders all over the place, sniffing out a topic. Fine. But when you write your final draft, you should have decided what you want to say and be able to take your reader directly to it. Look at each sentence, each paragraph, to be sure it serves your purpose. If it doesn't, cut it out—no matter how much you may like it.

Sometimes you may have to digress a bit to make your main point. If you write about Shakespeare's ideas about kingship, you may want to argue that his Richard II is a splendid poet but a bad king. If you go off on a long discussion of Richard's poetry, your reader may lose the thread. But if you give an example or two of Richard's beautiful language and then point out that Shakespeare may be making a distinction between good words and good deeds, you demonstrate to your reader that your apparent digression about Richard's poetry has a point. The principle is this: When you seem to digress, tell your readers why you are doing it and how what you are doing fits your argument.

5. A Good Essay Rests on Solid Evidence.

Some time ago I read an essay that compared the 1960s with the 1980s. It made some points that seemed more or less correct. The 1960s were more sexually free than the 1980s when AIDS became a frightening possibility to those with many sexual partners. The 1960s featured protest on campus; the 1980s were calmer. So it went.

But not once in the essay did the writer quote a text from the 1960s or the 1980s. Not once did he compare films from the two decades. Nor had he tried to compare the art, popular or critically acclaimed, from these two decades. He cited no statistics of any kind. He wrote as if he had only to make a generalization, and readers would accept it because it was a truth everybody agreed on.

In fact, most generalizations we make about reality are flawed. When we look closely at the evidence, we find that all of it does not conform to received opinion. One of the most important parts of your education will be to learn to question generalizations—to decide where they come from, why people make them, and who profits by them. If you keep your mind fixed on the specific, on evidence, you will gain the authority to question these generalizations and to enlighten yourself and others.

Dozens of people through the years have assured me with great head nodding and profound melancholy—and a bit of self-righteousness—that the reason students don't write well nowadays is that they don't study Latin in high school. All students once took Latin as a required subject. I have read a lot of nineteenth-century student papers in classes they took at my university when everyone studied Latin. I doubt seriously that students on the average today write any worse than their ancestors of a century ago. But suppose they do. Is the decline in Latin the cause of this declared decline in English? One way to test the proposition would be to look at journals published in classical studies. Almost everyone who writes articles for such journals knows both Latin and Greek well. Do they write English better? So far as I know, no one has ever made a careful study that would answer this question, but my own skimming of such journals does not encourage me to argue that they are brilliantly written. Lacking any serious study of how well those who know Latin write English, we have only sound and fury when the subject comes up.

One of the best habits you can develop as a writer is to provide a specific example to support every generalization or opinion you put in an essay. My best students pour factual information into their writing. To read their papers is to encounter a real world—the world of people and places, objects and events.

But all teachers read papers—often on topics like abortion, drugs, capital punishment, homosexuality, or whatever—written by students who seem to think that no one else has ever written on these topics. Most university libraries now have their catalogs on-line and available on monitors throughout the library buildings. In many libraries you can type a subject like "abortion" into the computer and find hundreds of books and articles written on the subject in both academic and popular journals. In this computer age, the first obligation of a writer considering a topic is to see what is available in the library on the subject.

Here are a few kinds of evidence to include in your writing.

Experience

As I have said, I don't ask students to write about their intimate experiences in student papers. But if you have had an experience that may enlighten the topic you are writing about, by all means use it. That is just what Montaigne did. If you write about violence in the public schools of America and you happened to have gone to school where kids brought knives and pistols to class, your experience is evidence. You may also have read stories of others who have encountered such violence. Their experience is also evidence.

This anecdotal evidence always needs to be fitted into a larger picture. Anecdotes may give a misleading impression. I was once robbed on a street in Naples, Italy. It was a most unpleasant experience, and the necessity of dealing later with the Naples police made it worse. I was startled by the robbery in broad daylight. I was infuriated by the attitude of the police. But it would be stupid for me to argue in an essay that my experience proves anything significant about Naples, the Italian police, or Italy. I've known a number of people who have been robbed in New York, New Orleans, and even Cambridge, Massachusetts. Nothing so bad has happened to me in any of these cities. One person's experience, related anecdotally, has a certain power in an essay. But don't try to prove too much by it.

Remember, too, that not all experience happens with the body alone; experience can also happen with the mind. Every book and article you read is part of your experience, and when you write, you should be continually on the look-out even in your most casual reading for something you can use in an essay.

Statistics

You often can fit your personal experience into a statistical framework and make the experience more worthwhile in an essay. If you have had a friend or a relative who smoked cigarettes and died of lung cancer, that anecdote in itself might not say much about the relation of smoking to cancer. But when you combine that experience with the overwhelming statistics that show that almost ninety percent of those who die of lung cancer have been cigarette smokers, you have compelling evidence of a relation between cancer and smoking. Other statistics are equally compelling. In baseball, statistics show that left-handed batters are much more successful against right-handed pitchers than against left-handed pitchers. Statistics from various standardized tests show that American students score much lower on average in mathematics than their Asian counterparts; but American students score number one in self-esteem.

Statistical data must be used with care. Someone has said that statistics don't lie but that liars use statistics. Medical researchers remind us continually of the dangers of using statistics improperly. For example, statistics show that adults who take vitamins are generally more healthy than those who do not. But the people who take vitamins are also likely to make a lot more money than people who do not take them, and people who make more money are likely to be more educated, to eat better food, and to have better medical care than those who make less. So statistics about vitamins alone are problematic.

And remember. Statistics seldom apply to every individual in the group. According to statistics, people who exercise regularly and eat and drink moderately live longer than those who don't keep fit and eat and drink too much. But we all know of people who have collapsed and died while they were jogging.

I have more to say about statistics in Chapter 4 in the section entitled: "The Argument from Similitude."

Quotations

If you interpret a literary or historical or scientific text, you must quote from it, providing the exact words that will help us hear a voice or catch a tone or reveal a theme. Vladimir Nabokov, novelist, essayist, and teacher, used to tell his students to begin their study of a novel or story by noting *exactly what the writer said.* This intense preoccupation with exactitude should guide the careful writer in the search for evidence. Study the text, and see exactly what it says. Quote from it to prove your point.

Here are reasons to use quotations:

1. Your source has said something in a striking and memorable way. "Money is sweeter than honey," Ben Franklin said.
2. The quotation confirms a point you have argued or will argue in your essay. News magazines use this technique frequently, and it can work in college essays, too. Suppose you want to argue that watching television is a

mindless habit of the American people. You can cite Jerry Seinfeld as he was quoted in *Time* when he decided to drop his long-running television show.

> "It's a habitual medium," he says matter-of-factly during the course of a long afternoon and evening's interview. "Most people aren't really entertained. What they need is they need to watch TV. Entertainment is almost a luxury item." As the day wears on, Seinfeld returns to the subject, this time even more adamantly: "Television is like a flyer somebody sticks on your windshield. Who gives a damn what's on it? It's iridescent wallpaper. Sometimes I think people just like the light on their faces."[3]

Authorities

Citing an authority on the subject can help you in defining the topics you use in essays. I have mentioned that when you use important abstract words in a paper, you should define them. Sometimes a quotation from an authority may give you the working definition you need. Authorities can also help support positions you take.

Scholars and researchers may be authorities. Authorities may be those who have spent their professional lives doing something of interest to you in writing your essay. The slogan from the 1960s applies here: "Question Authority." A renowned medical researcher is an authority on blood cholesterol. If he says cholesterol is not as dangerous as most medical scientists think, you can use his comment as evidence. But it is not conclusive evidence. The opinion of an authority is only another opinion, respected because we assume that the authority has done something worthy of respect. Authorities can be wrong; they often are. It is best to quote an authority only after you have given other evidence that supports the position you and the authority take.

And remember that an authority in one field is not necessarily an authority in another. Not long ago I looked through a book by a prominent lawyer who argued against Charles Darwin's hypothesis of biological evolution. I was not at all convinced that a lawyer had any scientific competence to denounce Darwinism as it has been developed by thousands of scientists since Darwin. Every working biologist I know of accepts Darwin's fundamental tenet of evolution by natural selection. When a working scientist denounces Darwin, I will take the matter seriously.

6. A Good Essay Considers Any Evidence That May Seem to Contradict the Writer's Major Argument.

If you write on a controversial subject, you will find that other writers have taken a view contrary to your own. You owe it to yourself and your readers to consider contrary evidence and interpretations that contradict your views. Careless or dishonest writers ignore contrary evidence. They imagine that they will weaken their case if they mention arguments that oppose theirs. The opposite is true.

Readers who discover dishonesty in a writer will never trust that person again. But to acknowledge contrary evidence and to deal with it frankly makes a writer credible and helps his or her argument. Yet every year thousands of writers in college courses argue important issues without considering contrary evidence and often without acknowledging that any contrary evidence exists. Important controversial issues seldom have all the good guys on one side and all the bad guys on the other. Papers that assume such a moral division convince only the naive. They do not change the minds of those in the thoughtful audience looking for guidance, the very audience you should be trying to persuade. If you write as if every opponent is a knave or a fool, fair-minded readers will dismiss you and your work.

My students often face a problem within their own heads. They think knowledge ought to be a seamless garment, that all its parts fit so closely together that they leave no room for disagreement among honest people. They want to pretend that they know everything. But knowledge is seldom so tidy, and it is never complete. Knowledge comes in pieces with rough edges and holes, and some pieces are always missing. Honest writers admit the difficulties.

Concession can be a powerful argument. Concede the truth of contrary evidence when you believe it is true. You may argue that it does not damage your case, that even if it is true, it does not mean that your argument is invalid. A California law now forbids smoking in bars. Smokers are outraged that a last refuge has been taken away. They argue that this law infringes on private behavior. You can certainly concede that the law is hard on smokers, but you can argue that the second-hand smoke exhaled by smokers has been shown to be harmful to nonsmokers who must breathe it in poorly ventilated areas. Government regularly intercedes when one's private behavior becomes dangerous to the public. Governments prevent people from playing radios and tape decks on public transportation, and governments impose severe penalties on drunk drivers.

You can also argue that your opponents have misinterpreted evidence that seems to oppose your own argument. Smokers argue that several companies now sell air filter systems advertised to purify air by removing cigarette smoke. You can concede that the filter systems are available and that the advertising does indeed claim miraculous results, but you can counter with the argument that advertising and truth are often two opposite things and that no scientific studies prove that these air filtration systems work.

Never be too proud or too frightened to make a concession. To concede when you must gives the appearance of fair-mindedness and confidence—an appearance valuable in persuasive essays. Strategic concession has been recognized since the orators of ancient Greece as a major strength to both speaking and writing. Those who argue vehemently and blindly for a cause sound like fanatics. Only fanatics listen to fanatics. Your aim should be to attract another kind of reader.

7. A Good Essay Is Written with an Audience in Mind.

Remember your audience, the readers you want to like your work. We have already noted some important questions about audience. What do your readers know? What do they not know? What do you share with them? What will interest them? How can you win their respect?

Test your audience by sharing your writing with friends. Ask them to tell you what your essay says. Don't ask them, "What do you think about this?" Most will reply, "I like it." Friends are like that. They may tell a white lie to make you feel good. When you ask them to tell you what they think you have said, they can't lie. You may then learn much more about your prose. If they can't tell you clearly what you've said, you have to work some more.

Most professional writers share their work with somebody. An acquaintance of mine says he writes for about five women he knows—all of them critical but tolerant. I write for my editor, who has worked with me for twenty-five years. She is a woman of taste and intelligence, not afraid to ask questions, not afraid to tell me she doesn't know what I'm trying to say or that she doesn't know why I'm telling her this or that. I believe that if I can interest her, I can interest others as well. She is also the kind of person I want to read my work, and my sense of her as an educated and intelligent human being makes my writing better than it would be without her.

Writing for an audience does not mean a hypocritical effort to please at any price. You have your own opinions, your knowledge, your ambitions for your writing. Express them to please and persuade people you know. You can take pride in making someone you admire say, "I like this. You have persuaded me."

Respect your audience. Make your audience respect you. Wayne C. Booth, a noted authority on writing, has said that every piece of writing has an "implied author," someone your readers find standing behind the words on the page. Your implied author may not be the person you want to be. Some inexperienced writers think they are being bold and superior when they adopt a slangy style only to discover that their readers find them arrogant, shallow, and tiresome. To reach the widest audience, your own implied author should be sincere, humane, persuasive, tolerant, interested, fair-minded, and honest, showing confidence in the intelligence and fair-mindedness of his or her readers. A little humor always helps.

Don't be cute or silly, but be lively. Write naturally. Use simple words rather than complicated ones—unless your thoughts can be expressed only with complicated words. Don't qualify sentences too much. Don't sound wishy-washy. Write as if you like and trust your readers. Don't show off; don't condescend. Be honest and forthright, simple and direct.

8. A Good Essay Makes Internal Connections and Transitions.

A good essay marches step by step to its destination. Each step will be clearly marked. It will depend on what has gone before, and it will lead gracefully to what comes afterward. Good transitions are essential to good writing. Your readers must follow the development of your subject, and transitions help them see the relation of the parts to the whole. As I said earlier, good transitions are like the yellow arrows painted on the road to show a biking group where it needs to turn to stay on route to the goal.

The verbal signs of these transitions are words such as *because, however, furthermore, so, therefore, and, but, thus,* and *nevertheless.* You do not have to write these words to make transitions. In fact you can kill an essay by writing *therefore, nevertheless,* and *however* too often. But you can imply these transitions in various ways. In a good piece of writing, a reader senses the connections and uses them to move smoothly from one part of the essay to the next.

Here again a good essay resembles a good story. In telling a story, we construct a chain of cause and effect. We say, "This happened, and because of it, the next thing happened, and because of that, yet another thing happened." We usually put down the events in order, and the mind leaps from happening to happening without having to be told, "Then this happened." Were we to leave out a step, the rest of the story would be confusing or incomprehensible or simply dull. Leave the wolf out of "Little Red Riding Hood," and you're left with a little girl who goes through the woods, delivers some cakes to her grandmother, and comes home again. It's as dull as watching a pig sleep. Good fiction involves a connected series of tension-building episodes beginning with the first and going forward to resolution at the end.

A good essay proceeds in much the same way. The essayist may imply something like this throughout: "*A* is true. Because *A* is true, *B* is also true. Because *A* and *B* are true, *C* is also true." Sometimes the connections are more tentative. "*A* is true. If *A* is true, *B* may also be true. If *A* and *B* are true, *C* may also be true." Whether the connections between *A* and *B* and *C* are certain or tentative, you can use them to hold your essay together, moving your reader step by step from one thought to the next. You should review your work section by section to be sure your reader can tell how the parts fit together, how one step leads to another. Each paragraph should flow smoothly out of the paragraph that comes before it. You can usually leave out words such as *therefore* or *furthermore* because your readers should be able to see the connections without them.

All this is to take for granted that the essay moves from point to point. Now and then I get an essay that tells me the same thing over and over again. "William Faulkner writes about a lot of alienated people who find that life is absurd." The statement is true. But too often the student will then do nothing but bring up one alienated person after another. Young Bayard is alienated in *Flags in the Dust.* Quentin Compson is alienated in *The Sound and the Fury.* Darl is alienated in *As I Lay Dying.* Joe Christmas is alienated in *Light in August.* A paper like this ends up as a catalog saying the same thing over and over again but describing different characters. As a reader I want to know what *alienation* means, and I want to ask some questions about the suppositions of alienation. What does it imply about religion, about society, about influences from other writers? And how is the alienation of Quentin different from the alienation of Darl? To read only that this person is alienated and this person is alienated and, oh yes, this person is alienated, too, is to make a list padded out with plot summary. And it is to eliminate the possibility that the essay can move from one level to another, step by step.

9. A Good Essay Does Not Drift without Clear Purpose from Item to Item.

This point is related to the last one. Frequently my students give me what I call the "museum-tour paper." They are the guides; I am the visitor. "Here is an impressionist painting by Renoir," they say. "And here is one by Manet. And look! Here is one by Monet. And look there—a painting by Pissarro."

The "museum tour" may be a plot summary of a literary text. The summary may be loosely united by a broad and general idea. The idea may be so obvious that no one needs to write about it.

> *Macbeth* shows the dangers of ambition. Macbeth is not ambitious until the witches tell him he will be king and that from his friend Banquo a long line of kings will come. After that he gets the chance to kill Duncan, and driven by his wife, he does so and becomes king. But ambition will not let him stop with Duncan. He must kill Banquo and try to kill Banquo's son because having fulfilled one part of the prophecy, he is eager to keep the other part from coming true. His ambition drives him to destroy all his rivals, and so he has the family of Macduff also killed.

All this is true, but anyone can read the play and see that it is true. To make an essay on *Macbeth* interesting, you must find some organizing principle that will help you integrate these various facts. You should not merely lead your readers from the beginning of the play to the end, picking out interesting facts along the way. Remember that a good story—like a good essay—works toward a climax where everything we have been told comes together in a resolution. It is not merely a collection of interesting facts; the facts are organized by the climax, the resolution, by the motive that makes you tell the story.

If you write about *Macbeth* you might take up one of the old definitions of tragedy that requires that we have sympathy with or pity for the tragic hero. In Shakespeare's other great tragedies, audiences feel sympathy for Hamlet's position as the son of a murdered father, or Lear's discovery that the two daughters who claim to love him most cast him out into a storm, or Othello's deception by Iago that makes Othello himself a murderer. But what sympathy can we have for Macbeth? Here is a question worth a paper.

The issue here is analysis. The word *analysis* means that something is broken down into its parts and put together in a different form. When we analyze a text, we break it down into various ideas to help us understand what makes it work. Once the work is broken down, we use it in our papers in a different form. Here is a tip to help you judge your own work to see if you are giving plot summary or a "museum tour." Beware if you find yourself following this pattern: Your essay begins with the beginning of the story or the document; the middle of the essay is about the middle of your document; the end of your essay is about the end of your document. It is not impossible to write a good essay following that pattern, but it is rare. I suggest that you always try to make the form of your essay different from the form of the document you write about.

10. A Good Essay Is Mechanically and Grammatically Correct and Looks Neat on the Page.

Telling a writer to use correct grammar, punctuation, and spelling is like telling a pianist to hit the right notes. We make lots of errors when we write drafts. But we have to care enough about our work to proofread it before we turn it over to the audience for whom it is intended.

The mechanical conventions of writing have developed historically, sometimes without much logic. English spelling seems especially illogical, and whether you spell well or not has nothing to do with your basic intelligence. Some people are bad spellers, and all that means is that they are bad spellers.

Even so, the mechanical conventions are essential symbols of communication, and you must observe them. Otherwise readers will struggle with your prose. If you do not observe the conventions, most readers will suppose you are careless, illiterate, or even stupid. They may also suppose you don't care enough about them to want to give them your best effort. In academe it's not good to make a teacher think you don't care.

By all means learn to use a computer. If you do not know how to do touch typing, learn. Learn to compose at the keyboard. Mark up your early drafts. But when your work goes to your readers, it should be neat, clean, and correct. If you do not respect your own work, others will not respect it either.

Ask your friends to correct your work. They may be able to see it better than you can once you have worked on it a while. I've been responsible for some strong friendships among my first-year students when I have paired them off to proofread the work of one another. Use the dictionary and the spell-checker on your computer's word-processing program. I keep by my keyboard the *Instant Spelling Dictionary* published by Career Publishing of Mundelein, Illinois. It contains 25,000 words without definitions. I can flip through it quickly to discover if I have spelled *dilettante* correctly. I also have a dictionary within reach at every desk and table where I work at home or in my office. Think of your readers. Misspelled words, bad punctuation, the odd use of quotation marks—all make reading hard. Observing the conventions is a form of courtesy.

And by the way. Number your pages. Since the advent of the computer and word processing, I find that most of my students neglect to number the pages of their papers. This is a baffling omission. For some of us it makes commenting on papers difficult, and there is always the chance that papers can be scattered. Computers make numbering pages easy and also mistake-free. Take the trouble to use the format option to insert page numbers.

11. A Good Essay Concludes Swiftly and Gracefully and Mirrors the Beginning.

Conclusions are difficult, and many writers have trouble with them. The conclusion should leave your reader feeling that you have indeed come to an end, that you have said everything that needs to be said, and that your essay stands as a unified whole.

You may conclude in many ways. But almost always your final paragraphs should reflect some of the thoughts you present in the beginning of your essay. An essay is like a snake biting its tail; at the end it comes back to its beginning. Here are the opening and closing paragraphs of a clever article about stamps in a recent issue of *Smithsonian*. The title and the subtitle help guide us to the meaning of the piece. The title is "Stamps—What an Idea!" The subtitle reads, "New commemoratives look like our first stamps which were slow to catch on in 1847." Here is the first paragraph:

> When the United States Post Office issued the first federal stamps 150 years ago, the public response was distinctly, well, lukewarm. No brass bands played. No first day covers were issued. Hardly anybody bothered to use the stamps, though they bore the images of Ben Franklin and George Washington. Up north in Portland, Maine, postmaster N. L. Woodbury didn't even know that the federal government had issued official stamps. He dashed off a note to U.S. Postmaster General Cave Johnson—mailing it without a stamp as was then the custom—to ask whether to honor these "apparently genuine" stamps.[4]

Here is the last paragraph of the article.

> Philatelists lament the arrival of e-mail, television, faxes, express mail and other stampless communication shortcuts, and the new appellation "snail mail" is certainly not a good omen. Nevertheless, the recently issued commemorative Franklin and Washington stamps sold 12,174,540 copies between them just in the 11 days during which the Postal Service made them available.[5]

From this beginning and ending we can tell that the article is about the history of postage stamps in the United States from when they began to be used in 1847 until recent times. We see in these two paragraphs the difference in reception between the first stamps, bearing the likenesses of Washington and Franklin, and a recent commemorative issue of similar looking stamps. The emphasis in the paragraphs is on the difference in the attitude toward stamps in 1847 and today, and we may surmise that the article will speak of other differences between the use of mail in that time and in our own, and so it does. To get this information, we have to read the paragraphs between the beginning and the end, but we can get the gist of the piece by reading those paragraphs alone. The conclusion offers a satisfying means of drawing the end of the essay back to its beginnings.

You may use several different kinds of conclusion. As John Ross does here, you may end with a piece of information that comprises your thesis. The skepticism with which stamps were received in 1847 contrasts remarkably with the over twelve million stamps sold in eleven days 150 years later. Quotations make good conclusions—as they make good beginnings.

It is not good to introduce surprising new information at the end, information that the essay itself has not prepared us to receive, information that provokes us to ask important questions that remain unanswered in the essay itself. If John Ross had concluded his essay with a sentence saying that the government had perfected its fingerprint file so that we now need only impress our thumbs on the corner of the envelope, and the Post Office would send us a monthly bill, many of us would sit up straight in our chairs and shout, "What?" This startling new information would seem to us much more important than a lighthearted history of stamps, but such a conclusion would leave us unsatisfied.

Avoid the blueprint ending, the deadly dull summary that is the consequence of lazy thinking.

> I have told you about the World Series. I have given the scores of all the games, and I have told you many interesting stories about players, managers, and fans, and I have told you which team emerged as world champion.

Ugh.

CONCLUDING REMARKS ON THE ESSAY

We take for granted our amazing ability to recognize different forms of literature when we read them. We recognize poetry when we see it; we know we are reading fictional prose or a play. We may not know whether the fictional prose is a short story or a novel if we read one page taken at random from the whole. But we know we are reading fiction unless the author has made a deliberate attempt to deceive us in supposing that he or she is writing about truth. Fiction usually tells us by its form that it is fiction.

We also know quickly when we read nonfiction, even if we pick up a piece and start in the middle without having any idea of the title or the author. We may not know whether it is an essay or a book, but we know that the author intends to make us think we are reading something "true" or "real."

The essay belongs to the general family of nonfiction. But it relies on fictional techniques in that like a good story it begins with something out of order and attempts to explain or fix the problem. Readers begin essays with certain expectations shaped by their previous reading. If they do not find these expectations fulfilled, they stop reading. I have tried to summarize these expectations in this chapter. Check your own essay against my list, and revise accordingly.

The essay will be useful to you throughout life, for in one form or another it is essential to business, to government, and to the professions. Develop the habit of studying essays you find enjoyable to see how the writers achieve the effects that make you appreciate their work. Check the advice in this chapter by studying any essay you enjoy to see how it is put together. As you become more aware of the habits of good writers, you will become a good writer yourself. Your own prose will reflect what you read. Be a good reader, and you will not need this or any other textbook to help you write well.

Making Arguments

All essays make arguments. A good term paper, an M.A. thesis, a dissertation, or a book does not merely report facts. The writer argues that the facts should be understood in a special way. Good writers interpret the facts, and all interpretations are arguments. Some writers have said that all writing argues that we should do something or believe something.

Such a general definition of an argument does not mean that to argue you must find a foe and attack. If you interpret a new author's work, one about whom little or nothing has been written, you do not have to attack other interpretations of that work, for none may exist. The most fundamental meaning of argument is an assertion of a point of view. "This is what the facts mean."

But by popular habit, argument usually does mean disagreement when we strive to prove that an opponent is wrong and that we are right. Some people dislike argument just because it may become pugnacious. But *argument* is a civilized term. We make arguments instead of war. In a democracy we persuade people rather than beat them into submission. Candidates argue that they are more qualified than their opponents. Elected representatives argue that their policies are better than the alternatives. Lawyers and judges argue about what laws mean and whether certain acts violate the laws or not or whether someone is guilty of this or that crime. Citizens argue with each other about what's wrong with society—or with music or with literature or with the Boston Red Sox or with the pastor, priest, or rabbi, or with American cars, or . . . The list is as endless as human interests. In tyrannies, arguments are limited. Democracy is unending disputation.

Argument depends on some form of logic, based on evidence, to reach plausible conclusions from the available evidence. Persuasion is a larger category, involving all the means of getting people to take your side. A logical construction of existing evidence indicates that cigarette smoking is dangerous to good health. The tobacco companies try to persuade young people to smoke by offering ads showing manly looking cowboys on horseback or else athletic women with tennis racquets puffing away with no ill effects that anybody can see.

Television, movies, advertising in the print media, roadside signs, and most political speeches as well as many other "texts" in our society try to persuade without offering much logic. They use subliminal techniques that vary from age to age—vivid or quiet ways of presentation that we take for granted merely because they are repeated again and again. In his absurdly paranoid film *JFK* on the assassination of President John F. Kennedy, Oliver Stone took up the fantastic conspiracy theory of a New Orleans district attorney named Jim Garrison. Garrison tried to prove that Kennedy was assassinated by a conspiracy organized by right-wingers afraid that Kennedy would withdraw American troops from the Vietnam War. Garrison also saw the assassination as part of a homosexual plot against Kennedy. In real life Garrison became a laughing stock, and a case he brought against a man named Clay Shaw was thrown out of court. But Garrison's fantasy became the stuff of Stone's movie. Kevin Kostner played the part of Garrison, and Stone gave him a house with a picket fence, a loving family, and a large shaggy dog that Kostner/Garrison patted at moments in the film. Stone's subliminal persuasion worked to argue that a man who likes dogs and lives in a house with a picket fence can't be a liar.

So in many ways argument works to counter persuasion. Argument presents carefully sifted evidence and a logical sequence of examination against the facile and often subliminal efforts of persuasion. Arguments must be explicit. A lawyer making a case for a client accused of robbery argues either that the client is innocent or that mitigating circumstances require judge and jury to consider this no ordinary robbery.

You cannot argue well against positions that no one defends. Few activities bore a hard-working college teacher more than to read papers that argue safe and obvious points of view. "Economics is important to society." "Shakespeare wrote some interesting plays." "Dickens often treated poverty in his novels." Few things please readers (including your teachers) more than papers that make original and unexpected arguments. "Some people may be allergic to exercise." "King Lear got what he deserved."

Finding a good argument is a function of reading carefully and thinking about what you read. In cultivating the ability to argue, you ought to read newspaper editorials, columns, letters to the editor, and the op-ed pages of newspapers. Here you will find lots of arguments about many matters. Read carefully to see what writers choose to write about, where their positions seem to be strong, and where they seem to be weak. It is often disappointing to discover that people who write arguments in newspapers, even professional journalists, often argue from flawed premises or with distorted versions of the evidence. It's a good habit to read with an eye to discovering the weakness in argument, for then slowly you will learn to make your own arguments much stronger.

WRITING A GOOD ARGUMENT

1. Begin on Ground That the Writer and Readers Share.

This step might be called, "Begin with premises you share with your audience." Premises are the starting points of arguments, and you cannot argue without them. They are the assumptions that stand behind many statements in ordinary language, and we must identify them before we can even have an argument.

Suppose I suggest we go to lunch and I say, "By the way, it's raining. Be sure to bring your umbrella." The premise of this statement is something like this: "Rain is unpleasant. You don't want to get wet from rain. Since umbrellas protect us from rain, you can avoid this unpleasantness by carrying one." But suppose you like rain and love being wet, even when you are fully dressed. For you at least the premise is faulty.

In fact most of us don't like to get wet when we are fully clothed, and the premise behind the statement, "It's raining; be sure to bring your umbrella," is a good one. The best arguments begin with premises the writer assumes are shared by many readers who must then be convinced that those premises lead plausibly to conclusions the writer wants to draw from them. In every worthwhile argument, some people have already made up their minds for or against the proposition being debated. The writer aims at the great undecided middle group and hopes to lead the people in it to the writer's side.

Never begin an argument by assuming either that everyone agrees with you or that everyone disagrees with you. Don't condescend, and don't scream in outrage. Don't treat your foes like fools or criminals. The best arguments assume that reader and writer share some values, some information, some interests, some purposes—and some premises.

I have already mentioned Dr. Martin Luther King's "Letter from the Birmingham Jail," written on April 16, 1963, when Dr. King had been arrested for leading nonviolent demonstrations against racial segregation in Alabama. A group of white ministers of religion had taken out an ad in a newspaper objecting to his tactics of nonviolent confrontation with the authorities—nonviolent at least on Dr. King's side and the side of his followers. These ministers of religion wanted to postpone racial integration of schools and other public places in the South, and in particular they opposed Dr. King's decision to make Birmingham a focus of the civil rights struggle.

Dr. King might have begun his response to these ministers with a withering denunciation of their hypocrisy. Could they believe in the loving God of Jews and Christians and support not only racial segregation but the lynchings, the police dogs, the beatings, the threats, and the mockery that enforced racism in the South? Dr. King could have made a head-on attack. He might have insulted these ministers with a sarcasm that raised blisters on their souls.

Instead he began gently by calling attention to the religious language he shared with these ministers. They all accepted the God of Judaism and Christianity. From this common premise, he argued that they should also share his goal—equal justice for all God's people. His argument and his gentle tone made this appeal a classic, one reprinted in countless schoolbooks.

Now and then you can make a frontal assault on your opponents, displaying anger, contempt, and righteous indignation. But you can do so only if you are sure that the readers you want to reach are already emotionally aroused about the issue and if you are sure that your evidence overwhelmingly supports your side. I don't feel that much good is served by being gentle with American politicians whose greed and dishonesty erode trust not only in our government but in democracy itself. I think most Americans feel as I do, and a smashing attack on such dishonesty might have the effect of rallying those of us who feel helpless and betrayed by our elected officials. And maybe reform would result. Winston Churchill's contemptuous assaults on Adolf Hitler united the English people against Germany during the gloomiest days of World War II. He balanced his invective with eloquent depictions of the peaceful and just world that would come with victory over Germany and Germany's allies.

But remember! Few arguments can count on this emotional support from those who read them. Most arguments are efforts to clarify issues on which honest people disagree. Most arguments about academic subjects are like this. Even an emotionally charged historical argument such as the American motives for dropping the atom bombs on Japan should, in the minds of most people, be approached with civility. When you enter such an argument, you look like a fool if you demonize your opposition. So look for common ground with your readers. Most readers hate shrill, discourteous, and angry arguments. Even when readers agree with you, most will feel uncomfortable with a diatribe. Remember that people want to believe that something in you, the writer, is akin to them. Not many of us want to believe that we are mean and ugly, ungenerous and spiteful. We like to think that we are reasonable, civil, and generous.

The tone of your beginning is as important as the premises you assume you share with your audience. Many speakers establish a common ground with their audience by beginning with a joke. Laughter unites audience and speaker and disposes the audience to listen to the rest of the speech. Writers seldom begin with jokes. But as you may see in Appendix 2, "How to Begin—and How Not to Begin—an Essay," writers may begin with stories, quotations, statements of fact, or interpretations of fact that will attract readers' attention and reveal common premises. The beginning says to readers, "We share something; we are alike; go with me and give me a chance to prove that I am right on this issue."

When you begin well, you dispose your audience to consider your position, and then your argument is half won. If at any time in your writing you break the bond between yourself and your readers by making unfair and offensive remarks, you will lose them unless your evidence and your arguments are so compelling that they must keep going.

I have spent so much time on this issue because, in my experience, incivility is the single greatest flaw in the arguments of inexperienced writers. Inexperienced writers seem often to feel that blazing emotion is the best way to victory, and they seem to take pleasure in pouring out on the page a thunder of passionate certainty that they would never use in conversation with adults whose respect they desired. I find that most such passion comes because the writer who uses it has not done his or her homework. Such emotional and insulting outbursts on the page remind me of the old story of the Puritan preacher's note in the margin to his sermon manuscript: "Argument weak here; shout like hell." Here the person who argues should remember one of the best pieces of advice given in the Bible: "In quietness and confidence shall be your strength." Good writers can be quiet and confident because they have worked hard to study the evidence and to present it in a reasonable and convincing way.

2. Be Precise and Fair-Minded When You Argue.

An argument moves from premises through argument itself and comes to a conclusion. Always define your premises and your major terms early in your essay. Be clear on what you assume you share with your audience. A sharp definition helps put you and your readers on common ground. Arguments often go astray because various readers define words differently. When you define your terms, you help yourself and your readers stay on track.

The art of definition can be tricky, and in most arguments definitions you pull out of a dictionary are rarely good enough to use. Words have histories, and essayists must consider the details of those histories much more fully than writers of dictionaries can cram into the small space allotted to a dictionary definition. The historical development of words gives them "connotations," hard or soft meanings that get attached to the root meaning of the word and so affect the way we understand it. *Ask, beg, demand,* and *require* all have a similar root meaning, but the connotations of each are different. I will ask a friend to come to dinner. I will beg my wife to let me buy a blue-tick hound. I will demand that my neighbor quit playing the tuba at three o'clock in the morning. I will require my students to write a paper every week. Dishonest writers often use catchall words that damn the opposition. Before the argument begins the words have bad connotations.

When I was in college in the 1950s *socialism* was a bad word, and the American Medical Association frightened people with the term *socialized medicine* when government made any effort to provide health care for American citizens. Now we have Medicare and Medicaid, popular government programs that no one calls socialism. Instead the bad word is now *liberal* or *liberalism,* and politicians avoid these terms as if they were profane or obscene or worse, some contagious disease that might infect both a speaker and everybody in the audience if they were spoken. As a Southerner I recall vividly that anybody below the Mason Dixon line who stood up for racial integration of the public schools and public transportation was likely to be called a *Communist.* In the 1960s students were likely to call anyone a *Fascist* who supported the presence of ROTC on campus.

These examples illustrate a danger to avoid in argument. Make your argument as specific as possible, and avoid large, general words that are more likely to confuse than enlighten. Fair-minded readers know that words like *liberalism* or *reason* or *gothic* or *baroque* or *socialism* or *communism* or *liberal* or *romantic* have historical connotations. To say that Johnson is *romantic* may mean that he has told his girlfriend that his love for her will outlast the mountains. But his English teacher could also say Johnson is *romantic* because he thinks he can write a paper on *Hamlet* without reading the play. In both examples, the word *romantic* implies something unreal, but the differences in the reality are considerable.

Be cautious in using terms that cannot be precisely defined, even if the terms are common. Someone writes, "Machiavelli's little book *The Prince* was a typical product of the Italian Renaissance." But what does *typical* mean here? And what was the Italian Renaissance? So many people have given so many different definitions of *Renaissance* that it is impossibly vague to say that any book was "typical" of the period. Spell out the definition you mean, and say something like this: "Machiavelli's *The Prince* describes the practice of Italian rulers during the Renaissance whose only value was to get and hold power." A brief, precise definition sets your argument better than the effort to use a vague label that may give a misleading or even dishonest impression.

Often the best definition includes ambiguities and other difficulties, and writers have to take these slippery matters into account in the same way that Professor Gilbert Allardyce introduces his article, "What Fascism Is Not: Thoughts on the Deflation of a Concept." Here are some of his ruminations about a definition, explaining why his article undertakes a much more precise definition of a much used word—*Fascism.*

> "Perhaps the word fascism should be banned, at least temporarily, from our political vocabulary," S. J. Woolf wrote in 1968. Historians who have confronted the problem of defining this mulish concept may sympathize with this modest proposal. Unfortunately the word "fascism" is here to stay; only its meaning seems to be banned. Nevertheless, the German philosopher-historian Ernst Nolte is probably correct in stressing that historians do not have the responsibility to invent new terms simply because the existing ones are inadequate. But they do have the responsibility to confess how truly inadequate the term fascism has become; put simply, we have agreed to use the term without agreeing on how to define it. This article is concerned with the reason for this unfortunate state of affairs.[1]

What Allardyce says about Fascism should be a warning to all of us when we are tempted to substitute labels for argument. To call somebody a "liberal" or a "conservative" or whatever else you might choose as a label does not win an argument; it usually only creates conflict. If you argue a controversial topic such as the place of prayer in the public schools, you don't get anywhere by calling those who want school prayer fanatics or those who don't want school prayer atheists. Such names hurled in print are the equivalent of a screaming contest in the street. Nobody wins.

Instead you have to ask questions like these: What do we want schools to be? The answer to this question—whatever it is—provides the fundamental premise to your argument. Does prayer contribute to what we want schools to be? Does it detract? It is a neutral matter? What are the consequences of having prayer? What are the consequences of not having prayer? These questions should be answered by specific examples, drawn from real life. They should not be answered by abstract reasoning. What have the courts ruled about school prayer? Why is the issue so emotional? What is the best way to deal with an emotional issue like this one?

Many more questions can be asked of this topic, but in the very effort to answer the questions, we cool the discussion down and start arguing toward some agreement. We stop shouting at each other in the street.

3. Use Evidence.

Here we return to a point made earlier in this book. Writers must know things. They must quote texts. They must tell stories about real people. They should use statistics. You should buttress your arguments with the testimony of experts who have spent years studying the subject or who have had direct experience with it. You cannot toss a good argument off the top of your head.

Let's read and then analyze an argument on a controversial subject— legalization of drugs in the United States. The argument was written by Milton Friedman, a senior research fellow at the Hoover Institution in California who won the Nobel Prize in economics a few years ago. Here is what Friedman says:

> Twenty-five years ago, President Richard M. Nixon announced a "War on Drugs." I criticized the action on both moral and experiential grounds in my *Newsweek* column of May 1, 1972, "Prohibition and Drugs":
>
> > On ethical grounds, do we have the right to use the machinery of government to prevent an individual from becoming an alcoholic or a drug addict? For children, almost everyone would answer at least a qualified yes. But for responsible adults, I, for one, would answer no. Reason with the potential addict, yes. Tell him the consequences, yes. Pray for and with him, yes. But I believe that we have no right to use force, directly or indirectly, to prevent a fellow man from committing suicide, let alone from drinking alcohol or taking drugs.
> >
> > That basic ethical flaw has inevitably generated specific evils during the past quarter century, just as it did during our earlier attempt at alcohol prohibition.
>
> **1. The use of informers.** Informers are not needed in crimes like robbery and murder because the victims of those crimes have a strong incentive to report the crime. In the drug trade, the crime consists of a transaction between a

willing buyer and willing seller. Neither has any incentive to report a violation of law. On the contrary, it is in the self-interest of both that the crime not be reported. That is why informers are needed. The use of informers and the immense sums of money at stake inevitably generate corruption—as they did during Prohibition. They also lead to violations of the civil rights of innocent people, to the shameful practices of forcible entry and forfeiture of property without due process.

As I wrote in 1972, "addicts and pushers are not the only ones corrupted. Immense sums are at stake. It is inevitable that some relatively low-paid police and other government officials—and some high-paid ones as well—will succumb to the temptation to pick up easy money."

2. Filling the prisons. In 1970, 200,000 people were in prison. Today, 1.6 million people are. Eight times as many in absolute number, six times as many relative to the increased population. In addition, 2.3 million are on probation and parole. The attempt to prohibit drugs is by far the major source of the horrendous growth in the prison population.

There is no light at the end of that tunnel. How many of our citizens do we want to turn into criminals before we yell "enough"?

3. Disproportionate imprisonment of blacks. Sher Hosonko, at the time Connecticut's director of addiction services, stressed this effect of drug prohibition in a talk given in June 1995:

> Today in this country, we incarcerate 3,109 black men for every 100,000 of them in the population. Just to give you an idea of the drama in this number for incarcerating black men is South Africa. South Africa—and this is pre-Nelson Mandela and under an overt public policy of apartheid—incarcerated 729 black men for every 100,000. Figure this out: In the land of the Bill of Rights, we jail over four times as many black men as the only country in the world that advertised a political policy of apartheid.

4. Destruction of inner cities. Drug prohibition is one of the most important factors that have combined to reduce our inner cities to their present state. The crowded inner cities have a comparative advantage for selling drugs. Though most customers do not live in the inner cities, most sellers do. Young boys and girls view the swaggering, affluent drug dealers as role models. Compared with the returns from a traditional career of study and hard work, returns from dealing drugs are tempting to young and old alike. And many, especially the young, are not dissuaded by the bullets that fly so freely in disputes between competing drug dealers—bullets that fly only because dealing drugs is illegal. Al Capone epitomizes our earlier attempt at Prohibition: The Crips and Bloods epitomize this one.

5. Compounding the harm to users. Prohibition makes drugs exorbitantly expensive and highly uncertain in quality. A user must associate with criminals to get the drugs, and many are driven to become criminals themselves to finance the habit. Needles, which are hard to get, are often shared, with the predictable effect of spreading disease. Finally, an addict who seeks treatment must confess to being a criminal in order to qualify for a treatment program. Alternatively, professionals who treat addicts must become informers or criminals themselves.

6. Undertreatment of chronic pain. The Federal Department of Health and Human Services has issued reports showing that two-thirds of all terminal cancer patients do not receive adequate pain medication, and the numbers are surely higher in nonterminally ill patients. Such serious undertreatment of chronic pain is a direct result of the Drug Enforcement Agency's pressures on physicians who prescribe narcotics.

7. Harming foreign countries. Our drug policy has led to thousands of deaths and enormous loss of wealth in countries like Colombia, Peru and Mexico, and has undermined the stability of their governments. All because we cannot enforce our laws at home. If we did, there would be no market for imported drugs. There would be no Cali cartel. The foreign countries would not have to suffer the loss of sovereignty involved in letting our "advisors" and troops operate on their soil, search their vessels and encourage local militaries to shoot down their planes. They could run their own affairs, and we, in turn, could avoid the diversion of military forces from their proper function.

Can any policy, however high-minded, be moral if it leads to wide-spread corruption, imprisons so many, has so racist an effect, destroys our inner cities, wreaks havoc on misguided and vulnerable individuals and brings death and destruction to foreign countries.[2]

Now let's analyze how Friedman's argument works. First, he is writing on the op-ed page of a newspaper that goes to readers who keep up with current events and know already many of the terms he uses because they have been the stuff of the daily news.

They know that "Prohibition" was the effort to ban alcoholic drinks from the United States by the Eighteenth Amendment to the United States Constitution ratified in January 1919. Gangsters such as Al Capone then took over the distribution of alcoholic drinks to millions of Americans who insisted on drinking despite the law, and murderous gang wars racked many large American cities. The Eighteenth Amendment was repealed by the Twenty-first Amendment ratified in 1933. Friedman's readers also know that "Crips" and "Bloods" are the names of street gangs that deal drugs in big cities. And they know that the Cali cartel is an organization that refines and transports cocaine and other drugs that originate in Colombia.

One premise of Friedman's argument is that drugs are bad and that we would like to keep people from using them. This premise is widely accepted by Friedman's audience. I can't imagine that his readers would accept a premise that drugs are great and that everybody ought to use them. He certainly would not attract me by such a premise, and I doubt that more than a tiny fraction of the readers of *The New York Times* would have patience with it either. Remember, an argument is like any other kind of essay. It begins by drawing a circle of agreement around writer and reader, and Friedman makes it clear that he is no advocate of drug addiction.

Another premise is that we should choose the means of control that does the least possible harm. This is a premise that might provoke more opposition, for the definition of "the least possible harm" might differ from person to person. Many Americans think that drugs are so immoral that to allow them any legality is to compromise the moral quality of society itself. But it's just this premise that provides the jump-off point for Friedman's argument. He wants to show us that in fact the war against drugs does a great deal of harm.

So his argument consists in this: To make drugs illegal does more harm than good. That argument is then supported by evidence. The evidence Friedman adduces is a collection of effects that he considers more immoral than legalizing drugs. That evidence includes seven pieces of factual information. Some of his evidence includes facts that are well known to readers of newspapers and viewers of televised news. Some of his evidence is statistical. Some of it is comparative. We have a great deal of information in this brief essay—some of it startling.

Note that his argument is limited. He does not suggest how drugs might be distributed legally or what counseling and other forms of education might be used to keep drugs from becoming more popular than they are now. These considerations are not part of Friedman's argument. He limits his argument to one major effort: To prove that making drugs illegal causes more harm than good.

Your arguments should follow a form that is at least roughly similar to Friedman's argumentative form here—even if you want to argue against his position, as you may very well wish to do. You should begin with a unifying premise and move from it to your argument, which you support by as many kinds of evidence as you can bring to bear in the space you have. Friedman has managed to compress a lot of evidence in a very small space—about three typed pages if you consider it in relation to assignments you may turn in to your teacher in a college classroom.

ARGUMENTS IN VARIOUS DISCIPLINES

I have always doubted that the requirements for writing in various disciplines were really different from one another. In my view, the writer of a paper on English literature makes arguments in much the same way as does the scientific theorist. Each gathers information by careful study, and each tries to discover some pattern as yet undiscovered by others. If the writer about English literature and the student of natural science study the data carefully, they come to a creative moment, an instant of illumination, when they see a pattern of connections and everything suddenly makes sense. As I say time and again, much of the study involves writing down observations in a notebook.

Charles Darwin kept notebooks all his life. In his youth, on the five-year voyage around the world in the ship *Beagle* (1831–1836), he noted—sometimes with the aid of drawings—small differences between the beaks of birds on the Galapagos Islands and their cousins on the distant mainland of South America. He wondered what caused those variations. The birds' beaks were by no means the only biological problem he found on those blackened volcanic chunks of land sticking out of the blue Pacific. But they loomed large in his mind. He decided that at some earlier time the birds on the islands had been identical to birds on the mainland. But through generations of isolation in a different environment, a new species had evolved, similar to the species on the mainland but differing from them in many features, including their beaks. Species were not fixed eternally. All living things were in continual random change through successive generations.

Darwin knew that changes from generation to generation were a normal part of life. Children resemble their fathers and their mothers, but no child is an exact copy of either parent. Darwin's next step was to assume that some of these random and natural changes aid organisms—plants and animals—in their struggle for survival. The organisms that survive have progeny that may likewise have a slight advantage in the battle to live and to produce offspring. These were the building blocks that he finally put together in *The Origin of Species,* one of the most revolutionary books of all times—and one of the most controversial. It is also a readable book. Darwin presents in it a staggering quantity of data in a style that allows readers with little scientific knowledge to understand his theory. Whether one agrees or not with Darwin, honest people seeking an understanding of the world of living things must take his work with the greatest seriousness. Our own creative insights must also come from wrestling with what we know, an effort to fit the pieces of our knowledge together in some unifying system that we can then patiently argue in a book or an essay.

The Origin of Insight

How does insight come? What makes information suddenly leap together to form a pattern in the writer's mind? No one can give a precise answer. "The light dawned" is a common cliché to describe what happens. Always the light dawns after hard work—observing, assembling data, thinking, worrying, proposing various patterns to see what seems to embrace most of the data and what theory provides the most plausible explanation for what we observe.

The creative process in any discipline depends on asking questions after close observation. Darwin noticed the differences in the beaks of birds, birds obviously akin to each other. The birds on the Galapagos Islands had developed differently from the birds on the distant mainland. Why? Other people had not noticed the differences. Darwin not only noticed but asked himself that important question: Why? Why? Why? Years passed before he had a theory that would give him an answer.

Literary scholars and historians follow much the same practice—close observation followed by an effort to account for the facts. Critic Cleanth Brooks, studying William Faulkner's novel *Absalom, Absalom!* in the early 1960s, realized that Faulkner does not tell us exactly why Henry Sutpen shot Charles

Bon to death at the end of the Civil War just as Bon was about to marry Henry's sister Judith. Two college boys, Quentin Compson from Mississippi and his roommate Shreve McCannon from Canada, take fragments of the story as Quentin knows them and try to make sense of them. They spin out hours of speculation and finally arrive at a plausible theory that explains what happened. But Brooks pointed out that we do not know finally if their solution to the mystery is correct.

Most of us reading *Absalom, Absalom!* for the first time overlook the significance of how the story is told. Brooks remembered the detective stories most of us read at one time or another in our lives. He said that *Absalom, Absalom!* is like them. But in the detective stories written by great practitioners such as Agatha Christie, all the clues are wrapped up in the end, and readers feel a satisfaction in knowing what happened. Brooks realized that Shreve and Quentin have a lot of clues, but that Faulkner does not let us know whether their "solution" to the mystery in *Absalom, Absalom!* is the right one.

So the book becomes a lot like our own lives where we know fragments of stories about our parents and their parents before them, but we do not quite know how those fragments fit together in a coherent whole. Why did my father decide to come to America? He told me a simple story which I later discovered reason not to believe when I had long talks with his brother and sister in Greece. To this day I'm not quite sure how to fit all I know together, although I have tried and have published the results. If we look hard enough, we can dig up fragments of mystery in all our families that we cannot finally resolve. And that is what Faulkner does in *Absalom, Absalom!*; he gives us a mystery that the young men work hard to solve, but we are not quite sure that they succeed. Brooks brought together his own experience of reading his detective stories and reading Faulkner, and he wrote a brilliant essay published first in the Spring 1962 issue of the *Sewanee Review.* The insight came to him after reading his sources again and again.

The question "What exactly happened?" posed by Quentin and Shreve— and by Cleanth Brooks in studying the book where they appear as characters— is not far different from the questions historians and scientists ask of their material. When the great ship *Titanic* sank on its first voyage in April 1912 after hitting an iceberg in the North Atlantic, a multitude of legends sprang up about the last hours of the ship. Hollywood made much of these legends in its many efforts to put the story on film. One was that women and children were put into the lifeboats first while men bravely stayed with the ship to the end. The legend is only partly true. Women and children were most likely to have been put in the lifeboats if they were traveling first class. Women and children who happened to be immigrants coming to the United States and traveling cheaply in steerage in the lower depths of the ship died at a great rate. The recent popularity of the latest *Titanic* movie shows the enduring power of many legends about the disaster. Historians try to penetrate those myths to discover what really happened, and although they can set aside some of the untruths of history, they are—like literary critics—left with unanswerable questions. To admit the unanswerable questions is part of the honesty of writing. You as a writer must search for the best evidence you can find in the best sources you can find, and you must try to tell the truth.

THE RHETORIC OF ARGUMENT

Evidence is the supporting stuff that makes an argument possible. What we do with evidence may be called the *rhetoric of argument*—how we present the evidence in a persuasive way. The rhetoric of argument is based on inference. (I discussed inference at length in Chapter 2.) We argue only when a conclusion is not obvious, and inference is our major tool in understanding things we cannot confirm by direct observation.

The "A Fortiori" Argument

A fortiori is a Latin term that means "to the stronger." Stripped down, the *a fortiori* argument reads like this: "If we know that *A* is true, it is all the more likely that *B* is true." In Chaucer's *Canterbury Tales,* the "poor parson of the town," explaining his longing to be virtuous, used this metaphor: "If the gold rust, what shall the iron do?" He counted the priests as gold in English society, the ordinary folk as iron. If priests become corrupt, how much more likely is it that the people to whom priests minister should also be evil. That is the *a fortiori* argument.

We use the *a fortiori* argument often in daily life. If we contemplate becoming medical doctors and almost fail organic chemistry, we are likely to take stock and say to ourselves, "Hey, if I barely pass organic chemistry, it's going to be a lot tougher for me to get through all those other complicated science courses I'd have to take in medical school." So we may decide to become writers instead.

Lawyers frequently use the *a fortiori* argument in court. "We know that the accused lied when he denied he was having an affair with the victim's wife. If he lied about the affair, isn't it even more likely that he lied when he said he shot the victim accidentally?"

The *a fortiori* argument turns up in advertising with monotonous regularity. A computer software company advertises that its update of a word-processing program includes 500 new features. The implied argument is this: If the program was good before, it should be much better now. And how many times have we seen on a box of soap powder or a tube of toothpaste, "New and Improved"?

The *a fortiori* argument influenced the course of American participation in the Vietnam War in the 1960s and 1970s. One American general said that American air power could bomb North Vietnam "back into the stone age." Foes of bombing pointed to the failure of heavy British and American bombing to break the will of the Germans in World War II or even to slow German war production. Many studies concluded that bombing German cities only increased the Germans' will to resist. Therefore, they argued, it was unlikely that bombing could reduce the will of the North Vietnamese. The *a fortiori* argument went like this: If heavy bombing failed to break the will of a concentrated urban population in an industrial nation in World War II, it is even more unlikely to break the will of a rural population living in widely scattered hamlets. The effect of bombing such a country will only be to make a lot of holes in the ground and to kill a great many civilians.

THE *A FORTIORI* ARGUMENT AND INFERENCES   The *a fortiori* argument is essential to the inferences necessary in writing history. The evidence historians rely upon is fragmented and incomplete, and history itself is a process of assembling a puzzle made up of broken and missing pieces. Historians fill in the blanks by making intelligent speculations drawn from inferences. They can know some things with a fair degree of certainty. We know that South Carolina subdued Fort Sumter with artillery in April 1861 in the first combat of the Civil War. Other things remain forever uncertain. Did Lincoln deliberately provoke the South Carolinians into becoming aggressors? Did he move quickly to trigger war because he feared that the British might recognize South Carolina's "independence"? Did he think that faced with armed conflict, the South Carolinians might draw back from war? Lincoln is not known to have expressed his thoughts about his motives to anyone. We can only infer them.

Historians assemble all the evidence they can collect and try to frame it into a plausible, coherent picture—just as we try to find meaning in our experiences in the present. Historian Barbara Tuchman describes this process of inference from her own research:

> If the historian will submit himself *to* his material instead of trying to impose himself *on* his material, then the material will ultimately speak to him and supply the answers. It has happened to me more than once. In somebody's memoirs I found that the Grand Duke Nicholas wept when he was named Russian Commander-in-Chief in 1914, because, said the memoirist, he felt inadequate to the job. That sounded to me like one of those bits of malice one has to watch out for in contemporary observers; it did not ring true. The Grand Duke was said to be the only "man" in the royal family; he was known for his exceedingly tough manners, was admired by the common soldier, and feared at court. I did not believe he felt inadequate, but then why should he weep? I could have left out this bit of information, but I did not want to. I wanted to find the explanation that would make it fit. (Leaving things out because they do not fit is writing fiction, not history.) I carried the note about the Grand Duke around with me for days, worrying about it. Then I remembered other tears. I went through my notes and found an account of Churchill's weeping and also Messimy, the French War Minister. All at once I understood that it was not the individuals but the *times* that were the stuff for tears. My next sentence almost wrote itself: "There was an aura about 1914 that caused those who

sensed it to shiver for mankind." Afterward I realized that this sentence expressed why I had wanted to write the book in the first place. The "why," you see, had emerged all by itself.[3]

Aside from being a splendid account both of the role of inference in writing history and of the use of one of the important journalistic questions, this story provides an *a fortiori* argument. If so many brave men wept in 1914, may we not all the more assume that the Grand Duke wept out of a sense of impending doom and not out of a fear of his personal inadequacy?

The *a fortiori* argument can be falsified—as all good arguments can. No baseball fan would make this statement: Since the great hitter hit a home run against the worst team in the league in a meaningless game, isn't it more likely that he hit a home run in the deciding game of the World Series? In rape cases, courts generally rule out the *a fortiori* argument: Since this woman willingly had sexual relations with several men before the alleged rape, isn't it likely that she consented on this occasion, too? Such an argument neglects the fact that the violence of rape is a thing in itself and has nothing to do with whether or not the rape victim has consented to sex before. A similar argument would be to say that because someone has eaten a lot of hamburgers during his life, he consents to food poisoning now and then and shouldn't be upset about it when he nearly dies.

The Argument from Similitude

The argument from similitude holds that because people or events are alike in some ways, they must be alike in everything or at least in a great many ways. Its data are often statistical, and many things I said in my earlier remarks on statistics apply here. The argument is indispensable for research in the social sciences, but it can lead to dangerous inaccuracies.

Some counties in the United States have a remarkable history of voting for the winning candidate in presidential elections. Pollsters flock to those counties before elections, assuming that if they can discover how the people in these counties plan to vote, the pollsters can predict the outcome of elections. Politicians being the sort of people they are, the polls of such counties may help candidates shape their campaigns to appeal to the inhabitants of these counties in the belief that they are representative of the country. These counties, for reasons no one quite understands, seem to be "typical," like the United States as a whole.

Some life insurance companies offer lower rates to nonsmokers. More nonsmokers live longer than most smokers. But no one would argue that every nonsmoker lives longer than every smoker. A few nonsmokers die every year of lung cancer, and you may have an Uncle Roscoe who smoked two packs of unfiltered Camels every day for seventy years and died at age eighty-five when run over by a truck while jogging home from visiting his fiancée. Comparisons that classify people by groups offer only probability to individuals within the groups.

The argument from similitude has often been used fraudulently when someone claims that because the people or things being compared are alike in

some ways, they are alike in all. Richard Nixon never lived down his slander-
ous use of this argument in his campaign for the U.S. Senate in 1950 in California. His opponent was Helen Gahagan Douglas, a member of the U.S. House
of Representatives from California. At the time Senator Joseph McCarthy of
Wisconsin was terrifying many Americans by his claims that the Communist
Party had infiltrated the highest ranks of government, the film industry, the
churches, and publishing. In the summer of 1950 the United States sent troops
to Korea to repel a Communist invasion of South Korea, and the terror of Stal-
inism still raged in the Soviet Union. So Nixon tried to make voters believe that
Douglas was a Communist sympathizer.

He did so with the argument from similitude. Douglas had served in the
House of Representatives. Nixon compared her voting record with that of one
Vito Marcantonio, a radical and now long forgotten congressman from New
York. Marcantonio had supported the Soviet Union's foreign policy through
every slippery twist. He was defeated in the elections of 1950 and disappeared
from the American political scene. In domestic policy he supported price controls, public housing, civil rights, and health insurance—positions taken by
many Democrats and Republicans in the Congress. But most people knew him
only for his hysterical speeches in support of the Soviet Union. He also happened to hate Douglas.

Nixon's staff isolated 353 bills in the House in which Douglas and Marcantonio had voted on the same side. Congress votes on several thousand bills
during a term, and the issues on which Douglas and Marcantonio agreed had
nothing to do with the Soviet Union or Communism. But Nixon claimed that if
Helen Gahagan Douglas had voted with Marcantonio on so many occasions, she
must agree with him in everything else. It was like saying that if Marcantonio
and Douglas both liked soda water, they must also agree on the Soviet Union.

Frank Mankiewicz, a Douglas campaign worker, pointed out that Nixon
himself had voted with Marcantonio 112 times in four years. Even the most
hysterical anti-Communist might, on reflection, doubt Nixon's implication that
353 bills submitted to the House of Representatives of the United States were
Communist inspired. But it was a crazy time, and few voters paused to reflect.
They voted their fears, and Nixon won the election. But he paid a fearsome
price—a reputation for deceit that got him the nickname "Tricky Dick," which
dogged him through his resignation from the presidency in 1974 to avoid being impeached and lingered around him until his death.

People do not forget or forgive dishonest arguments; remember that before
you make one.

Cause and Effect

The argument from cause to effect or from effect back to cause is one of the
most common in human discourse, one of the most necessary, and one of the
most dangerous. We want to know why things happened—why war was

declared, why cancer struck, why a President was accused of sexual immorality, why Hamlet called death the "bourne from which no traveler returns" when the ghost of his father had obviously returned to set the play in motion. In both narrative and exposition, arguments about cause and effect may appear in almost every paragraph.

On the surface the argument from cause to effect seems simple. But it is not. Why do black players dominate professional basketball? One school of thought holds that blacks have a muscle mass that enables them to jump higher and with greater agility than most whites. The argument—which to some seems racist—is supported by some respectable researchers and by numbers. Most great players in the National Basketball Association are black. But another school of thought holds that basketball is the only sport open to the poor urban child. It requires little space and simple equipment. Black children start playing it early and play it often while white suburban children are playing soccer and being driven to music lessons. With more black kids devoting much more time to basketball, more of them grow up to be professionals. On which side does the truth lie? We don't know.

This debate illustrates the difficulty of cause-and-effect reasoning: The causal relation between two events may be impossible to establish beyond any doubt. When the argument is emotionally charged—as any argument about race may be—the difficulties are all the greater.

MULTIPLE EFFECTS   Some causes produce more than one effect. It becomes misleading then to isolate only one cause and pin all the effects on it. No reputable historian would argue that World War I was caused solely by the assassination of the heir to the throne of the Austro-Hungarian Empire in 1914 when he visited Sarajevo or that the Civil War was caused only by the election of Abraham Lincoln in 1860. Good historians know that the great crises in history build up like gas escaping slowly from a leaking pipe in a basement. Suddenly a spark causes an explosion. But without the accumulated gas the spark would remain only a spark.

The scientific model of cause and effect may lead us astray when we treat human events. In the nineteenth century Louis Pasteur discovered that heating milk to a temperature slightly lower than the boiling point would kill harmful germs without ruining the taste of the milk. Here is a clear relation between cause and effect. Heat kills germs and bacteria. Pasteurization caused safer milk. That kind of certainty seldom comes in the humanities and in social studies. Only dishonest people claim that it does. Informed readers become impatient and annoyed when they see a writer making simplistic claims about cause and effect.

At the other extreme are those who find elaborate conspiratorial explanations for everything. Many people are unable to believe that President John F. Kennedy was murdered in 1963 by a lone gunman. In 1991 movie director Oliver Stone produced a film called *JFK* in which he argued that the Central

Intelligence Agency of the federal government did it in collaboration with Lyndon Johnson, who as Vice President succeeded to the presidency on Kennedy's death. No matter that the movie is filled with absurdities, made-up characters, and outright lies, easily refuted by anyone with any knowledge of the evidence. In our time movies have become the new opiate of the people, and millions believe Stone's "argument." But despite his obvious talent as a filmmaker, he has become something of a joke among late-night talk-show hosts and journalists.

People who make and believe elaborate conspiratorial arguments about anything often feel smug. *They* are not deceived. *They* stand above the gullible masses. Their arguments usually boil down to saying, "It could have been true." I suppose that it could have been true that Elvis Presley was bald and wore a wig and spent his mornings reading German philosophy, but since I have no evidence that any of these things happened, I don't think my reputation would survive any argument I might make in their favor.

PLAUSIBLE SUGGESTIONS   It is all right to suggest a plausible relation between cause and effect even if you do not have final proof—as long as you are careful to tell readers how tentative your arguments are. Many great scientific theories have been developed by careful observers who supposed that the facts could be accounted for if they assumed something unproven or even unprovable. Albert Einstein's theories led many scientists to wonder if huge stars might collapse into black holes—conglomerations of matter so dense that their gravity prevents even light from escaping from them. No one has ever seen a black hole with a telescope, for by definition a black hole *cannot* be seen. But evidence is accumulating that black holes do exist as astronomers observe the behavior of stars seemingly under the influence of immense forces of gravity outside themselves.

Plausible but finally unprovable arguments are a part of both historical and literary studies. When William Shakespeare wrote his plays between about 1590 and 1611, England was under Protestant rule, and Catholics were often accused of treason. Yet many scholars find it plausible to suggest that parts of Shakespeare's plays indicate that Shakespeare himself was sympathetic to Catholics and the Catholic Church. Some argue that Shakespeare did not himself believe in a life after death. Each of these arguments can lead to fruitful discussion of the plays, but in the end they can be made plausible rather than provable.

FALLACIES   Cause-and-effect reasoning abounds in opportunities for fallacies—mistakes in logic. One of the most common is called *post hoc; ergo propter hoc,* a Latin phrase meaning that because one thing happens after another, the first is the cause of the second. A few years ago I read in a Tennessee newspaper a passionate letter to the editor arguing that sex education in the public schools has caused an increase in violent sex crimes. The writer argued that before sex education in the classroom, sex crimes were much less frequent. Therefore, he said, sex education caused these crimes. Another letter writer quickly replied that the demise of the television program "Leave It to Beaver" was the "real" culprit. It could be demonstrated, this writer said, that sex crimes dramatically increased after that program went off the air.

It is easy to spot fallacies like this one because they are so obviously absurd. But many fallacious arguments are more complicated and subtle, and many people—including the writers who use them—may be deceived. Honest writers examine the evidence critically. If it does not support their case, good writers will say so; if it may be interpreted in different ways, good writers will say that, too, even while they argue that their interpretation is the best one. We may yearn for simple answers, but truth is always best served when we recognize how complicated some events are, how difficult they are to explain, and how mysterious they remain when we have done our best to understand them.

The Argument from Necessity

The argument from necessity holds that no choice exists in a matter requiring action. The writer or speaker says, in effect, "Things are as I say they are, and you must do what I say you must do." This is almost always the argument of those who call nations for war, for if we had a choice, most of us would prefer to stay at peace.

On Monday morning, December 8, 1941, President Franklin D. Roosevelt spoke to the Congress to ask for a declaration of war against Japan. He began by presenting an undeniable fact in an unforgettable way:

> Yesterday, December 7, 1941—a date which will live in infamy—the United States of America was suddenly and deliberately attacked by naval and air forces of the empire of Japan.

Roosevelt moved from this statement of fact to his argument from necessity—that the United States now had no choice but to declare war on Japan.

A more modern version of the argument from necessity arises from issues in ecology. We have considerable evidence that average temperatures around the world are rising. We call the phenomenon *global warming.* Experts in climate tell us that if the trend continues, our weather patterns will change, storms will become much more violent, and the sea level will rise as the polar ice caps melt. In time coastal cities such as New York, Boston, Los Angeles, Venice, and others would be drowned by rising water. One cause of these rising temperatures seems to be the pollutants that we pour into the air from the burning of oil and coal. The argument from necessity is that we must take dramatic action or face catastrophe.

The argument from necessity is always vulnerable from two angles. An opponent can say, "The facts are not as you present them" or "Even if your facts are true, your conclusions about what should be done are false."

During the Vietnam War, President Lyndon Johnson argued passionately that if South Vietnam fell to Communism, all Asia would become Communist in a so-called domino effect, as if these countries were a row of upright dominoes that would all topple if one were knocked down. Therefore, he said in speech after speech, the United States had to win the war. Opponents countered that the domino effect was a myth, that even if other Asian countries should become Communist, they could not act together to threaten the United States. In effect Johnson's opponents countered his argument from necessity by saying no such necessity existed, and later events have proved them right.

The argument from necessity embraces a contradiction. It assumes a choice; yet the argument is that no choice exists. I am asked to choose war and told at the same time that I have no choice but war; I am asked to vote for a candidate who promises a balanced federal budget. I am told that if I do not want the country to fall into ruin, I have no choice but to vote for such a candidate. The argument works only if the audience assumes that the necessity does exist and that people will do willingly what they are compelled to do anyway. It's a tricky business, and you should feel yourself on sure ground when you use the argument from necessity.

The Argument from Authority

Aristotle called the argument from authority the "ethical" argument. He meant *ethical* in the Greek sense—character. The ethical argument depends on our opinion of the person making the argument. It is important in all parts of life because people have reputations. For whatever reason we trust some people, and we don't trust others. In writing academic papers students can buttress their own opinions by quoting from scholars who have written articles that support positions the students take in their own essays.

We believe some people because they exude authority. We believe them because they have studied the issue that interests us, or they have had experience in the issue, or because we like them. The argument from authority may be the least logical of all arguments, but it may also be the most believable. Some religious groups depend on testimony and have great vitality. At their services, people rise and tell stories to the group—sometimes with great emotion—about what God has done for them. Such groups often win converts because those giving the testimonies seem so sincere and their experiences so vivid.

Yet we know that eyewitness testimony, the recollections of participants in events, can be flawed. Human beings naturally tend to give themselves the best motives when they explain themselves, and many writers of autobiography magnify their own importance or their goodness in recalling their roles in events. Historians and other writers who rely solely on the recollections of participants are likely to be deceived. I happen to think that William Faulkner was the greatest writer the United States ever produced. Faulkner tried to enlist in the United States army during World War I, but he was too small to pass the physical exam. He went to Canada, was accepted in the Royal Canadian Air Force, and claimed later on to have flown in combat against the Germans on the Western Front in Europe. Many of his stories and novels are about fliers. Early reviewers thought he had flown in combat. But the war ended before he finished his cadet training, and he did not fight in World War I. He did not even get to Europe.

You can gain your own authority as a writer by demonstrating that you have worked hard to gather the facts, that you have put them together carefully, considered their relations thoughtfully, and that your aim is to get at the truth. This sifting of evidence includes checking the eyewitness accounts to see if they seem to be true. Students can always help their own authority by quoting experts—scholars who have written about the topic or others who have some knowledge of the matter at hand. Teachers are impressed when you quote books or scholarly journals to support your own arguments. If you read such sources, you will find your own vision expanded and even inspired.

Readers are also impressed when you document your sources carefully and speak with a moderation that displays confidence rather than in a shrill, polemical tone that makes them believe you are afraid your arguments are no good and that you have to shout to make people overlook the weakness of your case.

ARRANGEMENT

I have chosen to call *arrangement* what others call *deductive* and *inductive* reasoning. I find it helpful to consider deductive and inductive reasoning as ways of arranging evidence. Some evidence and some forms of argument fit naturally into deductive reasoning, and some fit better into induction. Your choice of which to use depends on your evidence and how you decide to use it. You will use both deduction and induction in almost every good argument.

Deduction

The path of deduction rises from something we know to be a fact to a conclusion about something else. It involves inference. Deductive reasoning goes on in a form traditionally called the *syllogism.* Here again we meet our necessary friend—the premise—the assumption on which an argument is based. Syllogisms have three parts—a major premise, a minor premise, and a conclusion. The major and minor premises are statements of fact. The conclusion involves comparing or reading these two statements so that an additional statement of fact may be made about the minor premise. The following syllogism has been used for centuries to illustrate the syllogistic form:

Major premise: All men are mortal.
Minor premise: Socrates is a man.
Conclusion: Socrates is mortal.

This example makes deductive reasoning seem neat and easy. In practice such reasoning is usually much more complicated. Yet most arguments use syllogisms, and only a little study is required to unearth them. They occur in all disciplines. The planet Pluto, invisible to the naked eye and most distant of all the planets from the sun, was discovered in 1930 on the basis of the following syllogism.

Major premise:	The gravitational pull of a nearby planet may cause variations in the orbits of other planets.
Minor premise:	The planets Uranus and Neptune show variations in their orbits.
Conclusion:	Another planet may be out there, one we have not yet discovered.

Yet another syllogism might run like this:

Major premise:	Movie makers are in business to make money.
Minor premise:	Most people who attend movies are under 50 years old.
Conclusion:	Not many movies will feature love affairs between couples in their eighties.

In January 1998 when President Bill Clinton was accused of a sexual liaison with a young woman who had worked in the White House, *New York Times* columnist Maureen Dowd wrote a column titled "Not Suitable for Children" that boiled down to the following syllogism:

Major premise:	We know Bill Clinton has had extramarital sexual affairs in the past and has lied about them.
Minor premise:	He now says he did not have a liaison with a woman who says they had sex in the White House.
Conclusion:	He is probably lying.

These syllogisms may seem awkward when they are arranged in the bare bones that I have used here. Yet writers must be able to find such syllogisms in their own thoughts and in the thoughts of others. Once we have reduced a line of deductive argument to a syllogism, we should check the terms to see if the conclusion is plausible. Note that the syllogism does not necessarily prove anything beyond the shadow of doubt. It is a way of arranging the evidence so that the conclusion seems to fit what we know. The conclusions of syllogisms are usually *plausible* rather than final.

In most deductive arguments the major premise is not stated; it is only implied. A presidential candidate attacks his opponent for being inexperienced in foreign policy. The implied major premise is that no one should become President without having made decisions about foreign policy. A scholar may object to another scholar's use of Freudian psychology to interpret someone's life in the past. The implied major premise may be that Freudian psychology is invalid or that it cannot be used to psychoanalyze the dead.

PROBLEMS IN DEDUCTIVE REASONING   Deductive reasoning offers obvious problems. The major premise may be wrong or at least disputable. The presidential candidate who claims vast experience in foreign policy may have sat in meetings with neither ideas to contribute nor the authority to influence any decision that was made. Or if the candidate did have influence, he may have bungled and blundered on five continents.

The syllogism may incorporate a fallacy.

Major premise: Atheists don't pray.

Minor premise: My opponent opposes prayer in the public schools.

Conclusion: My opponent is an atheist.

The fallacy here is that as the syllogism is arranged, it seems that someone can oppose prayer in the public schools *only* because he or she does not believe in God. In fact many very religious people oppose prayer in the public schools because they fear that such a prayer may force the religion of the majority on a religious minority.

The lesson here is that deductive reasoning must always take observation into account. Deduction is crippled when it ignores observation and considers principles that seem logical when in fact they do not fit the facts. The ancient Greeks are often credited with the discovery of modern science. In fact they were more apt at working out logical systems than they were at observing nature, and some of their conclusions were off the mark. In the seventeenth century, the prestige of Greek philosophy stood as a wall against the progress of modern science based on observation and hypothesis. (A *hypothesis* is a theory that tries to explain what is observed.) Scientists seemed anti-intellectual. They did not read books; they looked at nature. When Galileo argued that the earth moved around the sun, he ran into the Greek logic of his adversaries. They put forward the following syllogism.

Major premise: People feel motion when they move.

Minor premise: We do not feel the motion of the earth beneath our feet.

Conclusion: Therefore the earth does not move.

Those lacking Galileo's mathematics and his telescope were reduced to Greek "logic" that has long since been proved wrong by scientific observation.

Yet our society is filled with false syllogisms that many people refuse to correct by observation. "Liberals are unpatriotic; Jones is a liberal; therefore Jones is unpatriotic." "The Marlboro Man smokes cigarettes and looks handsome and tough; I want to look handsome and tough; therefore I will smoke Marlboro cigarettes." "No sensible person can be religious; Smith is religious; therefore she cannot be sensible." "Multitudes adore Michael Jordan; he wears Nike shoes; I will wear Nike shoes and be adored by multitudes."

Many false syllogisms come from not observing enough. It's foolish to imagine that all French people are rude because a French clerk in a post office was rude to you when you yelled at her in English. Racial prejudice, religious prejudice, and class prejudices of various sorts arise from lazy observations.

Despite its abuses, deductive reasoning is essential in argument, and we see it and use it every day. "Computers are sensitive to slight changes in electrical voltage; surge protectors block voltage changes from the computer; computer owners should use a surge protector." "College graduates usually get better-paying jobs than do noncollege graduates; Jones wants a job that pays well; Jones should get a college education." "Democracy depends on the free flow of information; the press provides information; therefore the press ought to have freedom to print both facts and opinions that people in government may not like."

Induction

We have encountered induction in our discussion of fact patterns. *Induction* is the process of observing facts until we perceive relations between them. Induction has been at the heart of modern medical research. Pasteur observed that certain bacteria were present in milk and that people who drank such milk often fell victim to certain diseases. He concluded that the bacteria caused the disease—and his conclusion changed modern medicine for all time.

By the same sort of deduction, researchers in this century noted that lung cancer afflicted cigarette smokers at ten times the rate that the disease afflicted nonsmokers. They concluded that cigarettes caused lung cancer. Further studies have shown that cigarettes also cause emphysema, heart disease, and other types of cancer, and that smoking also causes skin to wrinkle prematurely.

In literary studies certain themes may come up again and again in a writer's work. "Honor" is one of Shakespeare's themes. Hostility to ministers of religion and to religious people is a constant theme in Mark Twain. Toni Morrison writes about the struggles of black women to achieve independence and dignity, and her characters often talk over meals. Faulkner's characters more often talk over whiskey. Study of these themes may lead to inductions that help explain some of the deeper meanings of their works.

By using inductive logic, we assemble clues that add up to the solution of a mystery. For the writer, induction requires the careful collection of facts and equally careful thought about how these facts are related to one another—if indeed there is any relation.

Induction and deduction go hand in hand. By induction, researchers determined that nonsmokers living with cigarette smokers ran a much higher risk of heart disease and cancer than did nonsmokers living with one another. Lawmakers in some cities deduced from this research that nonsmokers had the right to a smoke-free workplace and smoke-free areas in restaurants and in other public places. Once induction leads us to a conclusion, we deduce other conclusions from it.

LOGICAL FALLACIES

We've already noted some fallacies connected with different forms of argument. It is worthwhile to give a little concentrated attention to the topic. Writers lose all credibility when they argue fallaciously, and you should be aware of fallacies so you can avoid them in your own writing.

Fallacies of Deduction and Induction

As we have seen, fallacies of deduction come when a syllogism cannot stand up to observation or when the relations between the parts of the syllogism go awry. We will look at more examples of faulty deduction below.

Fallacies of induction most commonly occur when we try to draw conclusions from too few instances—as we do when we condemn all the French because of a rude functionary. An American fortune-teller included the assassination of John F. Kennedy in her list of predictions for 1963. For several years editors of tabloids sold in supermarkets paid her big money at the New Year to predict events in the next twelve months. She was hilariously wrong so often that she became a joke, her predictions about as accurate as darts thrown at a target in the dark, and she disappeared into obscurity. Among her thousands of predictions came one lucky guess about a national calamity, and the gullible rushed to believe that she could see into the future. It's always good to remember that even a stopped clock is right twice a day, and that more than one or two instances are usually required to make a case.

Sweeping generalizations about people in any group or time are likely to be wildly inaccurate. Often writers make such generalizations because they are too lazy to make distinctions. Evidence is much more complicated and contradictory than any sweeping generalization allows and therefore requires the writer to do more work to get it right. Sometimes my students write that this person or that was a "typical" renaissance person. To my mind the renaissance is so complex that I don't know what a "typical" renaissance person would be like any more than I know what a "typical" athlete or a "typical" professor or a "typical" student might be like.

Straw Men

A *straw man* is an argument one claims one's opponents are making when in fact they are not making that argument at all. One attacks the imaginary argument rather than face the real issue. The setting up of straw men that can be easily burned or pushed aside is a curse of our political life. Someone objects to a school board's decision to ban *Huckleberry Finn* from the library, and someone accuses her of racism. Someone opposes abortion, and someone else accuses him of wanting to enslave women. Someone favors a woman's right to choose abortion, and someone accuses her of being a murderer. A political candidate suggests that guns, especially pistols, ought to be registered just as cars are registered, and the National Rifle Association will spend huge amounts of money to defeat her, claiming that her goal is to prevent Americans from owning guns.

In serious writing, setting up straw men is an immoral act. Readers with their wits about them disdain this cowardly practice. Writers and speakers who set up straw men fear to face the arguments of their opponents at their strongest points. Yet candidates for high office happily burn straw men in their election campaigns, contributing to the indifference to politics that has spread through our society. Political ads on television rarely do anything but attack straw men. Don't be like politicians. Be brave enough and honest enough to face your opponents' arguments at their strongest point and make your case by reason rather than deceitful passion.

The "Ad Hominem" Argument

The words *ad hominem* mean in Latin "against the man," and the fallacy called by this name is an attack on a person rather than a serious effort to deal with his or her arguments. Like the straw-man fallacy, the *ad hominem* argument is all too common in politics. It has now become rare for candidates facing each other in an election to treat each other as honorable human beings. The presidential debates before a national television audience now give us examples of the lowest form of rhetoric every four years. The candidates stick labels on each other and call it politics. How sad it is!

The *ad hominem* argument usually resembles a faulty deduction:

My opponent is a homosexual; therefore nothing he says about national politics can be trusted. I consort only with members of the opposite sex; therefore my sentiments about national affairs are infallible.

Most readers recognize the obvious faulty reasoning in the example above. But what about this one?

My opponent was expelled for cheating when he was in college thirty years ago. Therefore you cannot trust him to be President.

The argument assumes that because the speaker's opponent did something dishonest thirty years ago, he is still dishonest and that dishonesty taints everything he says on any subject. It does not consider the opponent's life since the act of dishonesty, and it ignores his present views on important issues. It assumes a syllogism like this:

Anyone who cheats once in school will be dishonest ever after.

My opponent cheated thirty years ago.

My opponent is dishonest now.

In politics a person's character is a genuine issue. We don't want to elect to high political office someone practicing sexual harassment, child abuse, or flagrant dishonesty. We don't want a racist President or a bigoted secretary of state. But too often in our political campaigns, *ad hominem* attacks divert voters from the real issues. When that happens, the *ad hominem* argument is the rhetorical refuge of a scoundrel.

The Bandwagon

According to the bandwagon argument, since nearly everyone else believes or does something, we should believe or do it, too. It is often used in advertising. Since nearly all college football and basketball teams use Nike shoes and other equipment, we should use Nike, too. Since all the polls show that LeRoy de Lechers will be elected President, we should vote for him to be with the majority. In fact everybody may not be doing what we are told everybody is doing. But people who want to be the leaders of our band tell us that we should go along with this proclaimed majority.

The strength of the bandwagon argument stems from our desire to seek the company of our fellow human beings and to be accepted by them. Most of us hate to speak out against strong majority opinion. The bandwagon mentality makes some people hesitate to express an opinion until they know what others are thinking. A group of college students discussing a movie will often wait cautiously for someone to express an opinion. Then they may all agree. Likewise their professors hesitate to express dislike for a great literary classic for fear of being thrown off the bandwagon of academe. I greatly admired the courage of one of my English department colleagues for confessing to me one day that he found *Moby Dick* one of the most boring books he had ever read.

The bandwagon argument is often fallacious. Although public opinion supports a war or a political candidate or a social program or a piece of legislation relating to some moral issue, public opinion may be wrong. Remember, public opinion supported Hitler. Some brave writer or speaker may have to get off the bandwagon to try to stop it before it rolls over a cliff. The strength of the United States Constitution and our democracy rests on the freedom to stand alone. The mere statement of near unanimity of views does not mean that those views are correct. When I was a child growing up in the rural South, the bandwagon mentality said racial segregation was moral and desirable and that the "outsiders" or "Yankees" who wanted integration deserved to be condemned and even killed. The bandwagon for decades kept the region in economic and moral ruin.

Begging the Question

Another common fallacy is *begging the question,* setting up an argument so that it can lead to only one conclusion. The argument may affirm things to be true that on examination prove to be much less certain. Politicians and others often beg the question when they use moral arguments. American involvement in the

Vietnam War was often couched in moral terms. "We have made a commitment to the people of South Vietnam. We must keep our promises." But as the war dragged itself out over bloody years, things began to look more complicated. Had we made a commitment to the people of South Vietnam, or was our commitment to a government that had little popular support? The answer to that question proved to be complex. The government the United States supported in South Vietnam had refused to permit elections called for by a treaty between France and Ho Chi Minh's forces who had won a bloody war that ended French colonial rule in Vietnam. President Dwight Eisenhower explained why the United States supported the refusal of elections. Ho Chi Minh, said Eisenhower, would have won eighty percent of the vote.

So the continual repetition by four Presidents of the statement, "We have made a commitment to the People of South Vietnam" begged the question. It assumed that we had made a commitment to the people that most Vietnamese wanted. Some 58,000 American soldiers died before Americans understood that we had made our commitment to a corrupt government and not to the people who were not represented by that government. In large measure these men died as a result of fallacious reasoning by the United States government and by many of its people.

Argument by False Analogy

False analogies often corrupt thinking about the relation of history to politics. Again, the American involvement in Vietnam provides an example. American leaders who wished to continue the war returned time and again to the Munich agreements of 1938 when France and Great Britain agreed to give Hitler those parts of Czechoslovakia he wanted rather than fight a war with him. But within a year Hitler had not only taken all of Czechoslovakia but had gone to war with England and France anyway. The analogy seemed plain. The democracies should have resisted Hitler before he became strong enough to threaten all of Europe and the United States. Therefore the democracies should resist Communism before it became strong enough to threaten all of Asia. The flaw in the argument is that many things in Vietnam in the 1960s were different from the situation in Europe in the 1930s—so many that the analogy kept political thinkers and the American people from seeing the reality of the present rather than the history of an event in the past. Analogies can provide rhetorical flourishes. We love comments such as, "This administration represents morning in America," but we can't argue very well from such slogans.

CONCLUDING REMARKS ON ARGUMENT

Argument is essential to democracy, to public discourse, to scholarship, to daily life. From the smallest meetings in our neighborhoods to the greatest debates in Congress, argument helps us see our way. It is a high mark of civilization.

When people lose the ability to argue well or to follow the arguments of others, or when they cannot discern fallacies when they see them, all our democratic institutions are threatened. Never be afraid to argue. But always be prepared to argue well.

To argue well you must command information. You cannot create an argument out of nothing. You must also be honorable. Admit it when all the evidence does not stack up in your favor. Concede points where the evidence requires concession. Treat your opponents with respect. Marshal your evidence. Remember that the solution to many arguments is neither this nor that but some of both.

Here it is worthwhile to repeat something I have said before. Knowledge seldom has neat edges that fit together like the parts in a good jigsaw puzzle. It comes with ragged corners, with missing pieces, and with uneven sides. We make our best arguments in an attitude of confident humility.

Paragraphs

Paragraphs are a modern invention. Greek and Latin writers did not use them. Until the nineteenth century, written English scarcely noticed them. The word *paragraph* originally meant a pi mark like this π placed at the head of a section of prose to announce that the subject of the discourse was changing slightly. After the mark, the section might go on for several pages. Eventually the paragraph mark was replaced by an indented line. Even then, the indentation might introduce a long section of unbroken prose. The paragraphs of John Stuart Mill and Charles Darwin, both great prose writers in the nineteenth century, ran on for several pages. Only gradually did the paragraph assume its modern form—a fairly short block of prose introduced by an indentation, organized so that every sentence in it contributes to a limited subject.

Paragraphs help both writers and readers. They order our thoughts and make writing easier to follow. They break down our ideas into manageable units. They let us arrange an essay one step at a time. They allow readers to follow our thoughts along a stairway of prose that we build for them.

Paragraphs give readers a sense of pace. From paragraph to paragraph we see that the prose is going somewhere. They also provide relief for our eyes. The long gray columns of unindented type in early nineteenth-century newspapers look dark and forbidding today. Indeed, the most probable cause of the paragraph's popularity was the expansion of literacy fed by the penny press. Ordinary people—sometimes not well educated—wanted their cheap newspapers to be readable, and editors wanted their stories to be flexible for inserts and deletions that let a piece slip neatly into the space available. The practice of the shorter paragraph spread then into books and magazines—and to good effect. We hesitate to start reading unparagraphed material because we subconsciously think we can't get through it. By showing a piece of writing in small blocks, paragraphs give us confidence that we can absorb the piece one block at a time.

THE STRUCTURE OF PARAGRAPHS

A lot of nonsense has been written in writing textbooks about paragraphs, much of it not only wrong but harmful. Much of the nonsense arises from the false notion that every paragraph should be a short essay and that the thesis for the essay should be expressed in something called a *topic sentence.* Some textbooks teach that a topic sentence may come at the beginning, the middle, or the end of a paragraph. Many teachers command their students to underline the topic sentence, and the students dutifully underline a sentence whether the paragraph contains a topic sentence or not.

A good topic sentence is said to be a general statement supported by evidence contained in the rest of the paragraph. The topic sentence is supposed to promote unity. Paragraph unity is important. When we read, we don't like to be jerked from thought to thought without seeing any connection between them. Paragraphs reveal connections.

Sometimes a paragraph does indeed include a general statement that fits the standard textbook definition of the topic sentence. The other sentences in the paragraph support the generalization. Such paragraphs usually explain things. But in most other paragraphs, no topic sentence as textbooks describe it can be found.

Let us consider the textbook topic sentence first. Here is a paragraph that explains why olives grown in California are tasteless compared to olives grown in Europe.

> Americans are used to tasteless olives because that's what industrial processes yield. California olives are treated with lye to remove a very bitter substance called oleuropein (from *Olea europea,* the olive's botanical name). The lye also removes most of what gives the olives flavor, and leaves them bland and hard without being crunchy. Lye-treated olives need help to taste like anything; spices and herbs in the prime, a stuffing with mushrooms or almonds or anchovies or pimentos.[1]

This paragraph begins with a general statement—which we may call a topic sentence—that the rest of the paragraph explains. The writer expands on the topic and provides details that make us believe it.

But many paragraphs, especially paragraphs in narration or description, are not introduced by general statements. Here, for example, is a paragraph from the late James Baldwin's "Notes of a Native Son":

> On the 29th of July in 1943, my father died. On the same day, a few hours later, his last child was born. Over a month before this, while all our energies were concen-

trated in waiting for these events, there had been, in Detroit, one of the bloodiest race riots of the centuries. A few hours after my father's funeral, while he lay in state in the undertaker's chapel, a race riot broke out in Harlem. On the morning of the 3rd of August, we drove my father to the graveyard through a wilderness of smashed plate glass.[2]

We could summarize the paragraph above in a general topic sentence such as this: "Several interesting things happened to me between my father's death and his funeral." Such a sentence would be tedious and unnecessary. As Baldwin tells us what happened, we easily follow along. We see the unity of the paragraph as we read it.

How Paragraphs Work

But how do paragraphs work? What do paragraphs with topic sentences have in common with paragraphs that lack them? How do paragraphs achieve unity?

I believe that we write anticipating when we are going to make a slight shift in the subject. When we move to another point, another idea, another incident, we indent and write a sentence. The first sentence of the paragraph includes ideas we expand in the next sentence. We connect the two sentences by a repetition—a word, a pronoun, or a synonym for an idea in the first sentence. The sentences are thus woven together like a net with threads reaching from place to place in the fabric.

Let's examine that process in the paragraph from James Baldwin:

On the 29th of July in 1943, my father died.

Think for a moment of all the possibilities in this sentence. We have several key thoughts—"29th of July," "1943," "my father," and "died." Baldwin picks up the thoughts of the date and the father. The important topic is "when." He develops this thought in the next sentence:

On the same day, a few hours later, his last child was born.

"On the same day" is a repetition of the thought, "On the 29th of July in 1943," and "his" refers to "my father." Baldwin develops a thought of what happened on July 29, 1943. Now he develops a further thought, also related to the question "when."

Over a month before this, while all our energies were concentrated in waiting for these events, there had been, in Detroit, one of the bloodiest race riots of the century.

Two thoughts are picked up here: "Over a month before this" develops the thought begun in "On the 29th of July, in 1943," and "on the same day." Then he adds another piece of information that carries his story forward. That new information is about a bloody race riot in Detroit, a battle between black and white Americans that left many dead. So Baldwin, a black writer, begins to weave for us a story that is both about his father and about race in America. We see the standard pattern of American prose. Each sentence in a paragraph reaches back for something that has gone before, and then adds new information to carry us on to the next sentence.

> A few hours after my father's funeral, while he lay in state in the undertaker's chapel, a race riot broke out in Harlem.

Baldwin has moved us from his father's death to a race riot in Detroit a month earlier, and having mentioned a race riot, he moves us now to the race riot in Harlem on the day of his father's funeral. This Harlem event is the new information in a sentence that has several words reaching back to things Baldwin has already told us. So he develops the next sentence, again new information tacked onto words that refer to things he has already said.

> On the morning of the 3rd of August, we drove my father to the graveyard through a wilderness of smashed plate glass.

So we see in these sentences of Baldwin's paragraph interlocking connections that begin with the first sentence. The first sentence is not a general topic sentence. It is a simple statement of fact. The other sentences are similar statements, all tied to the first sentence by words that develop thoughts we read in it. Sentence by sentence we get new information tied to what has gone before by words that look back so that in the end every sentence after the first sentence in the paragraph gives us something new in the context of something we already know.

These are the qualities of all good paragraphs, whether they have a general topic sentence or not. They reflect the writer's mind advancing through his or her thoughts about the topic. If the writer had other interests, the paragraph would have gone off in another direction, but working with the interlocking thoughts that carry prose forward. Suppose someone had written this:

> On the 29th of July in 1943, my father died. I scarcely had time to notice the event because on that day, I was ordered to fly yet another raid against Hamburg, and we had to take off within an hour after I received the telegram from home. I was the navigator on our B-24 "Liberator" bomber and had to fly the mission because there was no one to replace me. It was our second raid on Hamburg in four days, and I was so tired I did not have the energy to grieve for a loss so far away.

Again we have familiar connections we expect between sentences. Each sentence after the first reaches back to pick up a previous word or idea and then extends the thoughts, adding new information. What makes the two paragraphs different? The different purposes of the writers. But the structure is the same—a looking backward and a moving forward in each sentence. If your own sentences do not connect with previous sentences and add new information, you should consider revision.

Remember this: The first sentence is all-important to any paragraph. The writer, setting it down, makes a commitment to develop an idea that it contains in the next sentence and in the next and so on. You will begin many paragraphs with a general statement to be supported and explained in the rest of the paragraph. You will begin many others by telling of an event followed by a related event and another and another through the paragraph. However you begin, connect the first sentence with the sentences that come after it in this network of repetition and development. *The first sentence is always the sentence that gives direction to any paragraph.*

UNITY AND DISUNITY IN THE PARAGRAPH AND THE ESSAY

An essay proceeds in much the same way as the paragraph. It moves from thought to thought carefully, keeping the later parts in harmony with the earlier. Every sentence in the essay looks back to something that has gone before and adds something that will be developed in the later sentences. Disunity in paragraphs often leads to disunity in the essay, for if one paragraph jumps the track, it may derail those that follow. Such disunity usually occurs because the later sentences in a paragraph do not flow naturally from the first sentence.

Writers may stumble into disunity when they are not sure what they want to say. Studying your evidence, thinking about it carefully, asking questions, trying to answer them will help you gain assurance that you do have something to say, and you can get on with it. But you can also help unify your writing by reading it over and over to see that it does hold together, moving clearly from paragraph to paragraph throughout. Read your work aloud. I repeat this advice continually to my students, and I follow it myself. Your ear helps you edit when your eye fails you.

Paragraphs seem to fall into two general structural forms. In one each sentence builds so tightly on the previous sentence that to leave a sentence out or to put it in another place damages the unity of the whole. The sentences are like the links of a chain. Break one link, and the whole chain is broken. Here is such a paragraph. Take out or move any sentence, and you create confusion. Each sentence is a link in a chain.

> The first time I went to Cuba, in February of 1989, I felt that I was on a secret mission. My "cover" (which, undramatically, was also one of my real-life jobs) was that of theological adviser to the Northeast Hispanic Catholic Center: I was helping to chaperone a pilgrimage. Among the center's other activities, it arranges for groups of Latino parishioners to travel to their countries of origin, and that year we had finally won approval from the Cuban government to send a group of visitors. The center's director and I were warned, however, that any religious objects we might bring would have to be for personal use only. The Cuban authorities frowned on the importing of Bibles, rosaries, or pious books with intent to distribute.[3]

This paragraph may be illustrated by a design like this:

First Sentence

+

Second Sentence

+

Third Sentence

+

Fourth Sentence

+

Fifth Sentence

But in some paragraphs, the first sentence is a general statement followed by a list of detailed statements that support the generalization. You can change the list around or even leave part of it out, and the paragraph will still hold together. Descriptive paragraphs often have this quality. Take a look at a couple of descriptive paragraphs Loren Eiseley wrote in an essay called "The Judgment of the Birds."

> It was a late hour on a cold, wind-bitten autumn day when I climbed a great hill spined like a dinosaur's back and tried to take my bearings. The tumbled waste fell away in waves in all directions. Blue air was darkening into purple along the bases of hills. I shifted my knapsack, heavy with the petrified bones of long-vanished creatures, and studied my compass. I wanted to be out of there by nightfall, and already the sun was going suddenly down in the west.
>
> It was then that I saw the flight coming on. It was moving like a little close-knit body of black specks that danced and darted and closed again. It was pouring from the north and heading toward me with the undeviating relentlessness of a compass needle. It streamed through the shadows rising out of monstrous gorges. It rushed over towering pinnacles in the red light of the sun or momentarily sank from sight within the shade. Across that desert of eroding clay and wind-worn stone they came with a faint wild twittering that filled all the air about me as those tiny living bullets hurtled past into the night.[4]

As in all paragraphs, the first sentence in each of these sets the stage for what comes later. But the sentences after the first sentence could be rearranged in almost any order, and each paragraph would maintain its sense. Each sentence reaches back to the first sentence of the paragraph to amplify a thought expressed there. A diagram for this sort of paragraph would look like this:

First Sentence
_____

+   +   +   +   +   +

TRANSITIONS BETWEEN PARAGRAPHS

Paragraphs should not only hold together within; they should also allow smooth passage from one paragraph to the next. To ensure this smooth flow, pay attention to transitions. *Transitions* are words or phrases in the first sentence that look backward, tying the paragraph to what has come before and reaching forward to what is to come now. Good transitions make life easier on readers; they also help writers with their own thinking, for they set up relations within prose that are essential to its shape and unity. Transitions prevent your readers from jumping the track, from suddenly asking themselves, "Why are we talking about this?"

Transitions come in two forms. The more obvious of the two consists of words that tell your reader that you are moving from one idea to another. Words like *therefore, however, moreover, furthermore, nevertheless,* and *so* say to your reader, "I'm going this way; come along with me."

We all use these obvious transitions now and then. But before we write one, we should pause. Do we need it? These are cautious, plodding words, words that leap quickly to mind when we are stuck. When we use them too frequently, they leave the rivets showing in our essays.

The best transitions are another kind, less obvious. Here, as always, check the work of your favorite published writers to test my advice. You can read pages and pages of *The New Yorker, Popular Mechanics, Sports Illustrated, Smithsonian,* and *The Atlantic* without seeing one of these obvious transitions. Here you see paragraphs smoothly welded together so you don't feel the bumps as you go over them. How do professional writers achieve these effects?

A good device in making transitions is to use a word in the last sentence of one paragraph that you repeat in the first sentence of the next or to refer to the previous sentence in some way. You can also begin a new paragraph by jumping back to an earlier point in your paper, making some verbal gesture that lets your reader know that you are making such a leap. Here are the first two paragraphs from an essay by John McPhee called "The Swiss at War":

> It seems likely that the two most widely circulated remarks ever made about Switzerland's military prowess were made by Napoleon Bonaparte and Orson Welles.
>
> Welles said, "In Italy for thirty years under the Borgias, they had warfare, terror, murder, bloodshed—but they produced Michelangelo, Leonardo da Vinci, and the Renaissance. In Switzerland, they have brotherly love, five hundred years of democracy and peace, and what did that produce? The cuckoo clock.[5]

We have two transitions here. The primary transition is the word *Welles.* It appears at the end of the one-sentence opening paragraph of McPhee's essay. It begins the next sentence, the first in a two-sentence paragraph. (McPhee's essay originally appeared as an article in *The New Yorker,* a magazine that prizes short paragraphs.) The second transition is the word *Switzerland.* It appears in the first paragraph and reappears in the second sentence of the second paragraph. These repetitions of nouns weave the paragraphs together and provide us with an unbroken tapestry of thought.

No book can show all the possible transitions in good writing. But the principle is obvious. Transitions work by looking backward and reaching forward, by repeating words and ideas. The repetition should not tell readers only what you have already told them. It should rather be a base from which you spring to tell them something new.

From what you have learned in this chapter, you should be able to analyze paragraphs in any book or magazine. Test your own skill by locating transitions that bind paragraphs together in some enjoyable piece of prose. Then practice by building your own.

LENGTH OF PARAGRAPHS

How long should a paragraph be? Journalists break their paragraphs every two or three sentences. Most newspapers and many magazines are printed in narrow columns. Copy editors indent frequently to break up multiple lines of type. In academic writing paragraphs may run on for a page of more. One rule of thumb based on visual effect holds that the length of a paragraph should not exceed its width. If you weave your sentences together by the patterns of repetition and development that I have shown in this chapter, you may indent in numerous places where you may not have thought to indent at first. I sometimes look at a page in my own writing and decide that I want to divide a paragraph that has become too long for my taste. I can always find a place where the flow changes just enough to allow a new indentation.

Whatever the length of your paragraphs, observe the first-sentence rule. Make your first sentence your introduction. Take a thought from it, and develop that thought in the next sentence. Then choose whether you want to make the third sentence develop a thought from the second sentence or whether you want to leap back over the second sentence and pick up something from the first. Always remember that an essay develops thoughts. Sentences repeat something earlier and push forward to something new.

CONCLUDING REMARKS

Your first efforts to build paragraph unity may be hard. But as you get the hang of analyzing your own sentences, the going gets easier. Writing is like dancing: Learning the first steps requires concentration, and you may well step on your partner's feet or—more likely in modern dancing to rock music—collide with somebody else on the floor. But suddenly, with practice, the knack comes, and you keep time to the music with your feet as if you had been born to it. When you write, pay attention to the development of your thoughts. Look at the relation of your sentences to one another, and the paragraphs will take care of themselves.

Fundamental Principles of Sentences

entences make statements or ask questions. We make sentences naturally
when we speak. Otherwise we would not be understood except in the
most simple of ways. Some people say we seldom communicate in complete sentences, but they are mistaken. In any conversation, we speak in complete sentences unless we are answering a question or adding information to
something we said or something somebody else said or agreeing or disagreeing. To say that a sentence is complete is only to say that it makes sense. Most
sentences make sense by naming a subject and making a statement about it.

> My son is asleep upstairs.

Here the writer names a subject, "My son," and makes a statement about
it: "Is asleep upstairs." The completed statement is called a *predicate* to the subject. A predicate is any statement we can make about something else. Once you
form a basic statement, clauses, phrases, and other modifiers may amplify it,
just as harmonies amplify the theme of a melody. The statement itself is primary. Sentences may go wrong because the writers lose track of the statement
they wish to make. To reduce the confusion, name your subject, and immediately make a statement about it. Once arrived at your basic statement, you can
weave clauses, phrases, and other modifiers around it. Sentences like this one
turn up in the early drafts of most of us now and then:

> Since the Japanese, a people whose artistic care for the daily life has always ex-
> cited Americans, live crowded together on their small islands, they have been
> forced to construct social customs to help them live in harmony in close quarters,
> which are the bases for much of their art, including their love of miniaturization.

The sentence loses us because it tries to do too much in too little space. Here is the main statement:

> The Japanese have made art from the necessity of living close together on their crowded islands.

Once arrived at the basic statement, we can do several things with it. We can add some elements.

> The Japanese have made art of the necessity of living close together in their crowded islands—an art that includes social customs and miniaturization.

We can break our thoughts into several sentences, expanding some of them.

> The Japanese have made art out of the necessity of living close together in their crowded islands. Part of that art has been their social customs that provide careful ritual forms for daily life. Another has been their fondness for miniaturization. Americans have always been fascinated by Japanese art—perhaps because its dedication to small things is opposite to their own taste for grandeur.

In writing each sentence, try to keep the core statement in mind before you start. Take a breath. Form the main idea in your head. Only then start to write. As you write, add some elements. Adding will be no problem if you know what the main statement of the sentence will be. Too many of my students appear to start sentences in the mood of a motorcycle rider who leaps onto his machine at night and, without turning on the lights, roars off into the dark, hoping that the gods of the road will help him get somewhere. They start writing without any idea of where they are going. The results are not hard to predict.

Think for a moment about what you want to say. What is happening? Who is acting? Who or what receives the action? Don't confuse readers by packing too many important details in a single sentence. But don't condense things so much that you leave out information required to complete your thought.

KINDS OF SENTENCES

English sentences make three kinds of statements.

1. A sentence may tell us that the subject does (or did, or will do) something.

> Jones rode the elephant.

The subject is Jones. He did something. He rode the elephant.
2. A sentence may describe a condition, telling the state of the subject's existence.

> Jones was proud.

In what condition was Jones? He was proud. Sentences describing conditions use a linking verb to tell what the condition is. The most common linking verb is some form of the verb to be. If we say, "She is tall," we describe her condition or some quality of her existence, and we link the subject with the adjective tall by using the linking verb is. But other verbs can also be linking verbs. "Jones seemed brave." "The elephant looked annoyed." "The spectators felt uneasy." All these verbs describe the condition of the subject. They link the subject to an adjective that describes it.

3. A sentence may describe an action done to the subject.

> Jones was trampled by the elephant.

When action is done to the subject, we say that the verb in the sentence is in the passive voice. The subject does not act through the verb. The subject is acted upon.

WRITING GOOD SENTENCES

1. Use the active voice.

In the strongest sentences, the subject does something. The verb tells what the subject does. Although the passive voice is a good and necessary part of the English language, it will deaden your style if you use it too much.

We seldom use the passive when we speak. We don't say, "Jack's car was driven into the reservoir Saturday night." We say, "Jack drove his car into the reservoir Saturday night." We want to know agents. Who did it? The passive does not answer that question. Bureaucratic publications, especially those put out by government agencies, often use the passive to evade responsibility.

> "Mistakes have been made in my office," Congressman Jack S. Swindler told reporters. "Somehow a great deal of money contributed to my last campaign was transferred to my personal bank account, and it was used to send me and my family on a cruise to the Caribbean. The persons responsible will be found and punished."

Congressman Swindler means that he took the money out of his campaign's treasury and used it to take a vacation with his family in the Caribbean. But the passive voice seems to let him escape responsibility. It makes the whole affair sound like a computer error. Inexperienced writers may use the passive because they think it sounds impressive. But the passive sounds impersonal—voiceless and often dishonest. Consider the following:

> Minor characters in Shakespeare's plays have often been studied.
>
> The book was highly recommended.

Who studied the minor characters? Who recommended the book? We want to know. Yes, you can add a prepositional phrase to provide the agent. "The book was recommended by the author's mother." But it is more honest to be simple and direct. "The author's mother recommended the book, but most reviewers said the only reason for reading it would be if the penalty for not reading it were a good beating."

Use the passive when the recipient of the action is more important for your purpose than the actor.

Hoover was elected in 1928.

Uncle Mike was hit by a bicycle as he left the saloon on Saturday night.

The *Mona Lisa* was once stolen from the Louvre in Paris.

Use the passive in paragraphs that make a series of statements about a subject. The writer wishes to keep attention fixed on one subject. To do so he or she may use the passive as Robert Caro does in this paragraph from his biography of Lyndon Johnson. Caro describes Johnson's first congressional campaign in Texas. The passive forms are in italics.

> The speeches were generally *delivered* on Saturday: traditionally, rural campaigning in Texas was largely *restricted* to Saturdays, the day on which farmers and their wives came into town to shop, and *could be addressed* in groups. On Saturdays two automobiles, Johnson's brown Pontiac and Bill Deason's wired-for-sound gray Chevy, would head out of Austin for a swing through several large towns. On the outskirts of each town, Johnson would get out of the Pontiac ("He thought it looked a little too elaborate for a man running for Congress," Keach says) and walk into the town, while the Chevy would pull into the square, and Deason or some other aide would use the loudspeaker to urge voters to "Come see Lyndon Johnson, your next Congressman," and to "Come hear Lyndon Johnson speak at the square"; to drum up enthusiasm, records *would be played* over the loudspeaker.[1]

The passive verb phrases—italicized in this paragraph—allow Caro to keep his focus. Now and then, as in the first sentence, he might have changed to the active: "Johnson generally delivered these speeches on Saturdays," but Caro probably wished to avoid repeating Johnson's name too often in his large book. He shifted to the passive here to give readers some relief from this repetition. Use the active whenever you can; when you use the passive, have a reason for doing so.

2. Make Most of Your Verbs Assert Action Rather Than Describe a Condition.

You can say this:

> Most Americans are believers in capital punishment according to polls.

But it is better to say this:

> Polls show that most Americans believe in capital punishment.

The first sentence states a condition in the phrase *are believers.* The second sentence has two action verbs, *show* and *believe.* You can say this:

> Many Americans are of the opinion that foreign cars are more durable than American cars.

But it is more vivid to say this:

> Most Americans *think* foreign cars *last* longer than American cars.

The principle comes down to this. Occasionally check your use of *to be* verbs—*is, am, are, was,* and *were*—by circling them on a page. When you see a lot of them, revise. Don't be a fanatic about changing them. *To be* verbs are vital to the language, and you must use them sometimes, but too many will dull your prose.

3. Don't Digress in a Sentence. Support Your Basic Statement.

Everything in your sentence should support your basic statement. Sometimes inexperienced writers throw needless information into a sentence to show how much they know or simply because the information is interesting. Look at this sentence.

> President Andrew Jackson, who married a woman before her divorce from a previous husband was legally valid, ordered the removal of the Cherokee Indians from Eastern Tennessee and Western North Carolina in 1836.

President Jackson's marital troubles are interesting. But they have nothing to do with Jackson's decision to move the Cherokee Indians from their homes to Oklahoma on what became the "Trail of Tears." In this sentence, drop the clause about Jackson's marriage. Keep a tight focus on your prose. Don't wander off into nonessentials.

4. Combine Thoughts to Avoid Choppy Sentences.

We usually apply the term *choppy* to a string of short sentences, but choppiness does not reside in the shortness alone. Choppiness occurs when a writer cannot subordinate minor thoughts to major thoughts and needlessly and monotonously repeats the same sentence forms. Choppiness may also result from a lack of connection between sentences. We read a paragraph like the following with increasing annoyance:

> We biked steadily uphill. We biked along the river. We were silent now. We were too tired to talk. The ridges above us were covered with trees. Most of them were conifers. They were dark green. They gave a tinge of melancholy to the day. A wind blew. It was soft. It whispered in the trees. Below us the river splashed over the rocks. It was in the valley floor. We heard the two sounds distinctly. The wind in the trees. The river splashing over the rocks. Another sound was the whisper of the bike tires on the road. The road was asphalt. The sound was scarcely audible.

Writing such a paragraph in a first draft might not be a bad idea. Setting down these impressions in order helps you pull your memories together. But in revising, you should combine and subordinate some thoughts to others.

> We biked steadily uphill along the river. We were silent now, too tired to talk. Above us the ridges were covered with conifers, dark green, giving a tinge of melancholy to the day, and a wind blew, whispering in the trees. Below us the river splashed over rocks in the valley floor, and we heard the two sounds and a third sound—the sound of our own breathing, ragged and hard. A fourth sound, scarcely audible, was the whisper of the bike tires on the asphalt road.

I have written of bonding sentences by repetition from one sentence to the next. But avoid *unnecessary* repetition that slows the pace of your prose. Don't make readers ask themselves why you are telling them something you have told them before. Repeat only enough to make transitions from your earlier thoughts to the essay.

5. Avoid Writing Too Many Dependent Clauses in a Single Sentence.

Dependent clauses help us write in a mature style. All good writers use them.

> *After he had done his Christmas shopping for others,* he bought a large gift for himself, wrapped it up in gaudy paper with a bright holiday ribbon, put it under the tree, and told visitors *that it was from his best friend.*

The italicized words represent two dependent clauses. The first, beginning with *After* is an adverbial clause, modifying the verbs *bought, wrapped, put,* and *told* in the main clause that follows. The final dependent clause, *that it was from his best friend,* is a noun clause, the direct object of the verb *told.* Every dependent clause serves as an adverb, an adjective, or a noun in another clause.

Too many dependent clauses will clutter your thoughts, weakening the force of your basic statements. Be aware of them, and avoid the temptation to stuff too many into a single sentence. The lean style now favored in American writing keeps dependent clauses to a minimum. One dependent clause in a sentence rarely makes trouble. But don't put one in every sentence. When you put two dependent clauses in a sentence, a little flag should go up in your mind. When you have three, the flag should wave back and forth, and you should examine the sentence to try to simplify it. Now and then you may say, "I need three dependent clauses here." Fine. But give your readers a break in the next sentence. Make it simple.

In a first draft you may write overcrowded sentences. As you revise, pull out distracting clauses. Make them into sentences of their own, or eliminate them altogether. Like the other principles in this book, this one is observed with wide variations among writers. Weekly news magazines provide readable prose. It is not a prose you should slavishly imitate in all your writing. But it is sharp and clear and demonstrates the principles of readability. Here is a paragraph from a recent issue of *Time.*

> Astronaut John Glenn used to dread going to NASA's Lewis Research Center in Cleveland, Ohio. As a rookie pilot in the space agency's Mercury program, the 40-year-old Marine would periodically be required to strap himself into the tiny pod of a spacecraft simulator and wait for technicians to set it spinning in three dimensions at speeds exceeding 30 r.p.m. Using nothing more than a joystick, Glenn would have to bring the tumbling cockpit to heel. If he succeeded, he would continue in the program. If he failed, he could be bilged.[2]

In this paragraph are only two dependent clauses, one in each of the last two sentences, *If he succeeded,* and *If he failed.*

You can often revise a dependent clause into a modifying phrase. Clauses beginning with *who, which, that,* and *what* can often be reduced to phrases. You may write this:

> The island, which had appeared as a spot on the horizon earlier, now broadened into a large land mass which had palm trees waving over a white beach.

But it's more concise to write this:

> The island, a spot on the horizon earlier, now broadened into a large land mass with palm trees waving over a white beach.

You may write this:

> Our captain, who was an arrogant young man who spoke to us as if we were ignorant children, pointed at the rocks beneath the surface.

But it's more concise to write this:

> Our captain, an arrogant young man, pointed to the rocks beneath the surface, speaking to us as if we were ignorant children.

You can write this:

> What is dangerous about the charge is not that he had a love affair with a young woman but that he lied about it under oath.

But it's better to write this:

> The danger of the charge is not that he had a love affair with a young woman but that he lied about it under oath.

6. Begin Most Sentences with the Subject.

The normal pattern for sentences is *subject + predicate.* Experienced writers follow this pattern in most sentences. Look through a copy of almost any book or magazine, and you will discover about four-fifths of the sentences begin with the subject, whether a noun standing alone or a subject phrase. Here are two paragraphs from Richard Ellmann's biography of the great Irish writer James Joyce. They concern Joyce and his father John.

> The food bill was managed with equal address. The family lived on credit from grocers who dwelt in the expectation of being paid at least a little of the debts they had foolishly allowed to accumulate. Once when John Joyce had collected his monthly pension at David Drimmie and Son, his daughter Mabel persuaded him to pay off the grocer, give up drinking, and start afresh. The grocer eagerly accepted the money, then closed the account. John Joyce vowed he would never pay off a bill again, and doubtless he kept his word.
>
> His oldest son surveyed this scene with amusement and spoke of it with disarming candor. He told Eugene Sheehy that when he entered University College and had to put down his father's occupation, he listed it as, "Entering for competitions," because John Joyce always hoped to triumph in a puzzle contest and so

get a windfall. John Joyce, for his part, was not pleased with his son's failure to continue winning scholastic prizes at the university. He would ask him what profession he planned to go into, journalism, the bar, or medicine, and get no answer. He prodded and taunted his son, but got nowhere. Neither of them contemplated doing anything about the family situation; it was irremediable, and they cultivated a disregard for it which the son carried off more easily than his father. There was not much tension between them, however, because James Joyce saw his father principally in the evenings, and sometimes, since they were both out late, John at the pubs and James walking with Stanislaus, Byme, or Cosgrave, did not see him at all.[3]

Ellmann's lucid paragraphs show a typical pattern in readable English style. Only two sentences do not begin with the subject. Both begin with adverbs—*Once* in the first paragraph and *There* in the second.

7. When You Do Not Begin with the Subject, Usually Begin with Some Form of Adverb—A Word, a Phrase, or a Clause.

Ellmann's prose is typical in that when he does not begin with the subject, he begins with some kind of adverb. Sentence opening adverbs almost always modify the verb in the main clause. Adverbs answer the questions *where* and *when* and sometimes *how, how often,* and *how much.* Let's look at other sentences from Ellmann that demonstrate sentence openers. Here is a sentence that begins with an adverbial clause.

> As May Joyce's condition became worse, James moved aimlessly about the city, waiting for her to die.[4]

Here is a sentence that begins with an adverbial phrase.

> In her last hours, she lay in a coma, and the family knelt about the bed, praying and lamenting.[5]

And we have seen in the two Ellmann paragraphs noted above, sentences may begin with simple adverbs such as *once, there,* and others such as *yesterday, then,* and *tomorrow.*

8. Begin Few Sentences with the Adverb *There.*

There often introduces an inverted sentence, that is, a sentence in which the verb comes before the subject as in Ellmann's sentence noted above, beginning, "There was not much tension between them . . ." Ellmann's example shows that to begin an occasional sentence with *there* is no sin. But don't begin sentences with *there* without giving it a second thought. I find only a sprinkling of sentences beginning with *there* in the prose I read for pleasure. All too often to begin with *there* leads to vagueness. You can say this:

> There were several reasons he refused to smoke.

But you can get to the point faster by saying this:

> He refused to smoke because he feared cancer, his wife and children hated the smell, and he once set fire to his bed with a cigar.

To begin a sentence with *it is* raises similar problems. We can say this:

> It is common for people who tan every summer to get skin cancer.

But this is stronger:

> Skin cancer is common among people who tan every summer.

Now and then we all use *It is,* just as we all begin some sentences with *There.* Be stingy with such beginnings, and your prose will be stronger for it.

9. Use Participial Sentence Openers Sparingly.

A participial opener always uses a participle as an adjective to modify the subject of the sentence. Professional writers sometimes use participial openers to compress information, especially in news magazines, where space is short. It used to mark the style of *Time,* so much so that it was almost a cliché of the magazine, but that journal has wisely cut back radically on the participial opening in recent years. Here is a participial opening:

> Rolling through Pennsylvania, the train swept by farms and small towns at sixty-five miles an hour.

Nothing is wrong with that sentence, but it is not the natural way we speak. Too many such openings make our prose seem stilted, unnatural.

Sometimes a participial opening uses an implied verb, and *Time* still makes use of this opening several times in an issue.

> A Louisiana native, Beene gave up studying medicine at 19, believing that he could best express himself through design.[6]

You might place the participial *being* at the beginning of the sentence, but it is here understood. The same form appears now and then in Ellmann's biography of James Joyce.

> Resentful and inert, angry and indifferent, Joyce watched the marionettes outside his house, and inside saw his mother slowly die.[7]

And now and then a participial opener may let a writer invert a sentence, putting the subject after the verb to obtain a pleasing variety. Here is a sentence from a story in *National Geographic* written by a mountain climber who scaled a difficult peak in Antarctica. The "porta-ledge" was a narrow plank thrust into a crack in the rock to allow them to rest.

> Dangling directly overhead was the porta-ledge that Gordon and Alex called home.[8]

But any study of modern professional writing will show that participial openings are rare. They violate the general rule that a readable written sentence follows the common patterns of speech. We rarely use participial openers in

❋

spoken sentences. We don't say, "Having been out in the cold wind all day, I'm nearly dead." We say something like this: "I've been out in the cold wind all day, and I'm nearly dead."

Participial openers must modify the grammatical subject; otherwise we get confusing sentences opened by dangling participles, participles that do not correctly modify the subject.

> Killed while crossing the road, police said the chicken was not able to outrun the beer truck.

A participle may also dangle when it seems to modify nothing as in this sentence:

> Flying every week between Boston and New York, it was hard for her to fear airplanes.

Was a mysterious *it* flying between Boston and New York every week?

10. Be Economical with Adjectives.

Mark Twain had a rule about adjectives: "As to the Adjective: when in doubt, strike it out."[9] Follow Twain's rule.

Adjectives add qualities to nouns and pronouns. Use them only when they are necessary. Too many adjectives clog prose and weaken sentences. Here is Philip Caputo, writing about the Vietnam War. I have italicized the adjectives.

> They had been together for years and assumed they would remain together until the end of their enlistments. Sergeant Sullivan's death shattered that assumption. It upset the sense of unity and stability that had pervaded life in the battalion. One-Three was a corps in the *old* sense of the word, a body, and Sullivan's death represented the amputation of a *small* part of it. The corps would go on living and functioning without him, but it was *aware* of having lost something *irreplaceable.* Later in the war, that sort of feeling became *rarer* in *infantry* battalions. Men were killed, evacuated with wounds, or rotated home at a *constant* rate. By that time a loss only meant a gap in the line that needed filling.[10]

In a passage with 140 words, we have only eight adjectives—a proportion of about one adjective to every 17.5 words. If any single quality marks the style of those counted as good writers in America today, it is probably stinginess in the use of adjectives. Weigh every adjective you are tempted to use, and follow Mark Twain's advice. If you don't need it, throw it out.

11. Don't Use Nouns as Adjectives.

Much official language from bureaucracies groans under the tyranny of nouns pretending to be adjectives. Proper nouns can sometimes serve as adjectives— the *Gettysburg* Address, the *Marshall* Plan, or the *Bowery* Bank. Some words have the same form whether they are nouns are adjectives—*volunteer, deputy, savage, poor,* and multitudes of others. But most common nouns—especially those ending in *-tion, -sion, -ism,* and *-ness*—do not work well as adjectives. A careful writer will avoid constructions like the following.

> The implementation committee decided on a program of book acquisition processes for the library.

> She was a management consultant interested in the optimization of minimal resource use.

> The reporters had learned scrutiny thoroughness.

A better writer would say:

> The committee decided on a program to acquire books for the library.

> As a consultant about management, she was interested in using as few resources as necessary.

> The reporters learned to scrutinize facts thoroughly.

Many writers in companies, government, and other bureaucracies use lots of nouns as adjectives in a mistaken effort to make their writing seem more important and profound. Instead their prose becomes stiff and unreadable. Here again normal speech patterns offer a standard. We don't say, "We want to implement these quality-control procedures in automobile manufacturing." That's a mouthful. We say something like this: "We want to set up some procedures to control quality in making cars." We should follow the natural inclinations of the spoken language when we can.

12. For Sentence Variety, Occasionally Use Free Modifiers and Absolutes.

A *free modifier* is a participial phrase placed at the end of a sentence after a comma but modifying the subject. Free modifiers may replace dependent clauses. The free modifiers in these sentences are in italics.

> Sonny's car rolled into the lake, *sinking out of sight beneath the muddy water.*

> He recited his poetry with his eyes shut in ecstasy, *allowing the audience to sneak out of the room without embarrassment.*

Several free modifiers at the end of a sentence, all of them modifying the subject, can provide a sense of vigorous action.

> The Tennessee River flooded for the second time in a few weeks, covering highways and sweeping one railroad bridge away, severing communication.[11]

The participles *covering, sweeping,* and *severing* begin free modifiers and provide a speedy sense of the river in flood.

Free modifiers carry a sense of progression, showing one thing happening after another, leading to a climax.

She inched her way up the face of the cliff, *feeling* for holds in the rock, *moving* with infinite care, *balancing* herself delicately step after step, not *daring* to look down, *breathing* hard, *fearing* exhaustion, *going* on, *wallowing* at last onto a shelf of rock, safe at the top.

Free modifiers appear again and again in American prose. Master the form—participle followed by phrase after a comma, coming at the end of the sentence, modifying the subject. Some free modifying phrases imply the participle *being*.

Those who knew the river always felt that it seemed a thing alive, with a will and a personality.

You can insert the participle *being* before the preposition *with,* and have a complete free modifier. But here the *being* is easily understood and so is left out.

Absolutes share some qualities and stylistic advantages allowed by free modifiers. Whereas a free modifier is a participle introducing a phrase modifying the subject, an *absolute* is a noun followed by a phrase, and together noun and phrase modify the whole clause in which the absolute appears.

Allen Ginsberg was an icon of the Sixties, *his poetry proclaiming the spirit of revolt that marked the time.*

The absolute is the phrase at the end. You might substitute two sentences for the sentence with the absolute: "Allen Ginsberg was an icon of the Sixties. His poetry proclaimed the spirit of revolt that marked the time." But use of the absolute turns two somewhat choppy sentences into one vigorous one. Absolutes express action well, making them useful in both fiction and nonfiction. Here is a paragraph from John M. Barry's *Rising Tide.* It describes a trip made by a commission made up of black Americans, led by Robert Russa Moton, to investigate relief efforts in the wake of the horrendous flood of the Mississippi River in 1927. I have put the absolutes in italics, including those where the participle *being* is understood but not written.

In early June in Memphis the Colored Advisory Commission met for the first time. Moton divided the members into small groups and sent each into different areas of the flood zone. Their trips were strenuous. One investigator reported: "Our train took six hours to go eleven miles, *the water up to the lower steps of the car; the train in utter darkness the lights having failed, the Jim Crow coach half occupied by whites, and the remainder packed with Negroes some sitting three to a seat, aisles filled with men standing and the noise of the water boiling over the track, terrifying one woman until she screamed* and put down the window to shut out the sound, with the people refusing to sing because of what seemed to be a sullen resentment at their treatment. It was an experience which will long cling to me."[12]

The anonymous report within this paragraph is filled with absolutes that convey the drama of the scene far better than a series of short, choppy sentences might do.

13. Use a Triad Now and Then to Write Effective Prose.

Teachers of speech in ancient Greece noted the power of triads—groups of three verbs, adjectives, nouns, and adverbs—in rhetoric. The Greeks called this form the *tricolon;* I think *triad* is more familiar and useful to us. Such triads are still effective and frequent in English prose today. My heart leaps up when I find one in student prose, for the triad betokens a reaching toward professionalism in writing. You should use triads like pepper on food. A little adds taste to the whole, but too much makes the dish inedible.

Triple compound verbs, where a single subject controls three verbs, show up again and again in modern prose, but I seldom see them in student prose. Here you should imitate professional writers without going overboard. Compound verbs of all sorts compress action and quicken the pace of prose. They are especially valuable in conveying a sense of movement in narrative.

> I moved to Rome, rented a room, and made the rounds of the seedy little nightclubs near the Via Veneto. I introduced myself as an American singer available for bookings, but the streetwise club owners and musicians just smiled, shook their heads, and told me I shouldn't be out alone at night.[13]

The triple direct object can provide a good end to a strong clause. This sentence comes from the common practice of dueling in nineteenth-century America:

> Obeying the code of honor showcased a man's *courage, integrity, and conviction,* and marked him as leadership material.[14]

The triple predicate nominative, describing the subject, is also common:

> The body of an adolescent girl was held sacred in the Victorian era because it represented *purity, civilized morality, and the future of the race.*[15]

A triple repetition can be useful (note that the second sentence contains two triads, the second being a triple object of a preposition):

> Herbert Hoover was a brilliant fool. He was *brilliant* in the way his mind could seize and grapple with a problem, *brilliant* in his ability to accomplish a task, and *brilliant* in the originality, comprehensiveness, and depth of the political philosophy he developed.[16]

A triad of clauses can make an effective sentence:

> On August 19, 1965, the court convicted seventeen of these defendants to prison sentences ranging from three years and three months to life imprisonment. *Three defendants were acquitted; one died before he could be brought to trial; another was excused because of illness.*[17]

14. Use Appositives to Speed the Pace of Your Sentences.

An *appositive* is a word or phrase written after a noun to rename or otherwise define or describe the noun. The simplest appositives are nouns or adjectives.

> McDougal had his meal, *a cheeseburger.*
>
> The monastery, isolated and quiet, became his refuge.

❋

Appositives can be longer phrases.

> The foreign press, *a chummy and highly competitive bunch,* emerged from its lair at the Hotel Inglaterra coffee shop and raced to the waterfront.[18]

An appositive can also be a phrase set off by dashes.

> During the day our house was as silent as a graveyard. I'd run aimlessly through the rooms—*those beautiful, immaculate, unused rooms*—past the polished antiques, the big grand piano, the voluptuous couches piled with pillows.[19]

Now and then an appositive clause may be set off by a dash for special emphasis.

> I didn't object to the presence of this stage villain—he could walk into a one-reel melodrama from 1912, no questions asked—because he reinforced the growing sense that "Titanic" is, for all its narrative dexterity and the formidable modernity of its methods, an old-fashioned picture.[20]

15. When You Must Write Long Sentences, Balance Them with Short Sentences to Give Readers Some Relief.

Readers search for the basic statement in every sentence. The longer the sentence, the more difficult it is to find the basic statement. We can all understand this sentence, although it is fairly long.

> Although the rain fell hard enough to strip the leaves from the trees, leaving the air thick with the smell of shattered foliage, the drought had been so severe that we still needed water after the storm had passed on up the valley and the rain had stopped.

Several sentences of such length running together on a page force us to slow down so we can absorb them. Much academic writing seldom reaches a broader public because the writers pile one long sentence after another in what amounts to a gray flood of print. Readers get tired easily. We can look down on them for that. But it would be better to communicate with them.

Readers usually read at a constant pace. So they usually keep their eyes moving whether they understand the sentences or not. They may skip over what they don't understand—and you lose your point. After a long sentence like the one above, a short one is in order.

> An inch below the surface, the ground was dry.

No one can make an ironclad rule about the length of sentences. Short sentences are more readable than long ones. But no one wants to write like the old Dick-and-Jane readers: "See Spot. See Spot run. See Spot bite the postman. See the postman beat Spot to death with *National Geographic.*" Our language is an almost infinitely complex pattern of different sounds that make sense because we give meanings to the differences. A cat is not the same as a bat or a hat or even a gnat. For reasons beyond the power of a mere writer to explain, we take pleasure in the differences between words, finding satisfaction in creating or hearing variety in language. This quality seems to be built into the human mind. Not only do we seek variety in our words, but we look for it in sentences, both in their structure and in their length. We do not want all sentences to be alike. We do not want them to be all the same length. We don't want the same form in all of them.

Good writers aim at clarity, but they should aim at more than clarity: They should try to give pleasure. Part of that pleasure comes from constructing sentences in different lengths that fit together naturally. At least we think the sentences are natural when we read or hear them. We absorb them with ease and sometimes with delight. All this is to say that a steady progression of short, clear sentences may convey the writer's meaning but crush readers with boredom because such sentences do not satisfy the craving of the mind for variety in language. Somehow as writers we must find the golden mean between a clarity that sounds childish or otherwise monotonous and a complexity that is beyond comprehension.

CONCLUDING REMARKS ON SENTENCES

Be your own critic and coach. When you read something you enjoy, take a moment to study the sentences. Look at both structure and words. Try to incorporate into your own writing some of the stylistic devices you see in things you like to read. Remember that the main job of the sentence is to make a comprehensible statement. You can write foggy sentences in your first draft; let the light shine in your later drafts. Ask yourself this question: What is the most important thing I have to say in this sentence? Be sure you answer that question clearly in one statement. That statement should form the core of the sentence.

Avoiding Wordiness

If I could reduce all my advice about style to one sentence, it would be this: Use as few words as possible to say what you mean.

Note that the advice is not to use as few words as possible. It is to use as few words as you can to say what you mean—exactly what you mean. William Faulkner meant to say more than Ernest Hemingway did; therefore Faulkner used more words to describe a moment of action. Note, too, that both of them wrote more fiction than nonfiction.

In modern nonfiction, efficiency is the rule. Good prose is lean and spare, and every word counts. Readers do not have time for wordiness; besides, wordiness confuses them. Long, convoluted sentences, senseless repetition, tortuous dependent clauses, and clumsy phrases all work together to make them throw down the book or the article.

Brevity does not mean mindless simplicity. You must use enough words to say what you mean. If you do not give readers enough information, they cannot understand what you say. Nor does brevity mean that you write without drama, richness, and variety. It does mean that you cut every word, every sentence, every paragraph that does not add essential information. As you write, rethink your purposes, and consider anew what you have to tell your readers and what you think they can understand.

I make a game of my own editing. I look at every sentence, seeing how I can trim a word here, a sentence there. Do I need this paragraph? Have I said this before? Do my readers know this fact already, or do I have to tell them? Can I rewrite the sentence altogether to make it shorter and sharper?

Here is a sentence that gets revised in a hurry.

> When we consider the millions of dollars given to athletes for their performance and skill along with the adulation of countless fans and the prevailing sense that they can do no wrong and that they are therefore above the laws that bind ordinary mortals, it may be concluded that we should not be surprised when a millionaire basketball player tries to strangle a coach who yells at him.

Scratching out a word or a phrase here or there is not enough to mend the problems. The writer must shift gears and rewrite.

> Millionaire athletes with adoring fans can easily believe they are above the law, and so we have the spectacle of a basketball star who tried to strangle a coach who yelled at him.

You don't have to say "When we consider," and we know already that athletes are paid for their performance. Once we take out those phrases, we must reshape the whole sentence.

Here is where reading your own prose counts. Cut out clumsy phrases. Don't say, "It may be concluded that . . . " Just give the conclusion—whatever it is. Don't say, "What I mean to say is that . . . " Just say what you mean to say without saying "I mean to say." Don't say, "It must be recognized." Say, "We recognize." Be natural. People who strain for effect often have the effect of straining the reader.

Institutional publications revel in unnatural styles. Professor Richard Lanham of U.C.L.A. calls it the "official style," and it seems to be everywhere. The writers in the official style have mixed motives. They want to communicate, but they want also to assert their own importance. Here is an example taken from a job listing in the official *Gazette* of my university:

> Network Engineer. Office for Information Technology. Responsible for the planning, design, and implementation of communications networks carrying data, video, and voice signals throughout the university. Evaluates the relative technical merits of alternative technologies and design approaches. Prepares initial system specifications and designs for proposed networks or subnetworks.

The author of this document intended to avoid ambiguity. Unfortunately, the result is the official style. Note words like *implementation* and *alternative* and nouns like *information* and *design* used as adjectives. Professional writers don't *implement* things. They *do* them. They don't talk about *alternative technologies*. They speak of *various* technologies or simply "technologies," assuming that the plural form of the noun includes variety. Neither do they use *relative* unless they are talking about kinfolks. Could the listing be translated into something like this:

> Network engineer wanted to design and install communications lines throughout the university. Should know modern technology and design.

We might eliminate the last line. Must a network engineer be told that she should be qualified to design and install various systems of communication?

Such abilities should go with the profession. We would not think of advertising for a dentist "who should be able to fill various kinds of teeth." Suppose we keep all the elaborate qualifications of the original. We could still write a less wordy announcement.

> Network engineer. Responsible for designing and installing communications networks for data, video, and voice signals throughout the university. Evaluates various technologies and designs. Prepares specifications for systems and designs for networks.

The official style rises from fear. Writers are afraid someone may blame them for something. Or they fear that readers will not take them seriously. They become like dancers watching their feet rather than listening to the music.

Many writers fear that what they say is not worth saying, but they believe that if they put it in a complicated language, others may think it profound. Here are a few sentences from a carefully researched article in a recent *American Sociological Review*, a journal aimed at sociologists. The authors investigated the "streaking" craze rampant on college campuses in the early 1970s. Students ran naked through the streets and sometimes across football fields during games. Why did people streak? The question might be of general interest, and the article is an intelligent work by two intelligent men. But it is hard to imagine that many readers could curl up with prose like this:

> The greater the complexity and heterogeneity of previous streaking events, the greater the probability that schools will adopt the fad. The innovation is more likely to be adopted when the complexity of the previous incidents of the fad in neighboring schools is greater. The complexity of streaking incidents is a stimulus for potential adopters. For example, if many males and females, students and non-students streaked repeatedly day and night, on and off campus, then many categories of persons in other nearby schools could identify with the faddish behavior. As a result, the events are no longer performed by the rowdy but become acceptable to many potential adopters.[1]

I believe this sentence can be translated into plain English like this:

> The more people streaked, the more people were likely to streak—especially if incidents of streaking were elaborate and widely publicized. If multitudes of students and nonstudents streaked day and night at a given school, streaking would not be limited to the rowdy. Many different kinds of students were likely to streak in a neighboring school.

Why do people write as authors do in the *American Sociological Review* and some other journals? The question deserves reflection. The *New England Journal of Medicine* and *Scientific American* both present complicated issues in readable prose. A major reason is that the journal itself (like the streaking in the article) feeds on habits created by the discipline. Several graduate students in sociology have told me they must write like this to be accepted into the field. One can riffle through the pages of any copy of the journal and find articles written in this well-nigh incomprehensible jargon. Any budding sociologist may be forgiven if she supposes that she must make her writing as turgid as possible before it will be accepted by the editors of the review.

Such a style is a mark of fear. Fearful writers try to avoid any hint of ambiguity—an almost impossible burden for prose to bear. No writing except the thickest legal prose is entirely without ambiguity. Take this sentence as an example: "The greater the complexity and heterogeneity of previous streaking events, the greater the probability that schools will adopt the fad." Why both "complexity" and "heterogeneity"? Evidently the writers feared that we might suppose complex events were not heterogeneous events. Some process like this must have gone on in their minds: "If we say, "the more people streak, the more others are likely to streak," we might not convey our feeling that the more *diverse* people streak, the others are likely to follow their example." Taking this fear of misunderstanding into account, they spell out some of the diversity— males and females, students and nonstudents, streaking on and off campus. Later they speak of "many categories of persons" because they seem to think that if they said "many people," we might not understand that they meant many *different* people. The authorial mind at work here is like a lawyer's, resolved to write a will that no one can break. The authors do not trust their readers. In seeking to avoid every ambiguity, they wrote a prose that is misery to read.

Good writing rises out of confidence. If you believe you have something to say, you can say it clearly—or at least as clearly as the subject itself will permit. Complicated ideas may require complicated explanations. If you study an issue, gather information about it, think about it, and resolve to make sense of your ideas by writing about them, you can be confident in yourself and your readers. Confidence helps build a sound style.

No one idea about brevity suits everyone. No easy shortcuts create a brief style. You can pick up the habit of brevity only if you go over your drafts again and again. Read slowly but steadily, and force yourself to read at least some of your work aloud. Give yourself time to think through every sentence, every word. Cut out vague words, verbose phrases, unnecessary modifiers. Combine sentences when you can unless the result is a long and clumsy sentence. Examine stock phrases to see if you can shorten them. Look at this sentence:

> In the final analysis, the Japanese victory at Pearl Harbor may be regarded as a disaster for Japan.

The stock phrases are *In the final analysis* and *may be regarded as*. Say this instead.

> The Japanese victory at Pearl Harbor was a disaster for Japan.

You might write this in a first draft:

> What was most important was Hamlet's decision to accept his fate.

Say this instead:

> Most important was Hamlet's decision to accept his fate.

COMMON PROBLEMS

No chapter in a small book can solve all the problems of wordiness. But here I will address some common problems. As you study them, you may become sensitive to your own style. Cutting the fat out of prose is a habit—like exercise. Cultivate the habit. Let it discipline your writing. Nobody will hang you if you use one of the expressions listed below. Many of them spring to the fingers of most of us sometimes when we write. Now and then you can indulge yourself. But prose fat with redundancies and wordiness becomes difficult or vaguely unpleasant for readers. The writer's job is to make the reader's task as easy as possible. (The writer's job may also be to make readers as uncomfortable as possible when thinking about the issues of concern, but that is another matter.)

When you eliminate or abbreviate writing, you must sometimes rearrange the whole sentence. You cannot always be content to change or delete a word or two. Study the following examples.

Absolutely/Basically/Incredibly/Immensely/Perfectly/Positively/ Utterly/Definitely/Really

These intensifiers pop up often in the prose of inexperienced writers to show certainty. "I absolutely want to take this course." "I really liked him." "The cyclist definitely bit the dog." They have the effect of shouting, and they can clutter prose. You can usually leave them out, and your prose will be stronger for their omission. They often substitute for specific statements that could make your prose stronger. You can say, "McDougal was immensely popular." But you probably provide a better sense of McDougal if you say, "When McDougal walked down the street, people rushed up to shake his hand and clap him on the back."

Area/Region

Don't say, "The weather in the area of the southwest is hot and dry." Say this: "The weather in the southwest is hot and dry."

Aspect

Don't say, "Another aspect of the problem that should be considered is the feasibility of the project." Say this: "We should also consider whether the project can be done."

At the Present Time/At This Point in Time/At That Point in Time

Use *now* or *then* instead, or let the present or past tense give the time you want.

Case/Cases

Try to cut these words. Don't say, "In this case we see Faulkner's use of an old woman as oracle." Say this instead: "Faulkner here uses an old woman as oracle." Don't say: "In some cases exercises can kill." Say this: "Sometimes exercise kills people."

Certainly/Assuredly/Surely/Obviously

Use these words sparingly. Paradoxically enough, we use them only when we realize that a statement may not be obvious or certain. "He refused to let the police enter his house without a search warrant; obviously he had something to hide." Did he have something to hide? We don't know, but the writer thinks so. These words have their place, but you should not use them unadvisedly.

Close Proximity

Use *near* instead. Don't say, "The driveway was in close proximity to the house." Say, "The driveway was near the house."

Completely Destroyed/Totally Demolished

If something is destroyed, it is destroyed. If it is not completely destroyed, it is damaged. *Demolish* has a stronger connotation; so to say something is "totally demolished" is to commit verbal overkill.

Consensus of Opinion

The word *consensus* implies opinion. Don't say: "The consensus of opinion among reporters was that the President brought his troubles on himself." Say: "The consensus among reporters was that the President brought his troubles on himself."

Considering the Fact That

Use *although* or *because* instead. Don't say, "Considering the fact that the postman fell on him, the dog escaped with minor injuries." Say this instead: "Although the postman fell on him, the dog escaped with minor injuries."

Different

Often used unnecessarily. Don't write this: "He had taught in seven different states and knew five different languages and had been fired by thirteen different travel agents." No one could imagine that the states, the languages, and the travel agents were not different. So you don't have to use the word.

Doubled Phrases

English has a special liking for doubled phrases such as *null and void, cease and desist, pick and choose*, and *advise and consent*. They come from the English legal system. Some authorities say they result from the merger of Anglo-Saxon and Norman French after the Norman Conquest of England in 1066 when judges had to use both Norman French and Anglo-Saxon words to be understood by everyone in the audience. In ordinary writing such doubling is unnecessary. So don't write, "First and foremost, he thought he could beat up his coach because he made millions of dollars more than the coach did." Better to say, "First, he thought he could beat up his coach because . . . "

Due to the Fact That

Replace with *because*.

Each Individual

Don't use these two as adjectives to modify a noun. Don't say, "Each individual member of the team has her own talents." Say, "Each member of the team has her own talents."

End Result

Say "result" instead.

Final Outcome

Eliminate *final*.

Free Gift

Eliminate *free*. If we pay for a gift, it's not a gift.

Full and Complete

This is a doubled phrase. Say "full" or "complete" but not both.

Future Plans

This is a favorite of flight attendants. "If your future plans call for air travel, we hope you'll choose Air Chance." But how can "plans" be anything but "future"?

If and When

Use *if* or *when* but not both.

In a Position to

Use *can* instead. Don't say, "She is in a position to help him if she wants." Say, "She can help him if she wants."

In a Sense

Often unnecessary. It quibbles. "In a sense you can say he died of alcoholism." Better to be blunt. "He drank himself to death."

Incumbent

In the official style, many people write this. "It is incumbent on our company to make a profit." Why not be clear? "We must make a profit, or we will go under."

In Effect

Usually omit.

In Other Words

Usually unnecessary.

Instrumental

Often wordy. Don't say, "He was instrumental in establishing the book club." Say, "He helped . . . "

In Terms of

Almost always wordy. "Antigua in terms of weather was dry." Say instead, "Antigua is dry."

In the Event of

Replace with *if*.

In the Final Analysis

Either say "finally" or make your final point without announcing that it is final. Your readers can see that for themselves.

In the Realm of

Usually wordy. Don't say, "It is in the realm of possibility that the train will be on time." Say, "The train may be on time."

It Is Possible That

Say "can" or "may" instead. Don't say, "It is possible that some cholesterol is good for us." Say, "Some cholesterol may be good for us."

Located

This is a common word in *journalese*—the language of unthinking reporters. Don't say, "The house was located at 35 Oak Street." Say, "The house was at 35 Oak Street."

Observable Fact

Usually omit. We know we can observe some facts but not observe others, but to be told that something is an observable fact may be a deceit. "It is an observable fact that most young people are not well educated." Is that so? Educated in what? The term smacks of phony assurance about complicated matters.

One of the Things That

Usually omit. "One of the things you need to do is practice revision." Say instead, "Revise your work."

On the Occasion of

Usually cumbersome. "On the occasion of her coming, we shall all proceed into the open to offer our greetings." Say instead, "We'll all go out to meet her when she comes."

Owing to

Use *because* instead. Don't say, "Coach Dixie was unable to win the Southeastern Football Conference championship owing to the fact that his university made football players attend classes." *Because* says enough.

Period of Time

Say instead "at that time" or "in that period."

Positive Effects

Pompous. Don't say, "The rehabilitation program has had some positive effects." Say instead, "The rehabilitation program has done some good."

Prior to

Replace with *before*.

Prove Conclusively

Omit *conclusively*. See *Different* above. Don't use words to express supposedly subtle distinctions that no one of ordinary intelligence would miss.

Situation

A good word that can lead to confusion. It is so vague that writers and readers can lose track of what it means. "The Washington situation is beyond redemption." Just what is the "Washington situation"? Is it something moral? Something about military affairs? Something about politics? Something about drugs and poor schools?

Take into Account

Use *consider* instead.

The Question of Whether

A common padding phrase. "We must ask the question of whether we want to clone human beings." Better to say this: "We must ask whether we want to clone human beings."

To Some Extent

Often redundant and always vague. Don't say this: "To some extent living in the cellar has some advantages." Say this instead: "Living in the cellar has some advantages."

Veritable

Almost always unnecessary and a little pompous. "College fraternities pose a veritable flood of problems to administrations and faculty." Better to say, "Fraternities pose many problems to administrations and faculty."

Voiced the Opinion

Say *said* instead.

What Was/What Is

Often wordy and vague when used to introduce a clause at the beginning of the sentence. "What was most important was to keep the quarterback out of jail until after the Orange Bowl." Better to say this: "Coach Dixie had to keep his quarterback out of jail until after the Orange Bowl."

With a View to

Revise to eliminate. Don't say, "She bought the boat with a view to fishing." Say, "She bought the boat so she could fish."

With Regard to

Revise to eliminate. Don't say, "With regard to sportsmanship, he was more interested in winning." Say, "He was more interested in winning than in sportsmanship."

Good Diction

Diction is our choice of words when we write or speak. Good diction helps intelligent readers understand us, respect us, and believe us. Good diction in our writing is part of the ethical argument. If we use the language well, readers will find us that much more worthy of attention and belief. Slovenly diction will turn readers away more quickly than any other single quality of writing.

Words are mysterious, puzzling, beautiful things, and although we use them every day, we never quite master them. They have histories, connotations, shades of meaning, associations with a long tradition of writing and speaking. If we call someone an *opponent,* we mean one thing. If we say he is an *enemy,* we mean another. If we say a man is *charming,* we usually mean a compliment; if we say he is *smooth,* we imply a slight insult; if we call him *oily,* we mean a stronger insult, and perhaps we mean to warn off people who may be taken in by him.

Finding the right word is one of the joys of language, defining our experience to ourselves, helping to convey it to others. Mark Twain is supposed to have said that the difference between the right word and the wrong word is the difference between lightning and a lightning bug. What word best describes the sun? Hot? Incandescent? Vengeful? Mild? Weak? Benign? Pale? White? Red? Every one of these words conveys a slightly different impression, useful under various circumstances.

People sometimes ask me what book I would take to a desert island. I always reply, "A good dictionary." No other book offers so many outlets to human sensibility or makes us better aware of the seemingly infinite shadings

123

of human experience. Sometimes we may feel a vague but powerful sensibility build up inside us like a reservoir of water, but how do we tap it to use? Finding the right word may help us discover a meaning that is new to us, one that the word will make vivid to our readers. We look at a face. It inspires feelings within us, but how do we express those feelings? When we find the right word to express them, we know the feelings better; the word may help us define our own attitude.

PRINCIPLES OF GOOD DICTION

Words are used with other words; they take meaning from one another. Because English is so gloriously flexible, diction has no rules, only principles. These principles are firm enough to enumerate. Careful writers observe them and apply them to interpret choices in language. As you review the following list, you will see that various items overlap. I mentioned some of them earlier in this book.

1. Use Words Efficiently.

We should not pad our thoughts. Some speak of *preplanning* because they think the word more impressive than homely *planning.* Almost every bureaucrat nowadays speaks of *preconditions* when *conditions* would do as well. The use of *prior to* rather than the simple *before* seems to have become a linguistic virus that infects every politician who speaks ponderously into a TV camera. So we get sentences like this: "Prior to the implementation of the recently recommended policies by my committee, certain preconditions have to be satisfied by the other side."

The most efficient language is simple and natural. It creates its effects by the information it conveys and by the grace of the writing rather than by a pretense of erudition. When you have something to say, say it. Tell a friend what you want to say. Then try to write your thoughts down with the same directness that you used in explaining them aloud.

2. Write within the Written Traditions of English.

Avoid words that might lead educated readers to suppose that you are ignorant of the traditions of the written language. Writing once enjoyed a supreme authority that carried over easily from handwritten copies of books to the revolution created by printing. Printing was restricted in all countries until recently. Even in the United States with its constitutional liberties, editors and censors regulated printing, giving almost an aura of holiness to the written language, reining it in before the limits of the unprintable.

Just about anything is printable now. "Acceptable usage" is much looser than it once was because we hear words spoken on radio and television and in the movies that once would have been considered inappropriate in polite society. Many writers now use these words in their work. I find words printed in *The New Yorker* that would have made my mother turn green and that editors refused to allow Ernest Hemingway and William Faulkner to use in the 1930s and 1940s. The speech patterns of talk-show hosts and television reporters and commentators have insinuated themselves into the written language. Sometimes clarity is lost in consequence. The television commentator can use tone of voice and facial expression to convey meanings not carried in his or her atrocious vocabulary or garbled syntax. Students exposed to such language from childhood do not understand that the written language must stand by itself, without a commentator to whisper the true meaning into the ear of the reader.

Standards of written English are more informal than they have been in a long time. Even so, some words are considered ignorant by many readers. *Irregardless* is one. *Regardless* is the accepted term. *Irregardless* is a double negative in a single word, for both the prefix *ir-* and the suffix *-less* convey negation. You will never find the word in a published essay unless it occurs in a direct quotation. Despite its popularity with high school and college students, *funner* is still not an acceptable synonym for *more fun*. Although many people now say, "Myself and Cleo are giving a party Saturday night," writers who wish to be taken seriously should say, "Cleo and I are giving a party."

Nor will you find the word *ain't* in normal literate discourse, although it occurs in quotations because all sorts of people use it in speech. For some reason, *ain't*—a Cockney English word that originated in the eighteenth century—never caught on. I think it should have. But the Cockneys were lower-class, and *ain't* didn't make it. Alas.

Slang lies in the twilight zone of language. I don't penalize my first-year students for using in papers the slang they speak in the corridors and at home because words are always coming into the language from the mysterious percolation of informal talk. Slang has traditionally been a special language that sets some people apart from others, especially young people from adults. A *cool cat* to my parents was an unfortunate feline left outside on a winter night. For my generation it was another young person, usually male, who knew his way around—whatever knowing one's way around was. This year's slang may be obsolete by next year. If young people are to be taken seriously by adults—including college faculty members—who read and write serious things, they should curb the impulse toward slang. It sounds, well, juvenile. We're back to the ethical argument again. Writers about serious matters should seem serious, part of an adult world, or else their work will not be respected.

3. Avoid Fads in Usage—Especially Pretentious Fads—That Impoverish the Language.

Akin to slang but more generally spread through the population is the fad word or phrase, usually some sort of metaphor. Someone calls a financial consequence "the bottom line," and suddenly millions use the "bottom line" as the synonym for the most important consequence of any action. "The bottom line is this: Did the President lie?" At the Watergate hearings, televised for the world to see in 1973 and 1974 as the presidency of Richard Nixon toppled, one witness after another stalled for time by saying—usually with great deliberation—"At that point in time . . ." Suddenly *time* ceased to stand by itself. It had to have a *point* attached.

In the same way weather forecasters on television cannot talk about something simple like *weather* or *ice* or *snow.* They have to talk about *weather conditions* or *icy conditions* or *snowy conditions.* And one can no longer *head* a committee; one must *head up* a committee.

Commentator Edwin Newman long ago noted the ease with which we tack *-ize* on the ends of nouns to make them verbs. People now *verbalize* instead of talk. They *concertize* or they *accessorize* or they *downsize.* When the radiators went dead in my office a few winters ago, dropping the temperature to just above freezing, a technician came in, felt the chill, knocked on some pipes, and told me his crew would quickly *prioritize* my office. I wanted him to thermalize it before my shivering finalized my teeth and traumatized my fingers and my nose. The tradition of turning nouns into verbs by adding *-ize* to the end is old, but we still run the risk of letting it swamp us.

Above all, avoid language that seems to say more than it does. Don't use words that make you seem to be part of an elite group that always uses a complex word while ordinary people use simple language that proves how ordinary they are. I've given many such words in the suggestions below—words like *implement* and *bottom line* and *parameters* and others that spring to mind because people try to be fancy when the needs of language cry out for decent simplicity.

4. Use Language Idiomatically.

Idiom is as important as any word applied to English usage. It refers to habitual usages in language that have no clear logic. No language is entirely rational, and English seems more irrational than most. Its irrationality may be a sign of the vitality of the people who use it, people who refuse to be squeezed into the bondage of excessive rules. Idioms are language at its most irrational. Foreign speakers learning English have trouble with idioms—and English speakers have similar troubles when they learn foreign languages. When someone says, "Why is such an expression wrong?" our only answer is, "That's not the way we speak English."

For example, to speak and write idiomatically, we need to know how prepositions are used. We recognize that if we make *up* with someone, we have become reconciled. But to make *out* with someone implies something else, and to make *off* with something implies dishonest dealing. To pass *out* means one thing, to pass *off* means another, and to pass *on* means still something else.

We are more likely to encounter ill-used idioms in less obvious ways. For some reason we do not guess *on* the answer; we guess *at* the answer—though logic tells us we might simply *guess* the answer. Habit makes us speculate *on* the outcome of next week's game rather than speculate *in* it, but bankers speculate *in* stocks and bonds. We can say the game is *up* and mean one thing and say the game is *over* and mean another.

When we say that a carpenter *cut corners* on a job, we mean that his work was shoddy, although we know he also cut the corners of planks with his saw. When we say the speaker *took the floor,* we don't mean he took it home with him, and I can *twist your arm* to get you on my committee and yet never touch you. We can be *up in arms* because of the poor food in the cafeteria without ever having raised a weapon, and even a bald-headed boss can *let his hair down* at the office party.

Idioms change. In nineteenth-century prose, the idiom *to make love* meant to propose marriage, and Anthony Trollope in his hilarious novel *Barchester Towers* has the odious and slightly intoxicated Obadiah Slope "make love" to beautiful Eleanor Bold in a carriage. Both the gentle Trollope and his Victorian peers in England would have been outraged at the modern confusion of students reading his work today.

Idiom involves a subtle feel for language, a sense of what is appropriate to the context and purpose. A student of mine writing a few years ago on the battles of Lexington and Concord in April 1775 announced that the patriots gathered on hilltops and *affronted* the British as they marched by. In Shakespeare's time *affront* meant *confront* or *oppose by force.* But when I read my student's paper I had a vision of lines of patriots mooning the British troops and of insulted British officers saying, "Don't pay any attention to them, men! What can you expect from Americans?"

5. Accept Change Conservatively.

From what I have said so far and from your own experience, you know that language changes. Now it seems to be changing more rapidly than ever before.

New words come into English with amazing frequency. Some innovations show vitality. One of my favorite books is entitled *9000 Words: A Supplement to Webster's Third New International Dictionary*—a collection of words introduced to English within the previous fifteen years. In it I find modern coinages such as *software, dunk shot, monokini, printout,* and *life-support system,* all signs of the nearly miraculous talent human beings have for finding names to describe and control experience. (Only a few years ago the ancestor to that book was called *6000 Words.)* Computers and other forms of technology continually bring in new words to the language. I bought a new television set the other day for the first time in thirteen years. I stood puzzled by a bank of glaring and blaring screens in the electronics store, asking the salesperson many questions about technical terms that puzzled me, such as "wave-table sound." He replied in tones one would speak with a child who walked into a music store and said, "Who was Elvis?"

I like a lot of the new words. A few years ago my students started using the word *ditsy* to describe somebody somewhat disorganized and maybe irrational without being crazy. It has a nice ring to it. Maureen Dowd, columnist for the *New York Times,* likes the word, too. She writes of "a ditsy, predatory White House intern who might have lied under oath for a job at Revlon."[1] But I still would not write in a formal essay on history that Martin Luther's rival Andreas Karlstadt was "ditsy." I like the word *underwhelming* as an ironic opposite to the common word *overwhelming.* It is a common word in newspapers. Sports writers coin words frequently or change the meaning of common words. A *hot dog* is not merely a sausage to be eaten on a long bun; it also designates an athlete who shows off—or *showboats.* And maybe in time some historian will write, "In the Iraq crisis of 1998 the American Secretary of State Madeleine Albright did a lot of diplomatic showboating, hoping to make Saddam Hussein back down."

So the language evolves, and we should all be happy that it does. But I remain a conservative in my unwillingness to use some new words in formal writing until they have passed the test of time. In the last edition of this little book, I noted that *Time* had reported on a new edition of the Bible in black "street language." In the *Black Bible Chronicles,* the serpent in Genesis tempts Eve to eat the fruit God has forbidden to her and Adam. Eve replies, "Yeah, snake, I can eat of these trees, just not the tree of knowledge or the Almighty said I'd be knocked off." The serpent replies, "Nah, sister, he's feeding you a line of bull. You won't die. The Almighty just knows that if you eat from the tree you'll be hipped to what's going down."[2] I wrote in the third edition, "I have the feeling that this Bible will not catch on." It did not.

Our language is a currency of meaning. Currencies work best when their values remain fairly constant and inflation is gradual. If too many words mean one thing today and another tomorrow, communication between generations breaks down. It is a great gift that an adolescent can enjoy Jonathan Swift's *Gulliver's Travels,* written over two centuries ago, and that the novels of Charles Dickens still live for readers almost a hundred and thirty years after Dickens died. American democracy rests on a constitution written generations ago that still makes sense to us.

In his novel *1984,* George Orwell invented the word *newspeak* to mean the terrifying loss of the common meanings of words. Tyrants in this century have used a perverted language to subjugate their people. The former Soviet Union established satellite states called "people's democracies." But in these "democracies," the people dared not dissent publicly from government edicts, and no election was honest. When the Soviet Union dissolved and these false "democracies" were overthrown, people rushed into the streets singing and rejoicing.

A perverted language where words are torn away by force from their traditional meanings will inevitably lead to cynicism and distrust. In the United States, something called "national security" has enabled our own government to invade the privacy of its citizens, burgle their houses and their offices, tap their telephone lines, limit their freedom of speech, and threaten them for having unpopular opinions.

Acceptable Change

Yet the language does change. Some conservative critics express themselves foolishly. In the introduction to this book, I referred to the critic John Simon's sentiments, uttered apparently with a straight face:

> Why does language keep changing? Because it is a living thing, people will tell you. Something that you cannot press forever, like a dead flower, between the pages of a dictionary. Rather, it is a living organism that, like a live plant, sprouts new leaves and flowers. Alas, this lovely albeit trite image is—as I have said before and wish now to say with even greater emphasis—largely nonsense. Language, for the most part, changes out of ignorance.[3]

Simon is a priest in the self-constituted church of linguistic Puritans who live in terror lest anyone appear to be enjoying language without obeying the rules. But usage is king. English is what people speaking it and writing it and understanding it understand it to be. The language is no more in decay now than it was in Shakespeare's time, or even in the time of *Beowulf.* It is only changing. Ambrose Bierce, early in this century, defined *laundry* as "a place where clothing is washed." He added, "This word cannot mean, also, clothing sent there to be washed."[4] Yet I toss my dirty laundry into a basket and at intervals lug it downstairs to the Maytag and toss it in without any feelings of guilt. If the ghost of Ambrose Bierce turned up, I'd ask him to put my laundry in the dryer once it had finished the washing cycle. Richard Grant White published *Words and Their Uses* in 1870 in the conviction that English was going to the dogs. He disliked the word *editorial* for the essays editors wrote expressing their opinions in newspapers. He condemned the use of *execute* as a verb meaning "to put to death," and he thought *ice water* and *ice cream* should be "iced water" and "iced cream." (I ordered *ice tea* in a restaurant once, and a stern friend corrected me. "It should be *iced tea*," said he.) Benjamin Franklin opposed the use of *advocate, progress,* and *oppose* as verbs, but we use them all now without hesitation. Franklin himself coined the word *harmonica,* and he used the word *mileage* when it was either unknown or uncommon.[5]

Many purists become angry at usages of which they disapprove. I don't like the habit of using *hopefully* as a synonym for "I hope" or "it is hoped." (See my discussion on the word below.) But I don't feel as vehement as the otherwise gentle poet Phyllis McGinley who has declared that " 'Hopefully' so used is an abomination, and its adherents should be lynched."[6] The linguist Puritans see language as the property of the superior and the educated, and a territorial imperative compels them to fight off the barbarians. Language is to them a measure of status, and it is hard to escape the feeling that they assault the common language of others as a means of exalting themselves.

But while I deplore the bad temper and the extremism of these Puritans, I sympathize with their intuitions. Language should not be sterile; but it should be stable—not only because a stable language allows us to communicate across space in the present but also for the reason that I have already mentioned: A reasonably stable language allows us to communicate across generations and provides a tradition that, in a fine phrase by Saul Bellow, allows the living to break bread with the dead.

The best advice about usage is to read good writers to see how they use words. Who are the good writers? A difficult question! The only solution is to read a lot, and to absorb from your reading informal standards of taste to guide your use of words. Good writers are good readers. Reading brings you into the community of those who love words and use them well.

LIVELY PROBLEMS IN USAGE

In the following pages you will find my opinions about some lively problems in usage. I am as aware as anyone that mine is the kind of list that may be ridiculed a century from now as unborn readers will accept words that make me wince. Usage commands the way we use language, and the most rabid purists must finally bow to it no matter how much they resist. Nature herself intervenes, for purists die, and the language goes happily on without them.

My own views change reluctantly as I see usage take over. In the first edition of this work I made a distinction between *insure* and *ensure*. *Insure* means to take out an insurance policy on something; *ensure* means to make sure. I still make the distinction in my own writing. But the *New York Times* has folded the two meanings into the one word *insure*. Its headlines regularly speak of efforts to *insure* the peace or the investigation or the election or whatever. Early I would have supposed that to insure the peace, one needed to take out a policy so that if peace should be damaged or killed, someone would have to pay the beneficiaries of the insurance. But no, the *Times* means that someone is trying to make peace sure. Who am I to stand against the august authority of the *New York Times*? I have dropped my quibble.

My suggestions remain on the conservative side. Many readers will disagree with me on this or that question. Good. The disagreements will make you think about language. My own commentary on usage—like all such commentaries—reflects my own reading and the consequent sense of the language that comes from it, including my experience and my prejudices. I serve on the usage panel of the *American Heritage Dictionary,* a task I enjoy despite its long questionnaires. But it is also an experience that makes me humble before anyone's opinions about this or that word. The *American Heritage Dictionary* provides percentages of members of the panel who vote on controversial usages, and these votes are never unanimous. Even so, I think the majority of professional writers and editors share my views. See what you think.

Affect/Effect

A perennial problem. The word *effect* is usually a noun, as in the phrase *cause and effect.* "The *effect* of her decision was to create a boom in the computer business." *Affect* is usually a verb. "My attitude always *affects* my students."

Occasionally *effect* is a verb that means "to cause." "Luther's revolt against the Catholic church *effected* a revolution in thought and a series of religious wars." *Effect* used as a verb carries with it the connotation of completeness, of having done something to the full.

All Together/Altogether

If you say, "The congregation gathered *all together* in one place," you mean that all the people in the church or synagogue were present. If you say, "They were *altogether* happy," you mean they were completely happy. The adverb *together* refers to some kind of collection; the adverb *altogether* refers to some kind of completeness.

Alot/A Lot

I had to change the "quick correct" button on my word processing program to be able to write the error, "alot." It is common enough to be part of the automatic correction tool on my program. It is a mysterious but common error among my own students. *Alot* is not a word, yet my students write *alot* as though it were *awhile.* Even the correct form, *a lot,* is bland. It is dull to say, "Custer discovered that he had stirred up a lot of Indians." It seems better to recast the sentence in a more vivid form: "Custer saw thousands of Indians riding down on him, whooping with anger, and he realized he had made a serious mistake."

Alright/All Right

Here is one I feel certain to lose. Advertising commonly uses *alright* to tell us that somebody's underwear is all right. I still prefer the old form, *all right.*

Alternative

Many purists say we can use *alternative* only when we have but two choices. They reason that since the Latin word *alter* means "the other," implying only two, the derivative *alternative* can never be used when we have three or more choices. Common usage has long since buried this etymological logic, and we happily speak of three or four alternatives. But *at least* two choices must present themselves if *alternative* is to be used sensibly.

Amount/Number

The distinction between these words is similar to that between *less* and *fewer.* You cannot divide an *amount* into units that you can count. You can count a *number* of things. You may speak of a great *number* of people, but a great *amount* of people sounds as if people were grains of sand. And you can have a great *amount* of sand.

Anxious/Eager

The debate about this pair goes back at least a century. It seems better to use *anxious* to indicate fear or anxiety, *eager* to show pleasure in some expected occurrence.

I am *eager* to attend opening day in Fenway Park every April.

I am always *anxious* to see if the Red Sox will fold in May rather than in August.

Anymore/Any More

The adverb *anymore* means *now* or *nowadays* and has been traditionally used only in negative constructions. You can say, "He doesn't smoke anymore," and everyone will understand that he once smoked but stopped and does not smoke now. *Anymore* goes at the end of the clause. Sometimes people say, "Anymore I drink tea rather than coffee." This misplacing of *anymore* confuses readers and hearers. On reflection we see that the speaker means she once drank coffee but now drinks tea. A negation is implied, but the form confuses most people accustomed to the convention that the adverb *anymore* comes after the verb it modifies. The more customary and clearer statement is this: "I don't drink coffee anymore; I drink tea instead."

Any more works as an adjective modifying a noun. "The world does not need *any more* millionaire athletes."

Apt/Liable/Likely

To say that someone is *apt* is to remark on a skill, especially one that seems somewhat common. "She is apt at math."

Liable has a legal connotation—always unpleasant. "He was liable for his sworn testimony that turned out to be a lie."

Likely refers to something probable. "The big star was *likely* to be suspended a few games after he strangled his coach. He was not *likely* to attend the coach's funeral."

As/Since

English writers commonly use these two words as synonyms. Charles Darwin did so in *The Origin of Species,* and Charles Dickens did the same in his novels. The American practice of making a distinction between the two words seems preferable. *As* used as a conjunction connotates a contemporary time, something happening while something else is happening. *Since* gives a sense of something happening *in consequence* of something else. These sentences do not confuse:

She waved at me *as* the boat pulled away from the dock.

As I commute to work by bicycle, the cuffs of my pants sometimes get stained by oil.

Does commuting by bicycle *cause* my cuffs to be blackened by oil, or does the staining happen mysteriously as I bike along?

> *Because* I commute to work by bicycle, the cuffs of my pants sometimes get stained by oil.

My advice may seem somewhat perverse. If you wish to indicate causation choose *since* over *as,* but choose *because* over both.

A While/Awhile

Awhile is an adverb used to modify verbs: "He stayed *awhile.*"

While is a noun expressing an unspecified but usually short period of time. It is often the object of a preposition: He stayed for *a while.*

The sense of the two forms is so close that good writers often confuse them. The meaning given by most dictionaries for the adverb *while* is "for a while." Careful writers should make a distinction—if only to call attention to their care. It is an easy matter. When *while* follows a preposition—usually *in* or *for*—make two words: *a while.* When *while* is used with a verb and without an intervening preposition, use *awhile.*

Between/Among

The standard rule is that *between* should be used to speak of two things, *among* of more than two.

> It was easy to make a distinction *between* the two words.
>
> She moved easily *among* the guests in the room.

So far, so good! But the difference between the two words sometimes gets fuzzy. We don't speak of the infield on a baseball diamond as the space *among* the four bases, and we don't say that a treaty banning chemical warfare was signed *among* most of the nations of the world. If I am sitting with four friends at a table and wish to share a bit of gossip, I say, "Just *between* us—I think his best friends hate him."

The best rule seems to be to let literate people follow their inclinations. We should not fear to use *between* with more than two when the intent is to show some kind of active participation of every party following someone's lead—as in signing a treaty. We should not fear using *between* to refer to an enclosed space and its boundaries, no matter how numerous those boundaries are. Even these rules are not sufficient to cover all the ways we can use *between* when we speak of more than two.

But don't write *between you and I* or *between he and she.* When I hear these constructions, I wince. *Between* is a preposition here, and the objects of prepositions should be in the objective case. You should say *between you and me* and *between him and her.*

Avoid the phrase *between each* as in the construction, "A wall was built between each of the rooms." *Each* is always singular; *between* implies more than one. It does not make sense to say *between each* unless you add another parallel noun: "A wall was built between each room and the one next to it."

Book/Novel

I've noticed that more and more of my students are calling any book a *novel*. But a *novel* is a work of fiction, a story a writer makes up. Other books are *nonfiction;* that is, they claim to be factual, not made up. Autobiographies of most politicians claim to be *nonfiction* when they are more like novels in all the heroism they claim for the writer. But a *novel* is a book that claims to be fiction and that is almost instantly recognizable as fiction.

Co-Equals

This one drives me up the wall. Two captains in an army unit are not *co-equal* in authority; they are merely *equal*. But *co-* words have become common, probably in imitation of the word *copilot*. The problem is that we often don't know whether *co-* signifies "equal to" or "assistant to." A copilot is assistant to the pilot on a plane and therefore second in command. If the pilot has a heart attack, the copilot lands the plane. Some high school football teams have a captain and a *co-captain,* who like a *copilot* takes over when the captain is unable to function. Other teams have no captain at all but rather have co-captains who are supposedly equal to each other in authority. The *co-* scene is a mess. The problem rises from the search for a brief word that expresses the idea of second in command, a need supplied for many years with the word *vice* as in *vice president*. I think it is better to abandon *co-* words except when we speak of copilots. Fortunately we don't have to speak of them often.

Common/Mutual

Many writers, and even more speakers, have used these words as synonyms since the time of Shakespeare and perhaps before.

In 1658 the English writer George Starkey wrote of "our mutual friend," and in the last century Charles Dickens wrote a great novel with that title—and incurred the scorn of many. Yet people commonly speak of "mutual friends" today, and the sky does not fall. But they are just as commonly silently condemned by many who hear them. Strictly speaking, we should use *mutual* for some reciprocal action, something going back and forth between two things or two persons. In *Measure for Measure,* Claudio comments wryly on "the stealth of our most mutual entertainment" that has made his lover, Julietta, pregnant. Sexual intercourse is indeed an example of the reciprocity implied in the more "correct" use of *mutual*. People can also have mutual affection or mutual dislike for each other.

If we share something like an interest in photography or friends, we should more properly say, "They had a common interest in photography," or simply, "They shared an interest in photography." Or they can say, "We shared a friend." But then in one story in February 1998 the *New York Times* used both meanings of the term. In a story about the similarities and differences between President Bill Clinton and Special Prosecutor Kenneth Starr, one headline read, "A Mutual Distrust Born of Differences." Another headline spoke of "A Mutual Tendency to Talk It to Death."[7] In the first headline, "mutual" shows that Clinton and Starr distrust *one another,* the traditional "accepted" meaning of the term. But in the second use, the "mutual tendency" is clearly a "common tendency."

The term *mutual friend* has become so embedded in the English (and American) language that it seems unfriendly to fight it. No one will hang you if you say, "You and I have a mutual friend in Arkansas." Even so I prefer to say, "You and I are both friends of Dee Post in Arkansas." As the *New York Times* demonstrates, the distinction is passing away, but I find it useful to preserve it.

Comprise/Compose/Include

These words often get mixed up. *Comprise* means "to embrace." So we say, "The Senate *comprises* 100 members." The 100 members do not *comprise* the Senate; they *compose* the Senate. They *include* lawyers, judges, farmers, business executives, and a fair number of men and women who will someday do time in prison. You could not say that the 100 members embrace the Senate; so you should not say that they *comprise* the Senate. *Comprise* calls attention to all the parts. When you wish to call attention to only some of the parts, use *include.*

Conditions

The high frequency of this word seems to originate with TV meteorologists. They speak of "snowy conditions prevailing in Minnesota" or "stormy conditions over New England." They cannot bring themselves to say, "Snow is falling in Minnesota tonight" or "Thunderstorms are causing floods in Arizona." Now we have traffic conditions, economic conditions, and housing conditions. When an Air Florida jet crashed during takeoff from Washington National Airport in 1982, one official said, "Weather conditions are such that they are not conducive to rapid recovery." He apparently meant that it was too cold to recover bodies quickly from the icy Potomac River.

We should have snow, rain, weather, traffic, and housing. We should reserve *conditions* to mean "requirements." And we should certainly not use the redundancy "preconditions." To speak of "preconditions" is like speaking of hot heat or watery water.

Contact

Many writers object to the use of *contact* as a verb. Strunk and White, in their classic little book, *The Elements of Style,* advise readers to telephone, write, or get in touch with someone but never to *contact* him. The objection seems oddly genteel to me, a bit like the prohibition of the word *legs* in Victorian society even when speaking of the legs of a table. *Contact* means "touch," and to use *contact* as a verb probably implied the kind of touching that seemed vulgar to Victorians. Nowadays thoroughly respectable people contact others, and writers have been using the word as a synonym for *getting in touch* for decades. Few of us object if someone contacts us about next week's meeting, although we may hate the idea of the meeting itself. *Contact* means that some of us may be telephoned, others written to, and still others hailed on the street and invited to come.

Continuous/Continual

Something *continuous* goes on without interruption; something *continual* goes on at intervals. The movement of blood through our bodies is *continuous* until death. The Kennedy family in Massachusetts is a subject of *continual* interest. So don't tell someone that you expect to be with him *continuously* unless you are a special prosecutor and never intend to let the poor guy out of your sight, even when he's in bed asleep or in the bathroom taking a shower.

Cope

People often use this word to give the impression that they are saying much more than they really are. If you must use the word, write "cope with" and follow the two words with some reasonable object.

> Many Americans embrace conspiracy theories because they cannot *cope with* the reality that a murderous lunatic like Lee Harvey Oswald could have killed President Kennedy on a whim.

Cope conveys an uncomfortable vagueness. If you must use it, be as specific as you can. To say "He could not cope" is to indicate some general inability, a frustration of some sort, but it does not locate the source of the frustration. It leaves readers and listeners, and perhaps the person using the word, in confusion. Usually the expression is so mild that the confusion is unimportant. But in writing, unimportant and confusing locutions are like mud on a bike chain. They are an unnecessary drag on the motion of prose. Neither you nor your readers have time or energy to waste on them.

Couldn't Care Less/Could Care Less

The original idiom had a certain force in my adolescence. "I couldn't care less about Matthews." It seemed straightforward and emphatic. I care so little for the insignificant Matthews that it is impossible to care less for him no matter what malice or absurdity he might commit next.

Now the idiom has become twisted into the nonsensical "I could care less." It seems to be everywhere, like the common cold. "I could care less about Matthews." If we take language seriously, this version of the sentence now indicates that the speaker does indeed care something about Matthews. Perhaps she admires Matthews. Perhaps she hates him. Whatever her emotion, for some unspecified reason she *could* care less about him. We wonder what Matthews might do to provoke such a lowering of her esteem. With an idiom like "I could care less," language becomes not communication but incantation.

Why not avoid the hackneyed expression altogether and come to the point? "I don't like Matthews." "I couldn't care less," even when used correctly, is a cliché, and we may as well bury it. Even so, the cliché that makes sense is better than the phrase that doesn't.

Crafted/Handcrafted

These are advertising words with almost no meaning, part of the dilution and falsification of language that advertising has brought about. They are also in the language to stay, but careful writers may recognize what they say and clean up the language a bit. *Crafted* and *handcrafted* mean the same thing—that something has been made by hand using a combination of strength and skill and that the handwork guarantees that the object has a special quality. We often say that writing is a *craft,* meaning that it is a manual activity—something we do skillfully with our hands, something we can improve by spending more time on it.

In fact, many crafted items these days are made by machine, and although a great many crafted or handcrafted items *are* made by hand, they are not necessarily better for that. If you buy a handcrafted shirt, you may be sure that the stitching was done on a sewing machine—probably by some sweat shop in Hong Kong. But even if the pieces of the shirt were cut out by a machine, somebody had to operate the machine. So advertising copywriters can speak of "crafting." We could speak of the "crafting" of automobiles since some of their manufacture is done by hand. We know that automobiles are probably more reliable when they are made by robots than by hand since robots don't have hangovers on Monday morning or rush to quit early on Friday afternoons.

Diametrically Opposed

Here is another example of language inflation. People who say they are *diametrically opposed* may imagine that they are on one side of a circle and their opponent is on the other, separated from each other at the widest point of the circle, its *diameter.* They are as opposed as they can be. The sense of the circle long ago passed out of the expression, leaving a husk that has become a cliché. If you are opposed to something, just say so—and tell why. Once you begin to give reasons—and to hear your opponent's reasons—you may discover you are closer together than you thought.

Different From/Different Than

Most editors recommend *different from* and consider *different than* to be bad English, but the distinction is fading. Most writers I know prefer to say, "Her tastes in literature are different *from* mine." *Different than* is often used before a clause: "Her tastes in literature are different *than* they used to be." I still prefer *different from* in both instances. "Her tastes in literature are different *from* what they used to be."

Dilemma

Properly speaking, we should use *dilemma* for a vexing problem that presents us with two equally unattractive alternatives and requires us to make a choice. Confirmed cigarette smokers face a dilemma. They can give up a pleasurable habit and suffer discomfort, prolonged nervousness, irritability, and perhaps a failure of concentration while they yearn for a cigarette every minute. Or they can keep smoking and die of lung cancer if heart disease, stroke, or emphysema does not kill them first, and while they smoke they will annoy most of their friends and many strangers.

Careless writers may use *dilemma* to indicate any serious problem, and the language is poorer in consequence. Use *dilemma* only when speaking of the need to make a choice between painful or dangerous alternatives. Then describe the contrary choices. Don't use the word *dilemma* unless you tell us what the dilemma is—or was.

> United Nations forces in 1991 faced a dilemma. They could continue the Gulf War until Saddam Hussein fell from power, but then face the danger that Iraq might dissolve into warring factions that would destabilize the entire Middle East. Or they could leave Saddam Hussein in power and face the danger that he might recover enough strength to threaten the region again, perhaps with weapons of mass destruction.

Disinterested/Uninterested

Perhaps we should retire *disinterested* from the language, substituting the word *impartial.* Much confusion might thereby be averted. Most of us take the disinterested person to have nothing to gain or lose no matter who wins an argument or contest. Juries, umpires, referees, judges, and teachers should be disinterested. Jonathan Edwards, the great American Puritan preacher of the eighteenth century, defined love as "disinterested benevolence," a benign feeling that sponsors good deeds to others without expecting anything in return. But a judge should not go to sleep during a murder trial. He should be interested and uninterested at the same time.

To be *uninterested* is to lack interest. I am uninterested in chess, professional football, and novels by Joyce Carol Oates.

The confusion of these words has been around for years, and it is unlikely to disappear soon. So I suggest that we send *disinterested* into retirement and use *impartial* instead.

Dubious/Doubtful

Things are *dubious* when they cause doubt. People are *doubtful* about dubious things. Athletic dormitories are of *dubious* value in educating the young men who are packed into them like gladiators. Some of us are *doubtful* that most coaches of football teams that go to bowls care whether their student athletes are educated as long as they win games.

The distinction between these words has long been recognized, although since the seventeenth century some have seen them as synonyms. It seems to be a distinction worth preserving.

Due To/Because

Willis C. Tucker, one of my journalism professors to whom this book is dedicated, used to say that the only safe use of *due to* was in a sentence like this: "The train was *due to* arrive at two o'clock." He thereby neatly avoided the annoying complexity of the debate over this apparently simple little phrase when it is used with nouns. Purists hold that the phrase should be used only as an adjective, as in the sentences "Her victory was *due to* her stamina" or "The heart attack that killed William Jennings Bryan was *due to* his overeating fried chicken." In this sentence, *due to* is a synonym for *caused by,* and nearly everyone will accept it as correct. Purists object to using *due to* as a preposition synonymous with *owing to,* as in the sentences "He won *due to* bribery" or "The mayor felt annoyed *due to* being jailed."

I object to the phrase even when it is formally "correct." It leads to clumsy constructions, especially when it is used as a synonym for *because* at the beginning of clauses. "She was late due to the fact that she fell on her roller blades." It is much simpler to say, "She was late because she fell on her roller blades."

The use of *due to* often makes a sentence vague. "He was convicted *due to* the pistol." What pistol? Why? Perhaps the context will spell out the details. But why not make the situation clear by writing another sentence entirely: "The jury found him guilty because ballistics tests proved that the murder weapon was the pistol the police found in his belt when they arrested him." Here is another example of the clarity you may add to a sentence by using enough words to state your meaning fully.

Even if *due to* is used only as the purists demand, as an adjective, it can be vague. "He suffered demotion *due to* incompetence." Whose incompetence? We want to know. Even the "correct" use of *due to* does not tell us. *Due to* often makes writers think they have said much more than they have in a sentence. Try to avoid the phrase.

Either/Both/Each

Either indicates choice between one or another, and it is most appropriately used with *or* where the choice is between two nouns. "You may choose *either* the cheeseburger or the tofu." Sometimes *either* implies the *or:* "You can look at *either* candidate and see a man whose mother probably dislikes him." The sentence implies a choice between two candidates. The writer says that whichever choice we make is unlikely to be good.

For many people the idea of choice becomes blurred, and *either* becomes a too simple substitute for *each* or *both.* Someone says, "Flowers are blooming at *either* end of the garden." No important choice is implied here. The statement

❋

would be clearer if the person said, "Flowers are blooming at *both* ends of the garden" or "Flowers are blooming at *each* end of the garden."

Enthuse/Enthusiastic

It always sounds a little hokey to me when people write that they are *enthused* about something. It is much more traditional to say they are *enthusiastic*. In the Greek world the gods *enthused* oracles with the divine spirit, and the oracles then became *enthusiastic*.

Factor

One of those much overused words, *factor* is a signal that writing will be dull. Like other such words its chief fault is not that it is wrong but that it prevents us from making a more specific statement. It lets us shilly-shally. "His character was a *factor* in the breakup of our friendship." Why not tell the truth? "He was a liar and a cheat, and so I ended our friendship," or "He was much more successful than I was; so I decided I disliked him."

Factor is one of those dull words like *implement* or *prioritize* that substitute easy writing for the hard work of finding words to express our thoughts exactly. It's better by far to ask yourself exactly what you want to say and say it precisely.

Feedback

This word, like *input,* has come into the language from electronics, and it's probably here to stay, like the common mosquito. It originally denoted a circuit by which part of the output of a radio source was brought back to its origin. Sometimes this feedback was unintentional, and the result was a high electronic shriek in the loudspeaker when a speaker got too close to the mike. To some of us that sound is as reminiscent of high school as the smell of fetid clothes in the dressing rooms of the gym. Now *feedback* is commonly used as a synonym for *response* when people talk about other human beings. It is common in bureaucratic language, uncommon in well edited books and magazines. I strongly object to mechanistic metaphors to describe acts human beings do with their brains. *Feedback* makes us sound like robots.

Feel Bad/Feel Badly

The confusion between these two is one of the most common errors in contemporary writing and speech. We *feel bad* when something makes us unhappy or when we are unwell. We *feel badly* if we have burned our fingers and damaged our sense of touch. If I say, "Loretta *feels badly* because Leo lost their cat in a poker game," I mean that Leo's rash bet numbed her fingers. If I say she *feels bad* about the loss of the cat, I mean that she misses the beast.

The verbs of sense used with several common linking verbs cause trouble because some writers and speakers mistake a predicate adjective for an adverb.

A predicate adjective modifies the subject of a clause. We do not have trouble with a sentence like this: "He looked healthy and happy." No one would write, "He looked healthily and happily." We also say, "Mary sat still in the house." We do not say that she sat *stilly.* That would be *silly.* We say, "He felt damp after being caught in the rain." We don't say, "He felt damply after the shower." We write easily, "He walked into the room resolute and angry," knowing that it is not his walking that is resolute and angry but that *he* is resolute and angry. We should close a door *tight* because we mean it to be tight in its frame. If we close the door *tightly,* we imply that we are drunk—or at least *tight*—as we shut the door. We say we have our steak cooked *rare* because to say we have it cooked *rarely* implies that most of the time we eat our steak raw but that once in a great while we cook it.

So we feel *bad* when something displeases us or when we do something foolish or thoughtless that we regret—just as we smell *bad* when we have not taken a bath in a month and smell *good* when we have washed ourselves with good soap. We feel *good* when our team wins, *bad* when it loses, *unamazed* when that team is the Boston Red Sox.

Flaunt/Flout

To flaunt something means to wave it proudly, even arrogantly, for everyone to see. The implication is that some witnesses will be displeased for all that waving, but the *flouter* breaks the rules and does not care.

> Saddam Hussein *flaunted* his contempt for the United States and *flouted* his agreements with the UN.

Flout means to disobey, to scorn, or to run in the face of some convention or legal agreement and to do so flagrantly, openly, arrogantly. Both *flout* and *flaunt* imply pride and even arrogance. The pride, combined with the similar beginnings of both words, accounts for their confusion.

For Free

Many advertising writers have begun to use this form.

> Senior citizens have been given their fishing licenses *for free.*

Leave out the *for.*

Former/Latter

Try to avoid using these words to refer to two preceding persons or things. They force your reader to look back to see which is which:

> David Halberstam and Neil Sheehan both became celebrated for books they wrote about the Vietnam War, the former for *The Best and the Brightest* and the latter for *A Bright Shining Lie.*

A reader cruising through prose that contains this sentence has to stop, go back, see that Halberstam is the *former* and Sheehan is the *latter.* I think it better to say this:

> David Halberstam and Neil Sheehan both became celebrated for books they wrote about the Vietnam War, Halberstam for *The Best and the Brightest* and Sheehan for *A Bright Shining Lie.*

Fortuitous/Fortunate

Something that happens *fortuitously* happens by chance or by accident and may be good or bad. "Their meeting on the airplane was *fortuitous.*" If something is *fortunate,* it is good.

Fortuitous, like *disinterested,* seems to have lost so much strength that you should consider using another word to avoid misunderstandings. I would not now write this sentence: "He was sick in bed, and so his presence in the house at the time of the burglary was entirely *fortuitous.*" I would substitute *by chance.*

Fulsome

Another word so often misused that its proper meaning may be lost. Until recently the common meaning of *fulsome praise* was praise so flattering that it could not possibly be sincere, the kind of thing one politician says about another. *Fulsome* meant "disgusting" or "obsequious" or "nauseating." Anyone receiving fulsome praise without protest was taken to be blindly arrogant or a fool, and anyone who gave fulsome praise was a boot-licking sycophant. Now *fulsome* often means "great" or "enthusiastic."

It is bad to lose the distinction, for our language will be impoverished by the loss of such an ironic and useful term. *Insincere* praise carries none of the scornful force of *fulsome praise,* but now the cult of exaggeration makes the simple offering of praise, or even lavish praise or high praise, seem inadequate. All our expressions must be inflated until they are sound and fury, signifying nothing much, depending on the exuberance with which they are delivered rather than on the plain meaning of the words. Writers and speakers who exaggerate everything are responsible for turning *fulsome* into yet another inflated adjective, and in their eagerness for emphatic utterance, they fail to see that the traditional and useful meaning stands opposite to their intention.

Head Up

People seldom *head* or *direct* or *lead* anymore. Instead they *head up* committees, bands, groups, classes, and clinics on hair loss. I don't know what *up* adds to *head* except specious bureaucratic importance.

Healthy/Healthful

Something is *healthy* if it enjoys good health, if it is strong, vigorous, and alive.

John kept himself *healthy* by walking three miles every day and by eating well.

Joe had a *healthy* arrogance.

Something is *healthful* if it contributes to health.

Oat bran is a *healthful* food supplement.

Nuclear weapons are not *healthful* to children.

Hopefully/Hope

Few words provoke more antagonism nowadays than *hopefully* used as a hanging adverb meaning *I hope* or *it is hoped.* Writers and speakers have used the word for centuries to mean "in a hopeful spirit" when it, like other adverbs, modified a verb, an adjective, or another adverb. But since about 1932 the word has developed a new and more general and objectionable meaning. The ninth edition of the Merriam-Webster *New Collegiate Dictionary* includes a scornful note against the "irrationally large amount of critical fire" toward the word when it is used as a synonym for "I hope" or "it is hoped," and it offers analogies with *interestingly, presumably,* and *fortunately,* which are often used as *sentence modifiers,* that is, modifiers of entire sentences.

While willing to admit that usage is king and that probably no great good is accomplished by opposing *hopefully,* I must still record my reservations. Some 76 percent of a usage panel assembled by Wright Morris, editor-in-chief of the *American Heritage Dictionary,* and Mary Morris, a distinguished authority on usage, said they would not use *hopefully* in the sense of "I hope" or "it is hoped." That such a lopsided majority should oppose the word should make us hesitate to use it.

The words *interestingly, presumably,* and *fortunately,* cited by the editors of the Merriam-Webster dictionary, offer little of the ambiguity of *hopefully.* If we say, "Presumably he joined the army," we know that the adverb does not modify the entire sentence but that it modifies the verb *joined,* and we have no ambiguity. It is presumed he joined the army; we do not know whether he did or not. But if we say, "Hopefully, he joined the army," we are left in confusion. Thanks to today's vague usage, we do not know if he joined the army with hope in his heart—the obvious grammatical meaning of the sentence—or if the writer of the sentence hopes he joined the army. It is just this ambiguity that makes foes of *hopefully*—including me—find the word unattractive.

Other adverbs are equally ambiguous. "*Briefly,* he was in prison for forty years." People use *briefly* as shorthand to mean that they will be brief in their statement. But the statement would be far clearer if authors of such sentences left *briefly* out altogether. "*Unhappily* the dog ate all the appetizers before the guests came." Who was unhappy? Doubtless the hosts. But I suspect the dog was as happy as he had ever been in his canine life. "*Thankfully* the terrorist died in a hail of bullets before he could injure anyone." The terrorist was probably not thankful.

So it is with *hopefully,* as in the sentence, "Hopefully the faculty will get a raise this year." Does the sentence mean that the faculty is certain to get a raise and will do so with hope in its collective heart? No. According to current usage, the writer of the sentence means that he or she hopes the faculty will get a raise. Is it too much to ask writers to tell us specifically who has the hope? "The faculty hopes to get a raise this year." "I hope the faculty will get a raise this year."

To use *hopefully* or any of its random kin among the adverbs in the sense under discussion is to create another disadvantage. Adverbs cannot be inflected. They have only one form for past, present, and future. Nobody says, "Hopefully, when I was young, I would be rich." We must say, "When I was young, I hoped to be rich." The verb *to hope* can be inflected to show when the hope occurs. If you want to use the past tense, you must say, "I hoped." Why not use the verb in the present tense to say "I hope" rather than use the lazy "hopefully"?

The main objection to *hopefully* is that it makes something abstract that is personal. Hope does not float in the air like nitrogen. Hope is an emotion we feel as persons, and we ought to locate its source and identify the people who have it. I hope readers will take seriously these comments on a common but unfortunate usage.

Illusion/Allusion

We make an *allusion* when we refer to something without mentioning it specifically. We create an *illusion* when we form an unreal image.

> When he told me that he wanted nothing but to lie down in green pastures, he was making an *allusion* to the Twenty-third Psalm.
>
> In our society we nourish the *illusion* that if we talk about emotions all the time we will be more interesting people.

An allusion is always indirect. It is not the same as a mention or a citation or a quotation. Literary allusions enliven writing by calling to mind other things that we have read. When we read, "All his ambitions were sound and fury," we recall Shakespeare's Macbeth and the hopelessness to which his ambitions led him, for Macbeth declares that life is a "tale, told by an idiot, full of sound and fury, signifying nothing." A writer does not have to mention Macbeth by name; we would think him pedantic if he did so. The allusion is sufficient. Like most teachers, I am startled and delighted when I find a literary allusion in a student's paper.

Impact/Impacted

For centuries *impact* was used only as a noun and *impacted* as an adjective. Our forebears spoke easily of the impact of hooves on cobblestones or the impact of a new revelation about the government. They never said, "Queen Victoria impacted her Parliaments but did not control them." The *Oxford Eng-*

lish Dictionary tells us that John Wesley, in a 1791 sermon, used the word as an imperative: "Impact fire into iron by hammering it when red hot." Wesley was old then and probably in less control of his language than he had been earlier in his career. Anyway, his meaning here is specific and means to force or to drive. Every other usage given by the *O.E.D.* under *impact* as a verb is in the past participle used as an adjective. For centuries the person who said "I am impacted" meant "I am constipated."

But of late *impact* has become a universal synonym for *influence,* and it follows our national habit of overemphasis. Polls impact elections. Reform movements impact welfare programs. Shun *impact* as a verb. It is pretentious language.

Imply/Infer

Here is another confusion that has lasted for centuries, and I can express only the majority opinion, not a unanimous verdict. We *imply* something by conveying a meaning in some way other than a direct statement. We *infer* a conclusion by reasoning out the evidence, although the evidence may not deliver the solid proof we wish. The writer or the speaker *implies;* the reader or hearer *infers.*

> By not including South Korea in the areas the United States would defend in 1950, President Truman *implied* that he would not oppose militarily a North Korean invasion. The North Koreans *inferred* as much and invaded—only to discover that they were wrong.

Cognates of *imply* and *infer* are *implication* and *inference.* Here we seldom find confusion. "I did not understand the implication of his words." That is, he implied something that I did not grasp. "The inference was that she did not want to tell me everything." That is, I inferred that she did not wish to tell me everything she knew.

Incredible/Incredulous

Something is *incredible* if we cannot believe it. We are *incredulous* if we cannot believe something incredible.

> He made the *incredible* statement that the ghost of Elvis Presley told him he ought to become a singer himself.
>
> We were *incredulous* when he told us that the ghost has also given him Elvis's autograph.

Indicate/Say

To indicate is much the same as to imply, although the connotation of *indicate* is usually stronger. That is, something indicated is nearly always true, but something implied may be true or false. Even this distinction between the two words is not always observed. *Indicate* is often used to show that something happens without any special intention on the part of the person who does the indicating. *Imply* is customarily used when the person doing the implying wishes to convey some meaning beyond the plain words.

Smoke indicates fire. The smoke is impersonal; it has no intention. It is merely a sign that a fire is burning even if we cannot see flames. A baby, laughing, indicates that she is happy. The baby may be laughing spontaneously without intending to show that she is happy.

Do not use *indicate* as a synonym for *say*.

> "Tuition will go up by 14 percent next year," the president said.

The president did not *indicate* that tuition was rising. She might have indicated such a thing if she'd said something like this: "So, you're having a hard time paying your tuition this year. Just wait till next year. You'll think this year's rate was a bargain." As it is, the president made a plain statement of fact, not softened by the weaker word *indicate*.

Individual

A much overused word. Use *individual* only when you are making a deliberate comparison of a single person and or object and a group.

> One of the great problems of political philosophy has always been to balance the rights of the *individual* against the rights of society.

It is stiff and pretentious to write, "Three *individuals* came to collect their bribes from the governor."

Sometimes for no good reason, the word *individual* is used with the pronoun *each*. "*Each individual* house on the block has a porch and a garage. A little thought shows that "each individual" is redundant. You get the same meaning by saying "each house."

Intensifiers

Words like *very, absolutely, definitely, incredibly, basically, certainly, positively, fantastic, terrific, wonderful, marvelous, dreadful, horrible, fabulous,* and many more are *intensifiers*. They are lazy and overwrought efforts by writers to show that they really, really, really, really mean what they are saying.

We live among verbal hucksters screaming for our attention, a Las Vegas mentality where gaudy and wildly moving electric signs deaden our senses—calling forth from their makers even more flamboyant displays. Advertising screams at us. The habit has carried over into the language of daily discourse like some sickness infecting multitudes. Intensifiers deaden prose. They sound like shouting, and if you shout all the time, nobody will listen to you. Resist!

Lay/Lie

Herein lies one of the most commonly violated distinctions. Both verbs are irregular in the past participle—a major reason for the confusion they cause writers and speakers. To complicate things still further, the past tense of *lie* is *lay*. No wonder even educated people mess them up.

I *lie* on the floor to take a nap every afternoon.

I *lay* a paperback book under my head as a pillow.

Yesterday I *lay* on the floor and took a nap.

I *laid* a paperback book under my head as a pillow.

I have often *lain* on the floor to take a nap.

I have *laid* a paperback book under my head for a pillow.

The *lay/lie* affair gets more complicated when we consider folk usages that have come down to us from the time when English reflexive verbs were more common than they are now. "Now I *lay* me down to sleep. . ." So begins an old prayer. In modern idiom we might say, "Now I *lie* down to sleep," but nobody should mess with beloved old prayers.

To add to the confusion, *lay* and *lie* are both used as nouns to indicate how something lies. The choice is entirely idiomatic; that is, it has no rules. We speak of the lay of the land but the lie of a golf ball. A friend tells me of playing golf with a new acquaintance who became nervous when he discovered that my friend was a high school English teacher. The acquaintance hit a ball off into the woods, was gone for a long time, finally hit the ball out, and emerged, apologizing for taking so long. "I had a bad lay in there," he said. He conveyed a different impression from the one he intended.

The only good advice about this one is this: Be careful. The distinction is important, and people with an ear for language notice when others confuse the words.

Less/Fewer

The same principles apply here that go with *number* and *amount*. We use *less* for things we cannot count individually, and we use *fewer* for things we can. We can have *less* flour, but we have *fewer* people.

Some idioms call for *less* when we might suppose that *fewer* might be preferred.

She gave me *less* than ten dollars.

Today's high temperature was ten degrees *less* than yesterday's.

In these idioms we sense a unity of quantity in the money and in the temperature, and we use *less* to indicate our sense of the wholeness of what we describe.

Like/As If/Such As

This distinction is changing before our eyes. The supposed rule, followed by most editors and writers, is that *like* should never be used as a conjunction. But in speech and in formal writing, educated people have been using *like* as a conjunction for decades. Charles Darwin wrote, "Unfortunately, few have observed *like* you have done." Similar usages appear regularly in *The New York Times.*

Many authorities want *like* to govern only nouns, pronouns, or a noun substitute such as a gerund. No one could object to this sentence: "I felt like coming in the summer." *Coming* is a gerund, a noun substitute, and can be governed by *like.* But many will object if you write, "I felt *like* I might come in the summer."

You will be safe from attack if you use *as if* instead of *like* to introduce a clause. But to many ears, *like* is a simpler and more pleasing choice. Here you should make up your own mind—knowing that if you use *like* as a conjunction, many people will be annoyed.

The confusion between *like* and *as if* is not as obnoxious as the ill-considered efforts of some dislikers of *like* to purge *like* from our vocabulary as if it were a tramp bringing shame to the club. It is correct to say, "The party included some distinguished guests, *like* the dean of the faculty and the donor who bought six quarterbacks for the team." The fastidious will substitute *such as* for *like.* Nothing is wrong with *such as.* But nothing is wrong with *like* either. The rule some writers follow in using *such as* is aptly phrased in one textbook that gives this advice: "When you are using an example of something, use *such as* to indicate that the example is a representative of the thing mentioned, and use *like* to compare the example to the thing mentioned." This rule would give us these sentences: "The party included distinguished guests *such as* the dean of the college" and "He aspired to be distinguished, *like* the dean of the college." The rule is harmless, but it is not binding.

A somewhat more troublesome use of *like* is in comparisons like these: "She sings like a bird; he walks like an elephant." The fastidious say that these sentences imply a verb after the final noun: "She sings like a bird sings", "He walks like an elephant walks." So, they cry, if the verbs were written out, the sentences would be using *like* as a conjunction and would therefore be formally incorrect. In fact the verb is *not* written, and we can let her sing like a bird if she can and let him walk like an elephant if he must. It would be a false note to have her sing *as* a bird and heavy-handed at best to make him walk *as* an elephant.

Literally

Often used as an absurd intensifier. The word should give notice to your readers that you are not using metaphor or hyperbole. You can say that your high school friends are scattered to the winds, and you are speaking metaphorically since your friends were not actually blown away by a hurricane. But when you say, "My papers were *literally* scattered to the winds," you mean that a storm blew your papers in confusion out of your hands or off your desk. When you say, "He did not have two dimes to rub together," you mean he was poor. When you say, "He *literally* did not have two dimes to rub together," you mean that his net worth was less than twenty cents.

Avoid using *literally* when you don't mean it. Don't say, "My blood literally boiled" unless your temperature rose to 212 degrees Fahrenheit, started to bubble, and gave off red steam. Most of the time avoid the word. Instead of saying "Literally thousands gathered to hear her speak," you can say, "Thousands gathered to hear her speak."

Masterful/Masterly

The distinction has been all but lost, and I regret its passing. *Masterful* once meant "domineering" or "overbearing"—acting like a master ruling inferiors. *Masterly* meant "with the skill of a master." If we say, "Coach Dixie did a *masterful* job preparing his team for the game with Alabama," we mean he treated his players like a chain gang. If we say he did a *masterly* job of arranging his schedule so his team would remain undefeated, we mean that he did supremely well what publicity-conscious football coaches do to ensure national ranking and go to a bowl. To confuse the words eliminates a fine distinction.

Me/I/Myself

We have already considered the phrase *between you and me* in the rubric dealing with *between*. The phrase should always be *between you and me. I* should never be a direct object or the object of a preposition in a sentence. Don't say, "He gave Rocky and I the key to the weight room."

Oddly enough, just as *I* has become misused in the objective case, *me* and sometimes *him* and *her* are often misused in the nominative or subjective case. Many young people say and write, "Rocky and me went to see *Titanic* the other night. Him and me had the movie ruined for us when a guy in the ticket line told us the ship sank in the end."

The same failures in proper case turn up in other forms. *Myself* is a reflexive pronoun; that is, it calls attention to a special emphasis on the subject *I* or indicates action by the subject on itself. So we can say:

I *myself* have often made that mistake.

I shot *myself* in the foot.

But don't say, "He invited Jean and myself to the party." Say, "He invited Jean and me." And don't say, "Myself and Abigail invite you all to our party."

Medium/Media

The word *medium* is a singular noun signifying anything that enables something else to work or appear. Until recently, its most common use was in the phrase *medium of exchange,* which means money or anything else that allows people to carry on trade. In recent times, the plural form *media* has come to mean all the instruments of mass communication that serve society. The media include radio, television, newspapers, and magazines—although the word seems to refer in particular to television. A connotation of the word seems to be something ephemeral, something that does not remain important for long.

Books are a medium of communication, but somehow they are usually excluded when we speak of the media.

Two objections may be raised against *media.* It is less specific—and therefore less vivid—than the words it replaces, and it is often misused in that it appears with a singular form of the verb or pronoun. You should not say, "The media *is* responsible for the shallowness of American politics." If you use the word, it should be with a plural verb.

But we should rarely use the word at all. It seems far better to say something specific. "The effort of candidates to shape their pronouncements to fit the four-minute sound bite on television news has contributed to the shallowness of American politics. Few people can be profound, complex, or informative in four minutes."

Militate Against/Mitigate

Mitigate means "to lessen," often for good reason. If your neighbor sues you for driving your power lawnmower through her tulips, you may claim the mitigating circumstance that tulips make you break out in hives. The judge may then mitigate the rigor of the law that applies in your case.

Militate is related to *military.* Anything that militates against an opinion offers a strong reason not to accept it.

> Her declaration that she would rather go to a party with a cabbage than with him *militated against* his hope that she would marry him.

To say that something *mitigates against* an opinion makes no sense, although people do say such things. The confusion arises because people want a hard *g* sound to go with both words in the phrase *militate against.* Here is a rare instance where spoken rhythms in English, otherwise so desirable, can lead us astray.

Model/Replica

A *model* duplicates the appearance of something else, but on a larger or smaller scale—usually on a scale so different that there can be no confusion between the model and the real thing. A model railroad duplicates the appearance of a railroad but will fit on a table. A model of the DNA molecule is millions of times larger than the real thing.

A *replica* must be like the original in every detail, including size. The replica of the *Mayflower* in the harbor at Plymouth, Massachusetts, is said to be exactly like the original ship. A replica of an ancient Greek vase looks exactly like the vase and is exactly the same size.

The term *exact replica* is redundant. A *replica* is exact by definition.

More Important/More Importantly

It is incorrect to say, "The Yankees lost the pennant, but more importantly, they lost money." In constructions like this one, a clause is implied—*What is more important.* This elliptical clause (we call it *elliptical* because some of its words are omitted) works as a noun rather than an adverb. In this sentence, a *Time* writer uses the correct expression:

> *More important,* he sat at Stengel's side, learning the game from one of its managerial geniuses.

Also avoid *firstly, secondly, thirdly, fourthly,* and so on. Say, *first, second, third,* and *fourth.*

Nauseous/Nauseated

When you are sick at your stomach and ready to vomit, you are *nauseated.* If you come on a dead horse and get sick at the sight and the smell, the horse is *nauseous.* Something *nauseous* makes you feel *nauseated.* Don't say "I'm nauseous" unless people habitually throw their hands over their mouths and vomit whenever you walk into a crowd.

Ongoing

A bureaucratic synonym for "continuing." *Ongoing* is another of those flat, dull words that usually signal bad words to come.

Oriented/Orientation

We live in a wealth-*oriented* society.

He was success-*oriented* as a child but leisure-*oriented* as an adult.

The suffix *-oriented* and the noun *orientation* turn up all over the place now. We hear that McDougal is success-oriented or that he has an orientation toward wealth or that people are discussing his sexual orientation. These terms are vague and colorless, keeping us and our readers from real thought. It is much better to say, "We live in a society that seeks wealth and that admires it too much." It's more concrete to say, "As a young man, McDougal aspired to work hard and earn a hundred thousand dollars a year, but when he grew older, he preferred to drink beer, play golf, watch TV, and read trashy novels."

Parameters

This word from the world of computers and mathematics has become a pretentious synonym for *limits. Limits* is a good, strong word that says everything most people mean by *parameters* and says it without pretense.

The only generally accepted meaning of *parameter* is as a constant in mathematics that may be applied to variable situations. It is most commonly used in computer talk. For example, you can set the parameters of your word-processing program to provide a margin of one inch on all four sides of your paper, and your computer will hold those margins page after page no matter what you write. If you figure compound interest on your credit card at 18.5

percent per year, your parameter is the figure 18.5, no matter what transaction you consider or how much you charge.

Parameters may well be used in other contexts. I can imagine saying, "Grace and courtesy have always been *parameters* of social success" or "Creativity is the intellectual *parameter* for all the great disciplines." But it is only pretension that makes some people say, "We want to carry out this construction project within certain *parameters.*"

Posture

A word like *conditions* and *case* and the intensifier *definitely*. It is popular—and says almost nothing that cannot be said more simply and more vigorously in other words. Instead of saying, "The President adopted a defensive posture during his latest scandal," say simply, "The President went on the defensive again today when the latest scandal broke over the White House."

Preplanning/Advanced Planning

Both these terms are *tautological*. That is, they say the same thing twice. *Preplanning* must take place before the thing that is planned. It is an unnecessary inflation to add the prefix *pre-* to something that is by definition about the future. Do you plan plans? I don't know how you do that. You may plan in stages, but that is still planning.

Presently/Currently/Now

The adverb *presently* most properly denotes something about to happen. "The actors will appear *presently.*"

Recently the word *presently* has become a grandiose synonym for *now* or *currently* so that pilots come on the intercom to tell us, "We are presently flying over Tuscaloosa, Alabama." It seems better to hold to the older meaning of *presently* and to say "now" when we mean now.

Yet *presently* as an inflated synonym for *now* may be here to stay. In the first edition of this book, some good soul in production wrote of me in the note "About the Author" that I was "presently working on another novel." When I read that announcement, I presently protested, and the wording was changed.

Principal/Principle

Principal has always had the connotation of "first." It is most often used as an adjective meaning "the first" or the "most important."

> The *principal* source of her irritation with me was that I had run over her cat with my bicycle.

But it is also used as a noun to designate a person of primary authority.

> The *principals* in the final drama of the Civil War at Appomattox were Ulysses S. Grant and Robert E. Lee.

Principle refers to an ideal standard of conduct or an underlying system that helps explain some things we see only in a superficial way until we think of them.

> Coach Dixie told us that fair play was great in *principle,* but we should not be so devoted to it that we lost football games.

> The *principle* behind the mercury thermometer is that mercury expands at a constant rate with heat and contracts at an equally constant rate with cold.

Quotation/Quote

I've lost this one, but I cling to it with absurd devotion. *Quotation* is a noun; *quote* is a verb. But alas, *quote* is not only used as a noun; it is often used as a synonym for *text* as in "The Bible begins with the quote, 'In the beginning God created the heavens and the earth.' " I still think it bad form to write, "Faulkner's *quotes* from the Bible prove that he knew it well." I want my students to speak of Faulkner's *quotations.* You can also say, "He *quoted* a price that I found irresistible" or "Dickens frequently *quoted* Shakespeare."

Respective/Respectively

Use these words only when some major confusion might result without them: "The winners of the literary prize and the math prize were Jack Rowdy and Meg Lena *respectively.* Without *respectively* we might think Jack and Meg shared both prizes. As it is, we know that Jack won the literary prize and Meg the math prize. In fact, it is probably better to say just that.

Simple/Simplistic

Often confused. Something *simple* is uncomplicated and unpretentious. People, machines, novels, movies, poems, and plans can be simple. Only ideas or utterances can be simplistic. The connotation of *simplistic* is always bad, implying that the person with, say, a *simplistic* idea has not thought very much about the issue. "There's a very easy way to end the drug problem in the world. Just say no."

A simple way to raise enough money to repair the American highway system might be to impose an additional tax of fifty cents a gallon on fuel. A simplistic idea would be to ban all motor vehicles from the roads and turn them over to bicycles.

That

This excellent, useful word has lately been pressed into service as a synonym for the adverb *very.* *Very* is a weak adverb; people want something stronger. So we get sentences like this. "He was not that good looking." The usage seems to be always in the negative, and the logical question is to ask what the referent of *that* might be.

We can understand the word if somebody says, "I have been sunburned through a shirt, but my son's skin is not *that* sensitive." But what of this sentence? "His skin was not *that* sensitive." As sensitive as what? As a baby's? As the hide of a rhinoceros? We have no context to tell us.

Perhaps the original idiom was *all that good* or *all that bad,* and by ellipses we shortened it to *that.* It was not a good idiom in the first place; shortening has made it worse.

This

Now and then we all use a vague *this* in our prose, usually referring to something we have said in the previous sentence.

> Frederick Bazille and Claude Monet started painting in the open air; *this* was the real beginning of French impressionistic art.

We have no trouble understanding that the *this* in the sentence above refers to the act of painting in the open air, described in the first independent clause. But the vague *this* can lead to confusion.

> In their war plans of 1914, the Germans assumed they would have a hard fight against millions of Russians on their Eastern borders but that they would have an easy time with France, especially if they sent an overpowering army crashing through Belgium to capture Paris quickly. With France defeated in a few weeks, the Germans could turn all their force against the Russians. This was why a local conflict became a general European war.

In a text as complicated as this one, the vague *this* causes trouble to the reader who does not already know the story. The last sentence would be helped by the addition of a noun after the *This*. "This misconception was why a local conflict became a general European war."

Thrust

Another lazy word like *factor.* We read of the *thrust* of an article or the *thrust* of an argument. Writers who use *thrust* are trying to tell us that they are so clever that they see many, many different issues but that by their superior wisdom, they see the outline of a major purpose amid all these complications. They protect themselves from the accusation that they have missed the point, and they provide room for themselves to whirl about and run the other way should anyone challenge them.

Tragedy/Calamity

Strictly speaking, a *tragedy* is a drama played out on stage or in life in which a great human being is brought down by forces beyond his or her control—forces within his or her soul or in the world beyond. Macbeth is tragic; so is Othello. Macbeth cannot control his ambition; Othello cannot control his jealousy. Tragedy has always been part of the human experience because it reveals glory and depravity in the greatest personalities and comforts us by showing us that we are not alone in finding both glory and depravity within ourselves.

The rise of modern sensational journalism has confused *tragedy* with *calamity, misfortune, disaster,* and *accident.* In consequence, the tragic sense, having nearly vanished from our language, may be in danger of vanishing from our sensibilities. Now an airplane crash is a *tragedy,* as is the wreck of a truck that kills somebody. I would like to see *tragedy* restored to its original noble meaning. Other words should be used to describe the consequences of accidents that originate primarily from simple carelessness or mechanical failure. But the word has probably been so diluted that its redemption is impossible. Alas!

Transpire/Occur

Transpire was originally a genteel way of speaking of sweat, a meaning the French verb *transpirer* preserves. From this meaning, *transpire* evolved into the sense of "passing from the hidden to the open," a useful concept in this sentence:

It *transpired* that high officials in the United States government knew by 1967 that the Americans could not win the Vietnam War.

To use the word *transpire* as a synonym for *happen* or *occur* is inflated discourse as in this sentence: "The game transpired on a golden autumn afternoon before 107,000 screaming fans in Knoxville."

Try To/Try And

The proper idiom is *try to* followed by a verb. Yet many educated people say and write *try and.* "They would try to force the issue" is logical. "They would try and force the issue" is not especially logical, but the use has become so idiomatic that it seems futile to fight it.

Unique

Unique means one of a kind, and it can be modified only by words like *nearly* and *almost.* Nothing can be *very unique* or *rather unique* or *the most unique.* Something is either unique or not. If something is not unique, you can say that it is *rare, uncommon,* or *unusual,* or you can say that it is *almost* unique.

Varying/Various

The distinction between these words gives unusual trouble. If we speak of changes in the same thing from time to time or place to place, the word is *varying.* If we speak of different things with attention to the differences between them, the word is *various. Varying* is usually used before a collective or singular noun, *various* before a plural. These sentences use *varying* correctly:

The *varying* weather made the day interesting, although not especially pleasant.

The *varying* talk wandered from intense argument to calm and slow ruminations.

The following sentences use *various* correctly.

Various friends confirmed her opinion.

The responses to my proposal were *various*

Verbal/Oral

A strange confusion has grown up around these words, making them synonyms. While flight attendants are giving their ritual safety instructions as the plane taxis out to the runway, they direct their attention to those sitting in rows by emergency exits. They tell us that in the event of an emergency we must be able "to verbally direct others to the exit." I ignore the split infinitive, but I wonder about *verbally*. If I am seated by an emergency exit, and if the plane makes a belly landing in a field, I suppose I could write notes to other passengers saying, "This way to the emergency exit." I would then fulfill the obligation of *verbally* directing passengers. The flight attendants mean that I should give *oral* instructions, that is, that I should shout at the top of my voice, "This way!" *Oral* instructions must also be *verbal* since they use words and not gestures. But *verbal* instructions may be written but not spoken.

Viable Options/Viable Alternatives

Both expressions are inflated discourse, designed to deceive readers into believing that something important is being said. Are *nonviable options* really options at all? If not, why should we speak of *viable* options? The word *viable* should be reserved for its proper meaning, as in the phrase *viable seeds,* meaning seeds that will germinate if we plant them.

Violent/Vehement

If your coach yells at you on the basketball court, he is being *vehement.* If you strangle him because he yelled, you are being *violent.* Language may be vehement or profane or outraged or loud or insulting, but it cannot be violent.

Which

In my chapter on false rules (Chapter 10), I reject the that/which rule, and readers interested in that oft-inflated subject can seek enlightenment there. But *which* causes another difficulty, similar to that of the vague *this* discussed earlier. When it does not refer to a clear antecedent, the reader often feels a baffling absence.

> In many universities writing teachers love teaching but work only part-time as adjuncts, without adequate benefits, at low salaries without much contact with the rest of the teaching faculty, *which* accounts for the low morale many of them feel.

The *which* clause here has no clear antecedent. We grasp the meaning only if we assume that the *which* clause does not apply to the statement "writing teachers love teaching." Morale may be low because of the other facts mentioned in the sentence. The sentence can be fixed by adding a noun that makes a clear antecedent to the *which* clause: "*disadvantages which* account for the low morale many of them feel."

Which should have a clear antecedent expressed as a noun or a pronoun. Such clarity will save readers the trouble of backing up and reading again to see if they missed something.

While/Although

Some writers use *while* as a synonym for *although,* with confusing results. "While McDougal was an athlete in college, he became as fat as a barrel after graduation." What does this sentence mean? It could mean that although McDougal was an athlete in college, he stopped taking exercise and became as fat as a keg—but remained an athlete. This example may be extreme, although if McDougal was a baseball pitcher, it is possible. *While* in the sentence conveys a brief confusion any time it is used as a synonym for *although,* and good writers should protect readers from brief confusions whenever possible.

Who/Whom

This distinction provokes acrimonious debate among writers and grammarians. Some want to get rid of *whom* altogether or else use it only immediately after a preposition. We would have sentences like these:

We did not care *who* he chose to take the cat to the pound.

She did not know *to whom* she spoke.

Whom does indeed seem to be withering away. My friend Richard A. Lanham, U.C.L.A.'s distinguished authority on grammar, begins one chapter of a good book with the title "Who's Kicking Who?" He says "who's kicking whom" sounds stilted to him. It does not sound stilted to me. You must make up your own mind. Many people will object if you don't use *whom* in its traditional place. No one will object if you use it in the traditional way.

If *whom* sounds stilted to your ear, revise your sentence to get rid of it. *Who* and *whom* clauses are often edited out of popular styles. You can read page after page of *Sports Illustrated, Time, Smithsonian, The New Yorker,* and *National Geographic* without encountering a *who* or *whom* clause. Many serious books follow the same stylistic pattern. Richard Ellmann's classic and readable biography of James Joyce goes for many pages at a time without using a *who* or a *whom* clause. Good writers seem to sense that such clauses introduce distracting elements into sentences. Everybody uses them now and then, but when you write one, see if you have to have it, and if you don't, revise the *who* or *whom* clause out of your style.

As in the great debate over *like* and *as,* purists want to preserve the distinction between *who* and *whom* but often don't know what the distinction is. They throw a *whom* into a sentence where *who* is correct. The rule is this: Use *who* or *whom* according to how the pronoun is used in the clause where it appears. If it is used as the subject of the clause, use *who.* If it is used as the object of the clause, use *whom.* So don't write this:

> The university president demanded a football coach *whom* he said could break NCAA rules without getting caught.

The writer of this sentence saw that *coach* was a direct object. He assumed that the clause modifying *coach* should begin with *whom* in the objective case. But the sentence should read like this:

> The university president demanded a football coach *who* he said could break NCAA rules without getting caught.

In the dependent clause modifying *coach, who* is the subject of the verb *could.* Therefore *who* must be in the subjective case. The short clause *he said* is parenthetical, inserted in the *who* clause but not governing the subject *who.* You can check such clauses by trying to replace the *who* or *whom* with *he* or *him* or *she* or *he* in a sentence constructed from the clause. We can say, "*He* could break NCAA rules without being caught." You cannot say, "*Him* could break NCAA rules without being caught."

We use *whom* when it serves as a direct or indirect object in the clause where it appears. So we would say, "We did not care *whom* he chose to represent us." We could say, "He chose *him.*"

Always remember parenthetical elements within a *who* clause do not govern the pronoun. These sentences are correct.

> The candidate *who* the committee thought would be the best librarian was rejected by the chancellor for wanting to buy more books.
>
> The assistant *whom* they believed Coach Dixie would select lost his chance when he was arrested for gambling.
>
> The trustees fired the president, *who* had been beloved by the faculty, because he insisted that football players attend class.
>
> · The man *whom* the trustees chose to replace the president said he would be guided in all his decisions by Coach Dixie and the Booster Club.

Whom is used if it is the object of an infinitive made of a transitive verb: "They wondered *whom* to send as their representative."

A continual mistaken use of *whom* occurs in the use of its associated pronoun, *whomever.* Here is a sentence that appeared a few years ago in a good book published by Yale University Press:

> Haskell sold land to whomever would buy.

The author and the editors at Yale Press must both have seen the preposition *to* and remembered the rule that the object of a preposition should be in the objective case. They forgot that the entire clause following *to* serves as the object of the preposition and that within that clause the pronoun is governed by how it is used in relation to the verb. The sentence should have read, "Haskell sold land to *whoever* would buy." *Whoever* governs the verb *would buy* and must be in the subjective case.

Who and *whom* should be used to refer to persons. You should not say, "The German generals *that* planned the war later tried to blame it all on Hitler." You should say, "The German general *who. . .* "

These rules may seem so complex that you will be tempted to accept Richard Lanham's advice and throw *whom* onto the garbage dump of language along with other obsolete words. I would say only that *whom* serves a useful purpose, and it is not obsolete yet, and if you want your work respected by habitual readers, you are better off with *whom* than without it. The *whomless* writer may suffer unnecessarily the slings and arrows of outraged lovers of traditional English.

But remember my earlier advice. Revise to eliminate both *who* and *whom* clauses whenever you can.

Whose/Of Which

Some purists insists that the possessive *whose* be used only when the antecedent is a person or group of persons. They object to any use of *whose* to refer to an impersonal antecedent. But even H. W. Fowler, a conservative authority of matchless purity, ridicules this notion. It would require us to write sentences like this: "The aircraft, the tail *of which* fell off, landed safely." How awkward! Write, "The aircraft *whose* tail fell off," and you will land safely in any publication. You can rewrite the sentence to eliminate the issue altogether: "The aircraft lost its tail, but landed safely." Although such would be my own preference here, in practice rewriting is sometimes not feasible, and we must choose between *whose* and *which*. Whenever we face this choice, we should be guided by the rhythm of the sentence, and that will lead us nearly every time to *whose.*

Wise

I'm in no hurry timewise.

Japanese cars compete successfully with American cars both safetywise and pricewise.

Here is another linguistic virus that erodes the language because it is used too much—tacking -*wise* onto nouns to make them adverbs. It represents a lazy mind, and you should flee it.

With

With should not be used loosely with the sense of *and* or *in addition.* Don't write this: "Chip took first place *with* Yoke coming in second." Write this: "Chip took first place, and Yoke came in second."

Figurative Language

Figurative language is the use of words in any but their literal sense. If I say, "She floated easily on her back in the swimming pool," I use the word *floated* in its literal sense. If I say, "She floated gracefully from guest to guest at her party, making everyone feel like an intimate friend," I use *floated* in a figurative sense. If I say, "The water *boiled* for tea," I mean that the water was heated to 212 degrees Fahrenheit, that it bubbled violently, and that it began to turn to steam. If someone says, "His condescending attitude made my blood *boil,"* the word *boil* becomes figurative. This particular device we call *hyperbole*—exaggerated speech to make a point emphatically.

Figurative language must do three things: (1) It must draw on some common experience that binds the writer to an audience; (2) it must be fresh and engaging—often surprising; (3) it must be appropriate to the context.

SIMILES AND METAPHORS

Similes and metaphors are among the most common figurative devices. They join two experiences so that one may be illuminated by the other. In the writing program I directed for many years, we had a metaphor for a certain kind of paper filled with quotations, demonstrating hours of hard work but lacking any ideas from the student writer. We called it "the model plane essay." You can buy a model at a hobby shop, spend hours or weeks putting it together, and at the end you have an impressive looking object that looks exactly like the picture on the box. You have contributed nothing of your own to it except your labor and your dexterity.

161

Most instructors want student papers that show careful labor, but they also want original thought, some fresh insight, something alive contributed by the student writer. The model plane metaphor helped our students understand the difference between writing a formally correct paper and producing one that shows that the writer has become deeply engaged with the material. Metaphors can drive thought home.

Specialists in rhetoric often make an unnecessarily sharp distinction between metaphor and simile. Simile and metaphor differ in their construction. A simile is a kind of metaphor. A metaphor speaks of something as if it were something else: "Johnson was a bulldog in argument." A simile tells us that something is *like* something else. We could say, "Johnson is like a bulldog in argument" or "Johnson is as tenacious as a bulldog in argument." Both times we isolate a quality of bulldogs—their legendary tenacity—and apply it to Johnson. We don't apply every quality of bulldogs to Johnson. He does not walk on all fours and bark and eat dog food and bury bones in the backyard and chase the letter carrier. He is tenacious; that is the only point we want to make in the metaphor or simile.

Both metaphors and similes depend on some shared experience between writers and readers. When I say, "Johnson is a bulldog in argument," I assume that my readers know something about bulldogs or at least that they think they know something about bulldogs. (Bulldogs are in fact gentle and loving creatures.) Their knowledge of bulldogs helps me tell them something about Johnson. If my readers were Siberian nomads who had never seen or heard of a bulldog, my metaphor would make no sense.

The balance between the reader's knowledge and the writer's intent is delicate. Suppose I said, "Johnson is a salmon in argument." Most readers cannot think of anything about salmon that would apply to arguments; so the metaphor fails. I might expand: "Johnson is a salmon in argument; he starts in one place and goes all around the world and comes back to where he began, no matter what contrary views we put in his way." But the explanation ruins the effect. Good metaphors work like jokes, not that they are always funny but rather that they make a sudden and vivid impression. Explaining a joke ruins it. Like good jokes, good metaphors depend on common experience. Most of us have failed to get a joke that convulses everyone else in a group. We don't get the joke because we lack the common experience that makes it funny to others. Unless we make metaphors out of the common experience of our readers, they will not get the point.

Three Kinds of Metaphor

Most metaphors may be classified under three general headings. (1) The *descriptive metaphor* helps us understand one concrete object by reference to another. (2) The *abstract metaphor* helps us understand an abstraction by reference to a concrete object. (3) The *embedded metaphor* substitutes metaphorical language for literal reporting. Metaphors that help us see one concrete entity by reference to another help us describe things; metaphors that use a concrete reference to illuminate an abstraction help us explain ideas; and embedded metaphors brighten our language in more subtle ways.

Descriptive Metaphors Help Us Imagine Scenes

> Six hundred feet up the cleanly hewn face of a mountain called the Razor, the wind gusting off the polar plateau coated my beard with frost. I paused in mid-ascent, dangling from a bight of half-inch thick rope, and attempted to shake the cramps from my aching forearms. The Antarctic ice cap lapped like a ghostly white sea against the base of the rock face, far below. On the horizon huge, jagged peaks bristled like granite quills from the vast sprawl of ice.[1]

All sorts of metaphors run through these sentences that introduce an article about scaling a barren mountain in Antarctica. The name of the mountain itself—the "Razor"—is metaphorical. The ice cap "lapped like a ghostly white sea." The "jagged peaks bristled like granite quills." We who have never been in Antarctica get some impression of the barren beauty of this vast and dangerous land.

The descriptive metaphor can be used in any kind of writing, fiction or nonfiction. Sometimes a metaphor can add powerful effects that become more intense the more we think of them. Philip Caputo, writing about his days as a Marine in the Vietnam War, describes the heat:

> It was noon, without a breath of wind, and the sky seemed like a blazing aluminum lid clamped over the world.[2]

Caputo's metaphor calls up a metallic, whitish sky of a sort that those who have experienced hot summers know is a sign of torrid heat. But his "aluminum lid" has deeper meaning; it recalls a pot on the stove, the lid set on the pot to collect heat inside. The day in Vietnam conveys the feeling of being trapped over a fire with the heat rising. The metaphor with extended meanings gives us a remarkable sentence.

Abstract Metaphors Help Us Understand Ideas   A different kind of metaphor and perhaps the most powerful helps explain ideas by attributing a concrete reality to an abstraction, making the abstraction more manageable. Such metaphors have been used for centuries, often in religion where the essence is worship of an invisible God. In Psalms we read, "My cup runneth over." In this statement the writer, feeling the blessings of God, uses the cup as a metaphor for the life that can receive God's goodness. In the Proverbs we read, "The candle of the wicked shall be put out." The "wicked" in this scriptural text live by a man-made light that will be extinguished, leaving them in darkness. Some people speak of "bearing a cross," meaning a suffering they endure through no fault of their own. Sometimes we speak of death as a person, recalling both the apostle Paul's personification of death as enemy in his epistles and the figure of the Grim Reaper with his scythe that has been with us since the Renaissance. A famous metaphor in economics was Adam Smith's "invisible hand," a term he used to explain how supply and demand works in the marketplace.

This kind of metaphor—the abstract metaphor—easily translates into political cartoons. Hunger becomes an emaciated skeleton devouring the world. War becomes a cruel warrior in classical Roman armor. Such metaphors have a long history. When Southerners claimed, before the Civil War, that every state had the right to "nullify" or disregard laws made by the United States Congress, Daniel Webster replied that if Southerners were correct, the federal union was no more than a "rope of sand." Abraham Lincoln some years later used a biblical metaphor when he spoke ominously of a country part slave and part free, declaring that "a house divided against itself cannot stand." In our own century, when Franklin D. Roosevelt proclaimed that his administration would give a "new deal" to the American people, the metaphor became one of the most powerful in American history. Millions suffering from the Great Depression felt they had been dealt an unlucky hand. The image of a "new deal" made them think that they might now have another chance, another deal of the cards of life. The metaphor suffered the fate of many good metaphors: It became a cliché. Now the term *New Deal* calls up the Roosevelt administration, and hearing it, few think of a new deal in a card game where every player gets another chance.

A good metaphor can help us think. Some argue that without metaphor some current scientific thinking could scarcely go on. Albert Einstein's theory of relativity deals with phenomena so removed from commonsense experience that most people can scarcely begin to understand it. Early in Einstein's career the *London Times* called Einstein's theory "an affront of common sense." Metaphors have helped explain it to the nonscientific mind.

Einstein tried to imagine how the universe would look to someone traveling at the speed of light. He made a pictorial leap in his mind similar to the kind of leap we make when we read a good metaphor. He began with the notion that the speed of light is constant, seen from any vantage point in the universe, whether the light is moving toward us or away from us. Einstein taught that nothing in the universe could move faster than the speed of light and that anything in motion at that speed creates a set of relations with other objects that is radically different from the relations of anything in motion at a lesser speed. The idea, so alien to common sense, called forth from English philosopher Bertrand Russell this metaphorical utterance:

> Everybody knows that if you are on an escalator you reach the top sooner if you walk up than if you stand still. But if the escalator moved with the velocity of light, you would reach the top at exactly the same moment whether you walked up or stood still.[3]

Because we experience motion at much lesser speeds than the speed of light, scientists and science writers after Einstein have had to use figurative language to enable the rest of us to understand what they are talking about.

THE EMBEDDED METAPHOR   The embedded metaphor is perhaps the most common metaphor—so common, in fact, that we may not even recognize it as a metaphor. The embedded metaphor uses a verb or a noun in something other than its literal meaning. Suppose I write, "The fire devoured the house." I might say, "The fire burned the house" or "The fire destroyed the house." When I use the word *devoured,* I employ an embedded metaphor to suggest that the fire is like a ravenous animal eating something up. The metaphor devoured treats the fire as an animal. Peter Gay, writing about Sigmund Freud's experiences in Vienna during World War I, told how Freud expressed deep pessimism that the world would ever be the same again. "His rhetoric is a little overcharged," Gay wrote, "but it records his dismay and mounting misgivings about his commonplace loyalty to the German-Austrian cause."[4] The word *overcharged* has an electrical connotation, an overcharged battery that gives off more than a normal quantity of electricity.

The interplay of metaphor takes place in much good writing—though it can be overdone. At times living things are likened to inanimate objects; at other times inanimate objects are given the qualities of living things. The purpose of the metaphor is always to make us bring two parts of our experience together so that the immediate object of our attention becomes much more vivid. The pleasures of a good metaphor are probably as great to the writer who creates the metaphor as they are to the reader. Metaphors provide another example of how writing sharpens thoughts that might otherwise be dull and commonplace.

Metaphors Create Atmosphere

Atmosphere, tone, and voice all refer to the complex and sometimes only partly conscious emotional response a piece of writing sets out to create in readers. How do we feel when we read something? Metaphors may condition our response. Suppose you wish to call attention to how thin someone is. One metaphor can create an impression of unhealthiness:

> Mr. Murray was so thin that he looked like a patient in a cancer ward.

Another can create a more positive impression:

> Mr. Murray was so thin that he looked like a long distance runner.

Some writers create atmosphere with stunning metaphorical power. Study the metaphors (I have italicized them for emphasis) in the following passage by Joseph Conrad, a master of the metaphorical art. Conrad's metaphors create a mood of awe and foreboding:

> You know how these squalls come up there about this time of year. First you see a darkening of the horizon—no more; then a cloud rises *opaque like a wall.* A *straight edge* of vapor lined with sickly whitish gleams flies up from the southwest, *swallowing the stars* in whole constellations; its *shadow flies over the waters and confounds* sea and sky into one *abyss of obscurity.* And all is still. No thunder, no wind, no sound; not a flicker of lightning. Then in the tenebrous immensity a *livid*

✳

arch appears; a swell or two like *undulations of the very darkness* run past, and suddenly wind and rain strike together with a peculiar impetuosity as *if they had burst
through something solid.*[5]

Few writers today would dare duplicate this rich and subtle use of metaphor.
The first image is of a cloud rising "opaque like a wall," then of a "straight
edge"—a ruler—of vapor lined with "sickly whitish gleams," as if the stormy
sky were a person sick with some tumultuous disease. Next the passage tells of
the vapor flying up, and we easily imagine some monstrous bird "swallowing
the stars in whole constellations." Then its "shadow flies over the waters," giving us another image of a bird of prey swooping over the sea after something—
perhaps a helpless ship—that it may find floating there. Afterward a swell or
two of the sea runs "like undulations of the very darkness." Those familiar with
the first chapter of the book of Genesis, as most literate people were in Conrad's day, remember the chaotic and utter darkness at the beginning when "the
earth was without form and void, and darkness was on the face of the deep"—
an image we are prepared to meet in Conrad's words "confounds" and "abyss,"
which recall the primordial universe before God created light.

Conrad gives us two worlds, the world of the storm on the sea and the eerie
world of imaginary association called up in his mind by the storm—a world he
transmits to us with his metaphors. The association includes in it not only what
we may have experienced of violent tempests but also what we have read and
thought of the biblical story of creation, where God struggles against the chaos
at the dawn of time. Conrad creates in us something of the primitive fear, probably lurking in the subconscious of most of us, a legacy of the terror of our re-
mote ancestors before the forces of nature. Without this string of metaphors,
Conrad's prose would not accomplish these effects. The metaphors are numerous, but we accept them because they are consistent, and they work together to
create an atmosphere of awe and gloom. It is a different view of a storm from
one we might see on the evening television news in our time, with a brightly
painted meteorologist with sprayed hair gesturing at a colored map, grinning
with an arena of teeth, telling us that a hurricane is coming.

In his inaugural address of January 20, 1961, President John F. Kennedy
delivered a series of metaphors that conveyed vigorous energy and made his
audience believe that a young and vigorous administration was about to lead
the United States. He said:

Let the word go forth from this time and place, to friend and foe alike, that the torch
has been passed to a new generation of Americans, born in this century, tempered
by war, disciplined by a hard and bitter peace, proud of our ancient heritage and
unwilling to witness or permit the slow undoing of those human rights to which
this nation has always been committed and to which we are committed today at
home and around the world.

Reading or hearing Kennedy's image of a torch passed, we think of Olympic
runners carrying the flame from one to another across countries and the world

until they arrive at the place where the games are held. The new generation of Americans is described as "tempered," which recalls the process of making steel stronger by first heating it and then plunging it into cool water. We are told that these Americans have been "disciplined by a hard and bitter peace," and we think of soldiers or athletes trained by hardship to do their duty. We are told that Americans will not allow "the slow undoing of . . . human rights," and we think of a carefully knitted garment being unraveled before our eyes by a perverse child or malicious adult.

So it goes through the speech, one vigorous metaphor after another conveying a total image of strength, vitality, endurance, and courage. Presidents provide some sense of what they think of themselves and their administrations when they use metaphors. You can read their speeches and see what they believe about their own leadership and about the people they try to lead. In your writing, the metaphors you use will tell readers much about what you think of yourself and of them.

Use Metaphors Cautiously

Metaphors should make one point sharply. Long extended metaphors seldom interest readers. You may think it clever to create an extended metaphor that likens getting a college education to climbing a mountain. Admission is like arriving at the base; enrolling in your first class is like putting on your helmet and climbing tentatively over the first rocks; social life is like rain on the side of the mountain because a little of it is refreshing but too much may wash you off the cliffs. You can go on and on with such metaphors, and your audience will find them cute, but cute quickly becomes tedious. Their worst quality is that they don't enlighten anyone about the college experience or anything else. By the time you get to the top of your mountain, most readers have left you. In Britain an overextended metaphor is said to walk "on all fours." This scornful expression mocks those metaphors that try to do too much and so become contrived and boring.

Don't base arguments on metaphors. To convert a metaphor into an argument may be inappropriate and dangerous. The so-called organic metaphor has long been popular in the study of history. Plants and other organisms are born; they enjoy youth; they pass into maturity and then into old age; finally they die. Edward Gibbon's eighteenth-century masterpiece *The Decline and Fall of the Roman Empire* accustomed generations of literate readers to thinking of the final centuries of the Roman Empire in the West as a decline, a sickness, much like the aging and death of a human being.

Gibbon's metaphor did no special harm in itself. But more recent historians such as Oswald Spengler and Arnold Toynbee made the organic metaphor into an argument. From it they constructed elaborate patterns that they claimed represented the course of human history. Both frequently twisted the historical evidence to make events conform to the design they had imposed on the past.

Spengler in particular wrenched history into a plantlike cycle whereby all civilizations were seen as passing through the same stages, every stage likened to a similar stage in the development of an organism. He provided a design for history in which no individual striving could make much difference and no collective effort could change the implacable pattern of rise and fall. History in his view repeated itself just as the life cycle of a plant repeats itself again and again in the members of a species. Because Spengler believed that the twentieth century represented the last stage in the organic life of western civilization, he provided no hope for the future. Toynbee, although more moderate in his judgment, fell into much the same trap.

Metaphors may therefore illustrate arguments, but they should not become arguments. Metaphors help us express ideas, but they should not take over our minds or our writing. In a fundamental way, metaphors are not real. Describing Cleopatra's barge in *Anthony and Cleopatra,* Shakespeare wrote:

> The barge she sat in, like a burnish'd throne
> Burn'd on the water.

We are supposed to imagine that Cleopatra's stage barge was so polished that it seemed to burn like fire on the water of the Nile. As one scholar has remarked, if we supposed that Cleopatra's barge were literally on fire with she and her sailors leaping into the water to escape the flames, we would have no metaphor.[6] When we make metaphors, we use our imaginations. We play with words. We take part of one thing and make it intensify our sense of another. But a metaphor takes only a part; it does not take the whole. Human history is not like a plant in all its particulars; to make the metaphor of growth, maturity, and decline an ironclad rule for how human societies develop is to confuse a metaphor with an argument.

Novelist Tom Clancy expressed his concern for the dangers of the metaphor "surgical strike" in the winter of 1998 when the United States government was contemplating a bombing campaign against Iraq.

> One term people frequently use is "surgical strike." But surgery is not done with bombs, is it? Surgery is done with small knives held in the hands of highly trained physicians. A 2,000-pound bomb will kill people standing in the open hundreds of meters away, and the bomb fragments will not care if that person is male or female, young or old. Before one drops such a bomb, therefore, it is vital to know what the target is and why the target is important enough to risk death or injury to any person whom chance places in harm's way.[7]

Metaphors brighten prose, and those who write with no metaphors at all may produce prose that is dry and dead. But avoid packing your prose with so many metaphors that they become confusing or ridiculous. *The New Yorker* used to run a little feature called "Block That Metaphor," a passage from a writer who has solemnly jumbled metaphors together without thinking of their total effect—like this passage from a review of James Michener's novel *Alaska.*

> Perhaps the problem is Michener has grown "formula" in preparing such all-encompassing works. But here at least, the fluffy snowdrifts thaw, exposing permafrost of substance. To survive the long polar night of prose, readers must dig in and await spring when the narrative thaws and the verbal tundra becomes hospitable. It takes a gold miner's stamina, though, to pan away, discard the trivial tailings, and be rewarded—not by a mother lode of meaning but by precious flecks of literary gold.[8]

What can this passage mean? I think the reviewer intends to say that in all the trivia of Michener's enormous novel one may find a few interesting things. But the language becomes so pompous with grandiose metaphors that it is easy to lose track of his meaning.

Your metaphors should make sense. Work on metaphors carefully. Think about them. Practice them in your notebook.

Appropriate Metaphors

Metaphors should be appropriate to the topic at hand. Here exercise good taste. Some writers feel comfortable using metaphors and similes that would annoy others. I would not like to read that General Robert E. Lee's theory of battle was to crash into his foes as if he were trying to drive a bulldozer through a brick wall. General Lee never saw a bulldozer in his life, and a careful reader, considering the incongruity of such a simile, might be annoyed by it.

In making similes and metaphors fit your subject, use your wit. In writing about the bizarre-looking work of portrait artist Chuck Close, Deborah Solomon used several metaphors.

> Close, too, favors frozen expressions. If he were a painter of criminals—of twice convicted burglars or petty thieves—one could understand his subjects' dead, reptilian eyes. The twist is that Close paints artists, who, according to popular notions, are supposed to look sensitive, not embalmed.[9]

You can be ridiculous by mixing metaphors. A memo handed out in my university a few years ago urged the faculty "to grapple with the burning issues." I rather hoped the administration would issue insulated gloves so the issues would not scald us. I once heard an inspirational speaker tell an audience of high school seniors that they could "climb the ladder of success only by keeping their noses to the grindstone." I thought of how painful it was going to be for these young people to lug that heavy grindstone up the ladder while keeping their noses pressed to it. *The New Yorker* picked up a hilarious and amazing string of mixed metaphors uttered in solemn seriousness by another speaker:

> But a fellow user pushing for stricter security counters: "Perhaps I am flogging a straw herring in midstream, but in light of what is known about the ubiquity of security vulnerabilities, it seems vastly too dangerous for university folks to run with their heads in the sand."[10]

You *can* use a series of metaphors effectively, as long as they do not clash. Here is Irving Howe describing the Jewish immigrant housewife in turn-of-the-century New York:

> It was from her place in the kitchen that the Jewish housewife became the looming figure who would inspire, haunt, and devastate generations of sons. She realized intuitively that insofar as the outer world tyrannized and wore down her men, reducing them to postures of docility, she alone could create an oasis of order. It was she who would cling to received values and resist the pressures of dispersion; she who would sustain the morale of all around her, mediating quarrels, soothing hurts, drawing a circle of safety in which her children could breathe, and sometimes, as time went on, crushing her loved ones under the weight of her affection.[11]

Howe's metaphors come so naturally that we may not at first recognize them as metaphors. But then we identify "oasis of order," "circle of safety," and the metaphorical phrase "crushing her loved ones under the weight of her affection."

Match your metaphors and similes to the tone and content of your essay. These examples drawn from Howe nicely fit his subject, the development of the Jewish mother. It is a serious subject but not a somber one. Don't force your metaphors; don't make them overwrought and unnatural. Don't crowd your prose with them. But do use them.

OTHER FORMS OF FIGURATIVE LANGUAGE

Metaphors form the broadest class of figurative language, but other forms are also important. The classical rhetoricians called these forms *tropes,* from the Greek word for "manner" as in "manner of speaking." Now and then they can enliven your work, but all have their dangers, and you should use them with brave caution. Many tropes overlap.

Hyperbole

Hyperbole is exaggeration so great that no one can take it literally. We have already mentioned the cliché "He made my blood boil." That is hyperbole. No one expects the person who says such a thing to emit red steam. American humor often depends on hyperbole. Here is Texas journalist Molly Ivins giving her impression of the invasion of Grenada, an island in the Caribbean, in 1983. President Ronald Reagan said he was sending in the troops to protect American medical students in a school on Grenada. Maurice Bishop was prime minister; he was arrested and put to death by his army, which may have had support from Cuba. Mocking various events of the Reagan administration, Molly Ivins writes:

> My personal favorite: On October 25, 1983, the United States of America (population 250 million), the mightiest nation on earth, invaded the island of Grenada

(pop. 86,000) by air, land, and sea. And we whipped those suckers in a fair fight. We sent in almost 7,000 fighting men, armed to the teeth, along with ships, planes, guns, missiles, and tanks, to face a situation that we had (1) helped create by ignoring Maurice Bishop's pleas for help, (2) was none of our business anyway, (3) did not involve American medical students, who neither needed nor wanted our help, and (4) at worst could have been handled by a couple of Texas Rangers. The local population was mostly armed with sticks, and the 800 Cuban construction workers who were supposed to be commie soldiers either dropped their guns or never got to them at all. According to the Pentagon's own post-invasion analysis, none of the sixteen Americans killed in the invasion died by enemy fire; they all died by accident. The press, for the first time in the history of the nation, was not permitted to accompany U.S. troops into action—and only would have reported that we had bombed the local mental hospital anyway. President Reagan slept through the whole thing, as was his wont in moments of national crisis. Nevertheless, he went on television that night, after we had defeated the entire military might of Grenada, a place smaller than Cleveland, and his voice trembled with emotion as he said, "This—is our finest hour." The army later gave out 8,612 medals for heroism in the great Grenada invasion, even though fewer than 7,000 men took part.[12]

Understatement

Understatement is the opposite of hyperbole. Understatement is effective in writing about passion-filled issues; because it seems slightly out of place, it is often humorous. In writing of Adam Smith, whose *Wealth of Nations* published in 1776 gave the theoretical justification for modern competitive capitalism, John Kenneth Galbraith says:

> After the local school Adam Smith went on to the University of Glasgow and then to Balliol College, Oxford, an experience that he celebrates in *Wealth of Nations* with a stern rebuke for the public professors, as they then were called, those whose salary was independent of the size of their classes or the enthusiasm of their students. Thus relieved of incentive, these professors, he alleged, put forth little effort, did little work. Much better, he thought that they are paid, as he himself would be later at Glasgow, in accordance with the number of students they attracted. Smith's views on this matter would not be well received in a modern American university.[13]

Galbraith's last sentence provides an understatement that pokes fun at modern university professors who might riot if any administrator suggested that they be paid according to the number of students who signed up for their courses.

Irony

Irony is a deliberate effort to say something that will be taken in a sense opposite to the literal meaning of the words. It is, I think, the most difficult of the tropes, the one most likely to be misunderstood, and if it is misunderstood, irony loses its point.

Irony involves contradiction. The person who has a flat tire on her way to the airport and knows that she will miss her plane and an important meeting may say, "This is a fine state of affairs." Her statement is simple irony, meaning the opposite of what she feels. If I say, "The President took a courageous stand against burning the flag," the statement is ironic because it takes little courage to condemn flag burning in the United States. I may actually mean that the President was trying to look courageous by making brave-sounding remarks that carried no risk to him at all.

We speak also of the irony of events. Romeo and Juliet die because of a scheme intended to help them escape their families and marry each other. The secret tape recordings of conversations in his office that Richard Nixon intended to preserve as a record of his presidency led to his forced resignation. Writers can call attention to ironic events, but the irony of figurative language is the rhetorical device that concerns us here. Ironic statements have been with us for centuries. Jesus, speaking of those who pray loudly in public to impress others with their show of piety, said, "Truly I say to you, they have their reward." He meant that their reward was that people saw them, not that God heard them.

Irony can be a simple statement, or it can be an extended work of prose or poetry. Probably the best-known ironic work in English is Jonathan Swift's essay "A Modest Proposal for Preventing the Children of Poor People in Ireland from Being a Burden to Their Parents or Country, and for Making Them Beneficial to the Public." Swift, writing in the eighteenth century and appalled by the desperate poverty of rural people in Ireland where he lived, proposed that poor Irish children be raised as food for the wealthy. "I have been assured by a very knowing American of my acquaintance in London, that a young healthy child well nursed is at a year old a most delicious, nourishing and wholesome food, whether stewed, roasted, baked, or boiled, and I make no doubt that it will equally serve in a fricassee, or a ragout."[14]

Mike Barnicle, a columnist for the *Boston Globe* and one of my favorite writers, is a master of irony, often mixed with hyperbole. Here he is during the winter of 1998 when stories swirled across country about President Bill Clinton's alleged scandalous involvement with a young White House intern. In the midst of the scandal, polls showed Clinton's popularity to be one of the highest for any American President since polling began. Barnicle wrote:

> It's time to "spin" everything. Paste a happy face on every sordid tale of woe and grief coming down the turnpike.
>
> You want to tell me about the homeless. I will tell you more people live in three-bedroom bungalows and apartments than live in a box beneath a bridge.
>
> You heard something sad; I heard something happy.
>
> Your mother got mugged. Mine didn't.
>
> You got carjacked? So did Bill Diamond. But under President Clinton, laughter now accompanies larceny.

Diamond is a 75-year-old lawyer. Last week, as he came out of his doctor's office in Medford, he was confronted by a rainbow coalition of car thieves: one white, one black, one Hispanic, and one knife.

The three dopes showed him the knife and then took his car. However, the crime occurred directly across from the Medford police station.

So Diamond merely had to wait for the light to turn in order to stroll across the street and report it. And when the police officer at the desk asked, "Where did this happen?" Diamond said, "Look out the window."

There, a squadron of cops saw the three kids. They had headed down a dead-end alley. No surprises that SAT scores are sinking.

They got caught. Clinton didn't.

They had no alibi. The president does.

They're heading for court. Clinton appears headed for Mount Rushmore.

Is this a great time, or what?[15]

Barnicle obviously does not think this is a good time, and he just as obviously is outraged that the President of the United States seemed at this writing able to get away with something Barnicle thought was wrong. But instead of preaching a sermon, Barnicle chose irony and ends by ridiculing both the President and the American people who do not object to scandal in the White House.

The difficulty of irony is that it must take the form of serious, literal statement, but readers must know that the author is playing with them, saying something that contradicts the literal meaning of the words. Readers must see the art. Some student writers have in my classes written essays intended to be ironic, but I took them literally because the irony was not sharp enough. I recall once reading what seemed to be a racist tirade, only to be told by the student that it was intended as an ironic attack on racism. Here is irony that shoots itself in the foot.

If you mean the opposite of what you say, but your audience does not see the meaning, you work against your purpose. That is the difficulty the nineteenth-century English writer Thomas Carlyle meant when he wrote to his friend John Stuart Mill, "Irony is a sharp instrument; but ill to handle without cutting yourself." When intelligent readers take your irony literally, you have failed. Yet despite its dangers, irony is one of the great tropes, and a paper that uses it successfully can be memorable.

Irony often points to an outrageous reality. When Swift wrote that poor Irish children should be raised as food for the wealthy, he called attention to rich English landlords in Ireland who worked their Irish tenant farmers into misery and starvation. In a metaphorical sense, these wealthy English aristocrats were devouring Ireland. When Swift proposed a literal devouring—cannibalism—he hoped to make readers think of the devastating economic devouring going on under the guise of Christian morality.

The ironic statement can provide a dash of wit to an argument. *Time* writer Michael Kinsley wrote ironically in an essay on the 1989 Supreme Court decision that opened the way for state legislators to debate what kind of abortion laws they would have:

> The disaster facing America's state legislators, and potentially its national legislators, is that they may have to address an issue of public policy on which many of their constituents have strong and irreconcilable opinions. This they hate to do and are skilled at avoiding, even though it is what they are paid for. They would far rather pass laws against burning the flag.[16]

Ironies abound in this short passage. As the essay develops, it becomes clear that Kinsley thinks the national debate about abortion will be a good thing. He does not mean that it is a disaster at all. But it is a disaster in the minds of legislators who, he implies, would much rather come out strong about uncontroversial issues such as protecting the flag than about bitterly contested matters such as abortion. The notion that our representatives are "skilled at avoiding . . . what they are paid for" is an ironic comment on politics. Members of Congress like to pretend that they are brave; Kinsley implies that they are cowardly. They do not like to do what their jobs demand they must.

Irony can be subtle—so subtle that some readers or hearers may not grasp it while others who understand laugh both at the irony and at the ignorance of those who take it seriously. In that respect irony is often treated by ethical philosophers as a moral problem. Should one mock others with ironies they do not understand? The only answer a writer can give to such a question is that indeed irony has often been used as a form of mockery. One must consider these moral issues when one uses the trope.

Other Figures of Speech

Other figures of speech enliven English poetry and prose. In *synecdoche* we make a part stand for the whole. We speak of thirty head of cattle. (*Head* here is an idiomatic plural.) The book of Deuteronomy in the Bible tells us that we do not live "by bread alone," making bread stand for food in general.

In *metonymy* we use some attribute to indicate the whole. We speak of the "top brass" when we mean the highest military officers who used to wear brass emblems on their lapels to indicate their rank. We may write of the "Blue" to indicate the Union Army and the "Gray" to indicate the Confederate Army during the Civil War. We speak of the "Big Orange" to indicate the University of Tennessee football team because its dominant color is orange.

Be on the lookout for figures of speech in your reading. Try to make figures on your own. Don't be extravagant, but don't be so fearful that you fail to use some of the rich figurative devices available in our language.

AVOID CLICHÉS

Figurative language should make your writing vigorous; the opposite of vigorous writing is prosing filled with clichés, expressions as predictable as a funeral sermon. A good metaphor surprises us. But when we hear the first word of a cliché, we know the whole expression. "The plan was as dead as a _____." We fill in the blank with "doornail" as we hear the first part of the sentence.

But what is a *doornail,* and what awful calamity killed it? We do not know. When we say "as dead as a doornail," we repeat a strong consonant *d* sound, and English is fond of such repetitions. In speaking we might put some emphasis into the phrase. But it does not mean anything no matter how we say it; it creates no picture in our mind of a poor little doornail lying dead on the ground with its feet in the air.

"The author waxed eloquent on the glories of his book." Why do people "wax eloquent"? No one seems to know. They seem to wax eloquent more often than they wax anything else except possibly their new cars. Wax as in *wax eloquent* means "to increase." So we know that people waxing eloquent are becoming more eloquent. People in the sixteenth century used to "wax old." The moon still waxes and wanes. But in modern prose, people seem only to wax eloquent.

"The cold, hard facts are these; it will be a cold day in July before I pull his chestnuts out of the fire." Why must disagreeable facts always be cold and hard? The expression must have had some power once. Facts may have seemed like cold pieces of steel—perhaps steel with which people made daggers. Unpleasant facts would not be warm and cuddly. But now everybody trying to sound tough and worldly uses the expression "cold, hard facts."

So it is with "a cold day in July." The expression might have seemed funny to someone living in a Tennessee valley where July is like an open furnace. It long ago ceased to be either amusing or striking. And it makes no sense in the mountains of northern Vermont where July days can be chilly.

And what living reader pulled somebody else's chestnuts out of a fire, risking burned fingers or a scorched face? Chestnuts are still around, and a few people may roast them in fireplaces. But I doubt it. This cliché happened to be a favorite of Joseph Stalin, the tyrant of the former Soviet Union. It's best to let it lie dead and buried with him.

Writers use clichés out of weariness or uncertainty or hesitancy. A writer sits at a desk, struggling to put something on paper (or on the screen), realizing, as we all do, that writing is hard work and that sometimes words don't come easily. A cliché pops up. "We want our university to be on the cutting edge" of research. The writer grabs "cutting edge" because it is there. No matter that it's as tasteless as secondhand chewing gum. It's there; it takes up space; it even conveys a rough sort of meaning. The writer uses it—and the prose where it lies sinks just a little under its dull weight.

A young reporter covers a congressional hearing where the president of a cement company urges construction of an interstate highway through Glacier National Park so more motorists can see the grizzly bears. The reporter writes that the company president "has his own ax to grind." Neither the reporter nor readers will think of the company president, bringing his ax to the community grindstone, forgetting all the other tools in the corporation, concentrating on his own interest. No reader has ever ground an ax; the reporter may have seen an ax only on TV. But the phrase pops up, and it feels comfortable. So down it goes on the page—and down sinks the prose.

We know that someone who "has his own ax to grind" is concerned with those motivated by greed to advocate high, even noble causes. Most clichés convey meaning. They don't convey images. They are dead metaphors—dead because they create no pictures in our minds. Clichés open no windows, let in no fresh air, provide no revelations, and give us nothing to remember. Good writing gives an impression of a bright mind thinking seriously but not necessarily somberly about a topic, saying something worth reading. We heed such writing because we enjoy it. Clichés grind us down and erode our respect for the writer. They are deadly to the ethical argument.

Clichés come in two packages. Some are dead metaphors, vainly puffing to call up an image; others are common phrases, including fad words and formulae. Dead metaphors include *tight as a drum, fit as a fiddle, sound as a dollar, white as snow, blue as the sky, quick as lightning, sharp as a tack, neat as a pin.* Common cliché phrases include expressions such as *to add insult to injury; pick and choose; tried and true; a deep dark secret; an undercurrent of excitement; an agony of suspense; bustling city; brutal murder; tragic death*—and row on row of others stacked up like counterfeit money in the vaults of our minds.

Fad words come and go like pockets of unpredictable air turbulence. Suddenly people start using them to show that they know what's going on. *Parameter* seems to have receded as a synonym for "limit" or "perimeter." *Feedback, input,* and *bottom line* cling to language like a chronic disease. Football coaches still tell us that the "name of the game" is defense or scoring touchdowns or good blocking or good tackling or whatever else the name of the game happens to be on a given weekend. I always thought the name of the game was *football.* Coaches hold onto clichés the way some children hold onto teddy bears—and for the same reason. Coaches say, "When the going gets tough, the tough get going." They say, "We came to play," when we thought they might have come to drink tea. Good players give "110 percent." Why not 130 percent? I don't know. Since we are now a computer-driven society, we hear that scholars in the English department must *interface* with people who teach writing. We also hear that some people are *programmed* for success and others for failure. Ever since the Watergate scandal in 1973 and 1974, we cannot say "At that time"; we seem driven to pretend to be more precise: "At that point in time."

Clichés ooze out of newspaper columns, academic essays, student papers, and memos that pass from office to office. The "tip of the iceberg" rises menacingly in Washington, D.C., almost every week, even in July and August. "Read my lips!" George Bush cried in the 1988 presidential campaign, promising not to raise taxes. What on earth does the expression "Read my lips" mean? Whatever it was, voters in 1992 read Bush out of office.

Yet you will not find clichés often in slick-paper magazines such as *The New Yorker, Time, Atlantic, Newsweek, Smithsonian, National Geographic, Popular Mechanics,* and others. You do not even find them often in *Sports Illustrated* except as reporters quote coaches and athletes for whom clichés are the only way they know how to communicate with their fickle fans. These magazines must be carefully edited for a literate public if they are to survive. Editors know that clichés kill prose and that dead prose does not sell. Here again we may look to good journalists and essayists as models for our own writing. Such writers try to seduce readers into spending time with them. Intelligent people are not seduced by worn-out old lines.

How do we know when a cliché jumps into our fingers as we write? They are so pervasive that we cannot always avoid them. But some inexperienced writers cannot even recognize them. I have given one clue already: Many clichés give themselves away because they are so familiar that the first word or two call up the rest of the phrase automatically. When you start to use such a phrase, sit for a few moments and think of another expression.

Weigh the words you use. We read in the morning paper that a thug shot someone in the street, and we are told that it was a "brutal murder." The reporter wishes to convey horror and outrage. But do we need the worn-out adjective brutal? Can we imagine a gentle murder? Perhaps a gentle murder is committed by putting rat poison in somebody's hot milk.

On a bicycle trip through the Pacific Northwest in 1993, I came on a stuffed female grizzly bear in a glass case in a hotel lobby in St. Mary, Montana. A politically correct sign told me that this bear had been guilty of several "brutal cattle killings" and had therefore been shot to death. I thought, "If only that poor bear had killed those cattle courteously and gently, the way we do with hammers in slaughterhouses, she might still be alive. Or better still, she should have stopped at McDonald's and ordered 1500 cheeseburgers and let someone else do the killing for her."

And what of those declarations that someone is a "personal friend." Are there impersonal friends? When flight attendants tell us to collect all our "personal belongings," do they mean that we should take our children with us but leave impersonal belongings like our bags behind? And what of those historians of the Renaissance who tell us again and again of those "bustling cities" in Italy! The term is used so frequently in history texts that we may imagine cart drivers, merchants, bankers, lawyers, priests, courtiers, prostitutes, beggars, and princes hurrying about in the streets shouting "Bustle, bustle, bustle, bustle, bustle."

Couples living together without benefit of a formal marriage ceremony tell us they have "a meaningful relationship," and when they break up, they tell us that their love affair was "a learning experience." Young people who learn their profession by apprenticeship are said to have hands-on experience. We hear that laptop computers are "selling like hot cakes," and we do not stop to think that most cakes we buy today are cold.

All this is to say that writing requires attention. If we are to write well, we must examine every word, measure every sentence, and tailor our expressions to fit our thoughts. When we revise, we should pull our clichés out of a text as we might weed a garden. The simplest way to deal with a cliché is to turn it into ordinary language. Cities don't have to bustle. They can thrive. We don't have to say that a murder was brutal. We can describe it and let our readers decide whether it was nice. We don't have to look at the bottom line. We can consider the consequences or decide what the most important issue might be.

No book can settle the problems of dead language. But to be a good writer you must try to make your words stir a response in the minds of readers. Good figurative language can create images, both for you and for your audience. Dead language cannot create those images or the resultant desired responses. Now and then we may all use a cliché without being hanged for it. But an avalanche of clichés will smother your prose, and your readers will conduct your literary funeral by refusing to read your work.

Appendix 3 of this book provides a short list of clichés. You will not find every cliché there, but you can open the book to these pages when you feel tempted to use a phrase and do not know whether it is a cliché or not. If you find the phrase in my list, find a different expression.

CONCLUSION

Use figurative language when it seems appropriate. Try to make it come out of your own experience; do not put an expression on paper merely because you have heard it before and because everybody seems to be using it. If you reflect on language and experience, notebook in hand, you can develop a talent for figurative language. It takes time. So does everything else about writing.

Remember always that the most important quality of writing is its substance. To use figurative language in an essay that has nothing to say is like trying to ride a painting of a horse. It's not going to get you anywhere.

I have read with enormous pleasure David McCullough's biography of President Harry S. Truman. McCullough is one of our best and most popular writers. He uses metaphors and similes only rarely and seldom uses understatement, hyperbole, or irony. He achieves his effects by his prodigious research and his sure eye for detail and by writing simple declarative sentences filled with facts. I read his work with the feeling that here is an honest writer leading me with great authority through ground that he has carefully explored. He has worked hard to learn something, and he wants to tell me what he has learned. Most of what he tells us comes in the strongest kind of prose in the English language—the simple, declarative sentence. You can be a great writer by applying the same conscientious standards to your own work.

False Rules and What Is True about Them

English has rules established by centuries of habit. They were not written by the moving fingers of God on tablets of stone. Some of them are irrational—as all habits are. But break them, and you make it hard for readers and yourself. When you violate the rules, readers may think you are ignorant and therefore not worth their time. Yes, that attitude is unfair, but as John F. Kennedy frequently said, life is unfair.

The good news is that the rules of English are much less complicated than most people think. When my students make mistakes, I often find that their minds have been running faster than their hands. They think ahead to the next word, the next phrase, the next sentence while they write. They may lose their concentration and make errors that they can easily catch if they go over their work—especially if they read it aloud. When I work carefully over my own early drafts, I find all sorts of dumb mistakes. I laugh at myself and correct them—although to my horror I discover now and then that some of them make their way into print!

Alas, many people—including too many teachers—complicate matters by making up false rules. I once asked a group of high school writing teachers to tell me the most annoying mistakes made by their students. One teacher said, "I had it when my students use 'pretty' as an adverb." I said, "In English it's pretty hard to avoid doing that." And I long ago lost count of the teachers who have told me proudly that they keep their students from splitting infinitives.

False rules oppress writers and may make prose sound stilted and somehow wrong. Any examination of published prose will show that professional writers break these false "rules" all the time. Yet they have a vigorous life.

179

Writing is a complicated business, one of the most difficult acts of the human brain. False rules seem to grant security, to reduce writing to a formula that anybody can understand, to make it less threatening, to reduce success to a formula or a recipe that anybody can follow. The people who tout false rules are like astrologers; they can always find an audience even if experience proves them wrong.

Writing is more than obeying the rules. Writing is observation and imagination, order and revelation, style and form. It means making a subject part of yourself. And it always involves risk. To multiply false rules is much like welding armor onto a car; in the end the car may be perfectly safe, but it may also be too heavy to move.

Although the false rules are wrongly expressed, they sometimes have substance buried deep inside them. People have devised them to deal with real problems. We should take this substance into account even as we reject the silliness and the pedantry of the extremes.

COMMON FALSE RULES

Here are some common false rules with a few notes about what may be true about them.

1. Don't Use the First Person.

Every college freshman knows this one because so many high school teachers order their students never to say *I* or *we*. So instead of the first person we get impersonal stiff constructions like these:

> It is the opinion of this writer . . .
>
> This writer would be forced to agree . . .
>
> This writer has shown . . .
>
> The reader is made to feel . . .
>
> This writer was hit by a truck when she . . .

The best argument for the first person is that we see it in all kinds of professional prose. It is used in reviews of books and movies to avoid the tedious repetition of phrases such as "the reader" or "the audience." Walter Jackson Bate, writing about Samuel Johnson, demonstrates the graceful use of the first person without recourse to the tiresome and impersonal form, "The reader."

> Even if we knew nothing of the state of mind he was forced to battle during this psychological crisis, the edition of Shakespeare—viewed with historical understanding of what it involved in 1765—could seem a remarkable feat; and we are not speaking of just the great *Preface*. To see it in perspective, we have only to remind ourselves what Johnson brought to it—an assemblage of almost every qualification we should ideally like to have brought to this kind of work with the sin-

gle exception of patience; and at least some control of his impatience, if not the quality of patience itself, might have been passable if this period of his life had not been so distressing.[1]

The first person appears in accounts of events the writer has observed or participated in. Here is part of a paragraph from one of the best books I have read about the Vietnam War, an account by an infantry lieutenant named Nathaniel Tripp. (A "slick" is a military helicopter.)

> Now and then a Ninth Division convoy would roar through the village at thirty miles an hour. If I heard them coming in time, I would go out to the street and watch them pass. I would look at the filthy, sad-eyed infantrymen sprawled atop the vehicles, slumped over the machine guns, and feel a great sadness and longing. I would look for the platoon leader or company commander, look for the one with the grease pencils and maps, try to meet his eyes with mine so that I could wish him godspeed. If our eyes met, his would quickly dart away again, like a wild animal. And when, now and then, a line of slicks would come fluttering over our village, infantrymen dangling their legs from the doors, my heart would bob up and down with them.[2]

We may expect any eyewitness narrative to use the first person. But what about more formal writing such as the kind we do in academic books and articles. Even here writers expressing opinions about a controversial subject use the first person to avoid any ambiguity about where they stand or as a means of noting their opinions in a controversial field—an opinion with weight because of the writer's experience and authority. Often nowadays writers enter their own work as conversationalists—as I have done in this book. The writers take positions and announce forthrightly that the positions are theirs and not some vague mass. In his book, *The Origins of Virtue,* Matt Ridley attacks one of the favorite views of romantics in the Western world—that "natives," the Indian peoples of North and South America, are kinder and gentler to the environment than Westerners and that therefore native Americans of various sorts are more virtuous than whites of European origin. He demonstrates that when Indians find a profitable occasion to exploit the environment, they do so as avidly as any of the rest of us. He ponders his finding.

> This is not to castigate Indians. It would be cheap and hypocritical of me indeed, sitting in my comfortable house dependent on immense quantities of fossil fuels and raw materials for my everyday needs, to be rude about an Indian just because he has found it necessary to sell some cheap logs for cash with which to buy necessities. He is endowed with vast reserves of knowledge about the natural history of the environment that I could never match—its dangers, its opportunities, its medicinal qualities, its seasons, its signs. He is a better conservationist than me in every conceivable way—simply by virtue of his material poverty. But this is because of the economic and technological limitations within which he lives, not because of some spiritual, inherent ecological virtue that he possesses. Give him the means to destroy the environment, and he would wield them as unthinkingly as me—and probably with more efficiency.[3]

✳

But what about scholars, writing hard-core scholarship? They, too, use the first person, especially in areas where many opinions contest against each other and the writer wishes to show his or her own view while respecting others. Here is Harry Berger, Jr., one of our finest Shakespeare scholars, writing about *Macbeth*.

> I would argue that this view of *Richard III,* which Burckhardt in effect ascribes to Shakespeare, cannot be applied to *Macbeth* in the same manner—that it cannot be ascribed to Shakespeare as *his* view of the play—but that it *can* be applied. As I suggested earlier, it is the view Shakespeare ascribes to the good Scots, Macbeth's enemies, and it is a view he presents critically as self-justifying, scapegoating, and simplistic. Thus we are asked to see their pietistic restoration view as contributing to the subtler evil that obscures the Scottish air and envelops the loyal thanes as well as the bloody dog and his wife. In developing this thesis I shall be carrying further some readings of the play that in recent years have begun to challenge the orthodox view.[4]

Yet modern writers do not use the first person indiscriminately. When you write, ask yourself this: "Am I writing about myself, or is my subject something else?" Don't get in the way of your subject. Professional writers do not say, "In my opinion, the Middle East is one of the most dangerous places in the world." They say simply, "The Middle East is one of the most dangerous places in the world." No one debates that thought. If a writer signs her name to an article, every reader with common sense will understand that the assertions in it represent the writer's considered opinion and not some universal truth agreed on by all. One needs to say "In my opinion" only when the statement is fiercely debated and evidence abounds on every side of the question.

My inexperienced writers sometimes seem to think that nothing is worth writing unless it demonstrates some powerful emotional transformation in the writer. Sometimes they add an emotional commentary at the end of a paper. They want me to know that their hearts are in the right place. Writing about passion has its place now and then. But most of the time the facts standing alone—sometimes starkly alone—have such weight and power that for the writer to add his or her emotions would be trivial and distracting. In the following text, British historian Martin Gilbert tells the story of a young Jewish boy's experience during World War II as a slave laborer for the Germans. (The initials SS stand for the German word *Schutzstaffel,* signifying special forces in the German army chosen for ruthlessness, unthinking obedience, and cruelty.)

> Roman Halter remembered a moment of supreme danger, such as many of the boys faced, each one coming very near to death in some sudden, bizarre, and cruel circumstance. "One day twelve of us were taken out in Dresden by the SS," Roman Halter recalled, "and placed against the factory wall to be shot. Each of us had an SS man behind him who pointed his rifle at our head. We stood there facing the wall with our hands up. I wept because my hip hurt. Normally before an execution the SS would pick on one victim and brutalize him or her.

"As we were led out of the factory down the front steps, which were lined with SS men—and SS women, because among the twelve of us who were led out to be shot, there were ten men and two women—one SS officer pointed me out to another SS man, who turned his rifle upside down and lifted it above his head like an axe. I saw all this, and so did Abram Sztajer who was next to me and said in Yiddish, 'Move' (actually the word means 'slide'—'ritz cech'), and in that split second, when the butt was over me in the air, I turned and hopped down one step. The blow slid down the side of my body and momentarily rested on my hip. I screamed. It hurt terribly.

"There was an SS woman on the opposite side, a couple of steps down. When she saw that her colleague had failed to crush my skull, she pulled me towards her and hit me with a sharp object on the side of my head, which instantly produced a gush of blood.

"We were waiting to be shot, and Sztajer, who was on my left, could see from the corner of his eye, the bloodstained part of my face. 'Cry quietly, don't let them know that they have hurt you,' he whispered. For some reason I did what he told me, and gave out intermittent and suppressed groans."

Suddenly the prisoners who were about to be shot were ordered back to their barracks. There was to be no execution. In a few terrifying moments Roman Halter had twice escaped death.[5]

Almost any normal human being reading this account will feel deep passion, outrage, and simple anger at the cruelty here reported. But Gilbert would have ruined the stark effect of his story if he had interjected his own passion onto the narrative. These cruel details in themselves imply a moral judgment. He trusts us to know what side he stands on, and he does not insult us by assuming that we have to be coached about the correct emotions to have before these horrors. He keeps the focus on his true subject—the story of brutality inflicted on a young Jewish boy. He does not turn it to himself.

Wayne C. Booth's "implied author" should come to mind here. Never write to show readers how noble you are. Don't brag, even about your modesty. Don't show off; avoid drawing unnecessary attention to yourself. Stick to the business of telling readers what you know about the story you tell. When we blatantly insert ourselves into a story about someone else, we are like thoughtless people who talk with each other during a play so that no one around them can follow what is happening on stage. Avoid giving the impression that when you say "I think" or "in my opinion" you install yourself in an impregnable fortress, immune to any counterargument. Many Americans suppose that all opinions are equal and that those who express themselves vehemently enough and sincerely enough deserve respect and even admiration. These people imagine that others are guilty of bad taste or at least discourtesy if they disagree with opinions strongly stated. Many an argument ends with the offhand and sometimes surly remark, "Well, you have your opinion, and I have mine." Implied in a remark like this is often another: "Don't bother me with the evidence."

Thank God we live in a free society where people can say any silly thing they please. But if you are going to influence thoughtful and fair-minded people, you must be able to defend your opinions by reasoning about them. Don't use the first person to avoid an argument. If you command evidence, you can argue your case without using the first person at all.

Follow the example of Harry Berger, Jr., in the section cited above from his work. When you deliver yourself of an "I think" or an "in my opinion," it should reflect your own careful statement of a point of view earned by your disciplined study of the issue and presented humbly, recognizing that others have studied with equal care and come to a similar conclusion. If you get in the habit of saying "I think" or "in my opinion" in an arrogant and challenging tone that does not consider the evidence, people will pay no attention to you.

So the false rule about the first person contains some truth. Avoid using the first person except when it is clearly called for. In the following instances, the first person may be in order. When you deliberately assume a conversational tone as in a regular newspaper column, a letter, or a book like this one, you may use the first person. The conversational tone may help you create intimacy with your readers.

Most books about writing share the assumption that we all perform the same task and that the author has something to share with others who write. Most books like this one are chatty—perhaps too much so. E. B. White, John McPhee, George Orwell, Joan Didion, Ann Tyler, and many other modern essayists use the first person as a matter of course. They write (or wrote) about what happens to them, their reactions, their conclusions. They share their experiences to enlarge our own.

Some subjects lend themselves to informality; some do not. You will not find a chatty medical book on brain surgery or leukemia. For such subjects informality would be in bad taste—unless the author happens to be writing about his or her experiences as a victim of either affliction.

For serious subjects, use the first person only if your experiences are essential to your essay. If you report on research that you have done alone or with colleagues, you may use the first person or the passive, depending on your own taste. Most scientific journals use the passive:

> One thousand people were questioned about their preferences for automobiles. They were asked whether performance was more important than economy, whether they needed a large back seat, and whether color might influence their choice of a new car. They were asked whether they had more confidence in American cars or in Japanese makes.

Some writers prefer the first person in such reports, making their prose more informal and lively. That is the style of *Consumer Reports,* the nation's most popular and most respected consumer magazine. Here is a paragraph from an article about tests on strollers for young children:

> Parents and other adults do the most to keep the perils at bay, of course, but they should have an ally in the manufacturer. Unfortunately, the companies whose strollers we tested for this report don't always bear their fair share of the load.

Although baby strollers have been significantly improved in recent years, more than 10,000 babies and children under five are injured seriously enough every year in carriages and strollers to require emergency hospital treatment.[6]

If you sign your name to a formal essay or report, you may venture an occasional comment in the first person. You may wish to assert your own choice among conflicting opinions. You cannot use the first person singular if you have not signed the essay. If you write a memo to represent the views of your university on a controversial issue like hate speech, you may use the editorial *we* to show that your thoughts represent the official policy of your institution. But you cannot say *I* since no one knows who you are if your name is not on the piece.

2. Never Write a Sentence Fragment.

This false rule should be amended to read, "Never write a sentence fragment unless you know what you are doing." If you cannot tell the difference between a sentence and a sentence fragment, get yourself a good English handbook and work on the problem until you beat it. But good writers who know what they are doing use sentence fragments for special effects. We can scarcely read any modern writer without running into sentence fragments, especially in narratives but often also in expositions. They provide a rapid pace, especially effective in the context of a series of events or thoughts or described objects. If the context is clear, fragments are both readable and efficient. They get readers quickly from place to place. Here is an example from *The New Yorker.* Writer David Remnick recalls a meeting with the late Isaiah Berlin, who had written about Joseph Stalin and the Soviet Union:

> Foolishly, I thought Berlin wanted to know what had been going on in Moscow. Not quite.[7]

Negative fragments like this one are common as reversals of something positive said in the previous sentence. Fragments are often used as answers to direct or indirect questions.

> I ask him about crime. Two incidents in two weeks.[8]

Sometimes you can begin with a series of fragments—a rapid-fire collection of facts that set tone and theme for your essay. Most fragments depend for meaning on the sentences that come just before them. That is how David Remnick uses the fragment in the text above. It is a quick negation of the supposition in the sentence that precedes it. Fragments can often be joined to the preceding sentence by a comma, a dash, or a colon.

> Surely the death penalty was meant for this: to extract retribution for a man whose limbs were mangled by an explosion as his mother watched through a window. For a father killed in his kitchen while opening a parcel that had nonchalantly been passed around by his family. For another man blown away by a mail bomb addressed to someone else, the work of a terrorist who would then scribble in his journal, "We have no regret blowing up the wrong guy."[9]

Instead of forbidding you to use them at all, teachers should tell you to use them with care. Care includes being sure that the fragment does not become tiresome because you use it too often or that it does not become confusing because you use it out of a proper context.

3. Don't Split Infinitives.

Before we talk about split infinitives, we should be sure we know what they are. An infinitive can be split only by inserting a word or phrase between the infinitive marker *to* and the verb that makes the infinitive. The split infinitives below are in italics.

> Red Sox Manager Stuffy O'Neal begged his team *to really and truly try* not to fold until August this year.
>
> McDougal's daily exercise was *to strenuously and rapidly* lift a four-pound chocolate cake from his plate to his mouth until the cake was consumed.

These are not split infinitives:

> To be truly understood, Paul wanted his life to be an open book.
>
> Unfortunately, the pages were far too dull to be read.

Many people who know nothing else about grammar know about split infinitives and don't like them. For their dislike they reckon on a literalistic understanding of the infinitive form. In most languages, the infinitive is one word. *Hacer, faire,* and *facere* are infinitives meaning "to do" in Spanish, French, and Latin respectively. Each is one word. Purists insist that an infinitive in English should be considered one word and that to split an infinitive is barbaric. Their reasoning seems confirmed by our use of infinitives in English, especially by our habit of referring to an infinitive with the pronoun *it:* "To write was everything to her; it was a compulsion that sometimes alarmed her friends." The pronoun *it* refers to the infinitive *to write,* a singular entity used as a noun. The purists believe that to split an infinitive violates an integrity of the noun the infinitive may represent.

Nevertheless, common sense tells us that English infinitives are not one word but two, and even the most casual observation reveals that good writers occasionally split infinitives. Split infinitives appear in almost every issue of *The New York Times* and *Time,* for better or for worse huge influences in the way we think of correct English.

> The anthropologist Laura Betzig, surveying these early civilizations, has rendered the Darwinian opinion that politics has often been "little more than reproductive competition"—men using power *to better spread* their genes.[10]

Writing is governed by flexible standards set by editors. Most editors nowadays publish split infinitives, and I find it futile to rave against split infinitives as if they represented decadence and sloth.

Still moderation is in order. Although professional writers may split infinitives, they do so only occasionally. Several split infinitives in a short essay begin to sound clumsy. They seem to break down the natural rhythms of speech that make for clear writing and easy reading. We rarely split infinitives when we speak. We should be moderate in splitting them when we write.

Beyond rhythm is efficiency. Most split infinitives are not bad because they violate a sacrosanct rule but because the adverb that splits is unnecessary. Suppose you write, "He wanted to really work hard." You can drop the really and have a better sentence. Really here is a pointless intensifier. The same is true of most split infinitives; the adverb that does the splitting is unnecessary, and dropping it makes the sentence stronger.

Remember, too, that many people detest split infinitives with an irrational passion. I once knew a university president who scorned any letter to him that split an infinitive. He never wrote a book in his life. But he was convinced that anyone who split an infinitive was ignorant. People like him are surprisingly numerous in the world, and you should at least know that they exist when you write.

I don't split infinitives. Split infinitives disturb some delicate sentence balance in my head. Perhaps my reluctance arises from the lingering memory from my sweet-tempered seventh-grade English teacher, Mrs. Hattie Simmons Witt, in a rural Tennessee school. She believed firmly in God, brushed teeth, soap, and unsplit infinitives, and we loved her. Whatever caused it, my aversion to the split infinitive is so strong and so habitual that I do not fight it. I revise sentences to eliminate split infinitives, and something old-fashioned (and probably pedantic) in me makes me notice when others split them—although I don't correct them on student papers.

You are much more likely to find split infinitives in journalism—newspaper and magazine writing—than in trade books. The more time editors take with a manuscript, the more likely they are to cut split infinitives. But the split infinitive is so common nowadays in so many things we read that writing teachers become a little foolish when they accuse splitters of high crimes and misdemeanors against the English language.

4. Don't End a Sentence with a Preposition.

Prepositions are short words that never change their form no matter how they are used. They connect nouns or pronouns in prepositional phrases, and these phrases serve as adjectives or adverbs in a sentence. Prepositions allow the strength of nouns and pronouns to modify other elements in a sentence.

In the night he dreamed of horses.

The prepositional phrase *in the night* works as an adverb modifying the verb *dreamed;* so does the prepositional phrase *of horses.* Without prepositions, we could not easily express these ideas. *Nightly he dreamed horsely,* we might say. Some scholar might reveal the meaning of such a sentence, but it would be difficult.

The dictionary *on my desk* is my favorite book.

The prepositional phrase *on my desk* serves as an adjective modifying dictionary, a noun.

To place a preposition before its object follows the general rule of English syntax that related elements in a sentence should be as close to each other as possible. To end a sentence with a preposition deprives that preposition of a natural object on which to rest, and this apparent disorder may be unsettling. "The committee voted against." Against what? "The hamburger came with." With what?

But often it seems unnatural to be strictly formal in putting prepositions before their objects. We can easily say this: "That was the decision I fought against." We can change the sentence to read, "That was the decision against which I fought." But only a robot or a flight attendant would talk like that. You can revise the sentence to read, "I fought against that argument"; but if you have been talking about several arguments and want to identify the particular one you have fought against, you may wish to say, "That was the argument I fought against."

In developing our style, we choose between alternates that sometimes differ only slightly from each other. I can see a difference in emphasis between the sentences "That was the argument I fought against" and "I fought against that argument." Context would determine which one I used, but I would quickly use the former if I found it convenient.

5. Don't Begin a Sentence with a Conjunction.

I once had an angry letter reproaching me for this sin. Conjunctions join sentence elements—words, phrases, or clauses. The common coordinating conjunctions—*and, but, for,* and *or*— join equal elements. Other conjunctions, such as *if, although, whether,* and *even,* join dependent elements.

I do not know the origin of the false rule that sentences should never begin with a conjunction, but it is quoted to me frequently, usually by men over sixty. Yet any glance at a newspaper or magazine shows that professional writers frequently begin sentences with conjunctions. John F. Kennedy used conjunctions to begin fifteen sentences in his short inaugural address in 1961. E. B. White, one of the finest essayists of our times, uses conjunctions to begin many of his sentences. So did Lewis Thomas, one of our best writers about science. So the false rule would seem to have little validity among those who write English best.

Using a conjunction to begin a sentence emphasizes the connection between the thoughts of two consecutive sentences. With a conjunction to open a sentence, you say something like this: "Pay attention. This sentence is closely related to the thought in the sentence immediately before it. But it is important enough to stand by itself, to begin with a capital letter, so you have to take careful note of it."

As I have pointed out earlier, most sentences develop some thought in the sentence immediately preceding them. Although you may wish to emphasize such connections now and then, your readers will become immune to the effect if you use the device too often. Too many conjunctions at the start of a sentence begin to look like a verbal tic, an eccentricity of style that can become as annoying as the steady kicking of a restless child behind you against your seat at the movies. Used with circumspection, the device of beginning an occasional sentence with a conjunction can make your prose a little more fluid. But remember the implacable habit of most writers: around eighty percent of all sentences begin with the subject.

6. Avoid the Pronoun *You.*

If you have read this far, you know I have violated this false rule again and again—for a reason. I have written these pages in an informal, conversational style, and in conversations we address readers as *you*. We do the same in letters.

In more formal writing, to say *you* may seem out of place. No good writer would produce this sentence in a formal essay on cancer: "If you study cancer long enough, you discover that it is not one disease but a large group of diseases that share certain lethal qualities." It's much better to say this: "Cancer is not one disease but a group of related diseases." Nor do professional historians use the pronoun *you* in essays about history: "You have to sympathize with the Germans in World War I, facing as they did powerful enemies in both the east and the west." Say something like this: "In World War I, Germany faced powerful enemies in both east and west."

Even in informal writing the second person should be used sparingly. I dislike a sentence like this: "To serve in one of the first submarines, *you* had to be brave or foolish or both." Your readers did not serve in one of the first submarines; you cannot meaningfully include them in your sentence. Say this instead: "Crew members on the first submarines had to be brave or foolish or both." Nor can you say this: "When *you* have been a famous athlete most of your life, *you* sometimes feel miserable when the cheering stops." Most readers have not been famous athletes all their lives. Write this instead: "Famous athletes sometimes feel miserable when the cheering stops."

It's all right to say *you* in various informal contexts. Articles that give advice or describe processes often use *you:* "Most automatic cameras give *you* no choice in the exposure. A few, however, have a backlight switch, which lets *you* correct the exposure when strong light is coming from behind a subject."

Personal books or essays often address the reader. But in a formal, academic essay written for the college classroom, a research paper in history or philosophy or literature, you should use the second person sparingly if at all. By the conventions of written English, the second person is too informal for such purposes.

7. Avoid Contractions.

Here much of the advice about the pronoun *you* can be repeated. Contractions do well in informal or semiformal prose—like the prose in this book. You may sometimes loosen stiff prose by using contractions. Most teachers accept contractions in college papers, and contractions serve well enough in letters or personal essays. Contractions also serve well in books and articles about personal experience. Nathaniel Tripp in his fine saga about his experiences in Vietnam writes informally.

> Was he a midnight gardener, trying to get a leg up on the weeding? Either he *didn't* know we were there, or he knew us better than we thought, knew we *wouldn't* shoot him.[11]

Contractions serve less well in formal essays. I feel uncomfortable using them in scholarly books and articles because I find them a little too conversational, a little too informal for a serious subject that I want to be taken seriously by the audience who will read the piece. It comes down to tradition. Serious readers about serious academic subjects are not accustomed to seeing contractions in academic writing and in formal trade books about subjects other than personal experience. I do not see contractions in dissertations, in formal books about history or philosophy or literary criticism, in business reports, or in articles in medical journals. Less formal publications such as *Sports Illustrated* and *Time* use them but not excessively. Of course when you quote a source that uses contractions, you quote exactly as the words were written.

8. Use *That* to Introduce Restrictive Clauses, *Which* to Introduce Nonrestrictive Clauses.

Restrictive clauses add essential information to the core statement of the sentence; nonrestrictive clauses add information that may be parenthetical, interesting, and valuable but not essential to the meaning the writing is trying to convey. You cannot leave a restrictive clause out and preserve the meaning of the core statement; you may omit a nonrestrictive clause without damaging the core statement. The restrictive clause in the following sentence is in italics:

> Of all my teachers, the one *who gave me the lowest grades* taught me more than anyone else ever did.

Leave out the italicized clause, and you do not have the sense that the writer conveys in the sentence as it is. In fact you have little sense at all. Grammarians call this clause *restrictive* because it restricts the noun it modifies. We are not talking about just any teacher; we are talking about the one teacher who gave me the lowest grades.

Here is a nonrestrictive clause, one that does not restrict the meaning of the noun it modifies but merely adds some information.

> My English teacher, *who was also my next-door neighbor,* knew me from the time I was born.

Now we have a clause that can be deleted from the sentence without harm to the main statement. The clause is parenthetical; it adds interesting but unessential information. It does not restrict the noun *teacher.*

Many people, especially those older than sixty-five, believe that restrictive clauses should be introduced with *that* and that nonrestrictive clauses should be introduced with *which.* At times they become irate when anyone suggests that this rule is only a foolish and cumbersome false rule that few writers observe or even think about. We have just seen that in clauses that refer to people, *who* can introduce both restrictive and nonrestrictive types. Why all the fuss?

Back in 1906, the English grammarian H. W. Fowler hit on the idea of using *that* to introduce restrictive clauses and *which* to introduce nonrestrictive clauses. He rightly believed that writers should make a clear distinction between the two types. Fowler wanted people to write sentences like these:

> The song that Sam played in the movie *Casablanca* was called "As Time Goes By."
>
> The ocean, *which* we could see from our house, changed color according to the shifting light of the sun through the clouds.

Because the distinction between restrictive and nonrestrictive clauses is necessary and because Fowler was an English gentleman, many Americans who would love to be like English gentlemen have taken his suggestion as a law of language. Fowler himself knew better. Calling restrictive clauses "defining" and nonrestrictive clauses "nondefining," he wrote the following:

> If writers would agree to regard *that* as the defining relative pronoun, and *which* as the non-defining, there would be much gain both in lucidity and in ease. Some there are who follow this principle now; but it would be idle to pretend that it is the practice of either most or the best writers.

Fowler was much more charitable than his modern disciples who have turned the *that/which* "rule" into an absurd fetish. After the first edition of this little book appeared, some outraged readers called my office to express their fierce indignation that a writing teacher should be so decadent as to deny the "rule" any authority. The fact remains that few writers and editors care much about it.

We use *that* or *which* according to some indefinable sense of which one sounds better in the sentence. Most writers always have done the same. The rule is impossible to observe in sentences such as the one immediately preceding this one or in common usage such as this: *That which* makes the rule invalid is its impossibility. Neither can the "rule" hold in *who/whom* clauses, and it cannot help us in restrictive or nonrestrictive phrases.

But recall the motive of the "rule": You must make a distinction between the two kinds of clauses. The only sure way is by proper punctuation. Restrictive clauses are not set off by any kind of punctuation; nonrestrictive clauses are usually set off by commas, although you can also use parentheses and dashes.

On occasion the meaning of the sentence changes according to whether the writer uses commas to make a clause nonrestrictive or does not use them to make the clause restrictive. Here is an example:

The novel, which he wrote in Virginia, sold more than 30,000 copies.

Here is a nonrestrictive clause, one that gives some added information about the novel under discussion. He seems to have written only one novel, or at least in this sentence one particular novel is under consideration. He happened to write it in Virginia. But here now is the sentence with the nonrestrictive clause turned into a restrictive clause by the omission of the commas.

The novel which he wrote in Virginia sold more than 30,000 copies.

Now we are talking about one novel among many. Other novels not written in Virginia may have sold more or less. The one written in Virginia sold more than 30,000 copies. The restrictive clause marks off this novel from others, and it is therefore not set off by commas.

The *that/which* rule is false, and few writers observe it. But you must be conscious of whether your clauses are restrictive or nonrestrictive, and you must punctuate accordingly. Otherwise you may confuse your readers by obscuring your meaning.

CONCLUDING REMARKS ON FALSE RULES

Don't be seduced by false rules, but don't go to the other extreme and suppose that English has no principles and conventions at all. Consider the motives behind the false rules, and observe the cautions that I have mentioned here. Always be aware of your audience. If, for example, you don't know if your teacher will accept contractions, ask her. Try to be efficient in your writing. That is, always use as few words as possible to express as clearly as you can the meaning you want to convey. I revise again and again, trying to cut out excess verbiage—and I always feel at the end that I have not cut out enough. The principle is a good guide for all of us. It will help you cut needless intensifiers out of prose—especially those that split infinitives. More important, it will make you reflect on the choices in your writing that we often make unconsciously. The way to good writing is always by reflection on what we do as writers sentence by sentence, phrase by phrase, word by word. Read carefully and thoughtfully to learn the practices of other writers. Use common sense and observation.

Grammar and Mechanics

Most Americans, given half a chance, will moan loudly about their ignorance of English grammar, sometimes in tones that smack suspiciously of pride. To some, grammar seems almost effete, a collection of puritanical rules that ought to be ignored by hearty men and women. Others take an opposite view. They believe that grammar is the soul of writing, and that schools ought to be marching students through grammar drills in lockstep, teaching all the parts as soldiers are taught to name the parts of their weapons.

Truth resides here and there in both views of grammar. Yes, we ought to know grammar, but how do we learn it? Grammar drills isolated from writing itself accomplish almost nothing. The soul of writing is to have something to say. If you have nothing to say, no one will read your prose merely to savor its flawless grammar. Students of every age gain much more by forming the habit of writing than they do from grammar drills and filling in the blanks of workbooks. How do they learn then?

The bad news is that writers ruin their prose when they make mistakes in grammar. Readers lose respect for them, and their writing becomes confusing. The good news is that most of us know more grammar than we admit. We learn grammar as we learn to talk. When grammar works, children communicate with their families. When they communicate, they get what they want. As they succeed, they remember the speech patterns that gave them success, and they use the patterns again to satisfy their next desire. Most of us continue to use the grammar we picked up as children. We get it from our parents. We may not recall the technical terms. Not many educated people can name the parts of speech, but they use them well enough. Few can make a lightning distinction

ebonix in beginning

between a conjunctive adverb and a conjunction, but they use without difficulty conjunctive adverbs like *moreover* and conjunctions like *and.*

Since about 1890 the grammar of literary English has been remarkably stable. It works in print and on radio and television and in our daily utterances. We can understand Australian movies and English newspapers. A few differences crop up. The English usually write this: "If one persists in betting on the horses, one will lose one's shirt." An American will usually write this: "If one persists on betting on the horses, he will lose his shirt." The English use plural verbs with many collective nouns. They say this: "The team are fighting with their fans again." Americans say, "The team is fighting with its fans." Yet Americans also say, "The majority are sure of themselves." These slight variations do not seriously harm communication between Americans and Australians or New Zealanders or the English or the Scots or the Irish.

Grammar cannot be a science. Like the rest of language, it is a collection of proved conventions and patterns that allow communication. Despite the best efforts of scholars on linguistics, we do not know just how those patterns developed. Why have we rejected *ain't* as a contraction for *am not* or *is not?* Why is *he don't* wrong and *he doesn't* right? Why can't we write this: "Thomas Jefferson and Karl Marx was both heirs to John Locke"? The only worthwhile answer is that the "erroneous" sentences are contrary to conventions developed over the centuries.

These conventions used to be much looser than they are now. The coming of mass literacy and the newspapers and magazines that feed literacy have created a much more inflexible grammar than Shakespeare or Chaucer used. Mass production requires standardization. Standard forms are easier to teach and easier to learn and also easier to recognize. When only a few people could read and when readers read aloud—as they did in the late Middle Ages when modern English was developing—grammar could be much more flexible. But when readers rapidly scan print in silence, irregularities trip them up and make them go back to read a line again before they can understand it. A standard grammar—like any standardized tool—helps a mass society work.

A few writing experts contend that to enforce the conventions of grammar smacks of elitism. They say that conventional English is only one dialect among many and that all dialects are equal. No humane person should scorn those whose dialect learned at home is different from conventional English. But it is a serious misreading of both past and present to say that all dialects, including conventional English, are equal in a large and literate society. Those who do not learn to use conventional English are at a lifelong disadvantage.

Television and other mass media are homogenizing the conventions even more. In the rural South where I grew up, the word *ain't* is fading. Neighbors my age still use it; their children use it less. Why is it going? I suspect that it is passing away because people are not hearing it on television, and the thousands of hours the average American child spends before the tube affect language more than all the English teachers in America combined.

Students may have problems in grammar because writing is so different from speaking. They get lost in the physical process of writing, of moving a pen or a pencil laboriously across the page, so that the brain runs off and leaves the hand. Writing goes so slowly and painfully for them that they lose track of their sentences. If you have problems in grammar, try reading your work aloud to yourself. You will pick up most of your errors. Writing with a computer liberates us from much of the physical toil of writing and allows us to see errors better and revise them away.

You can also buy yourself a good English handbook of a sort used in composition programs throughout the nation. Handbooks usually summarize all the major conventions of grammar and provide an index that lets you find items quickly.

But the best way to learn to write is to write and to have other people—including your classmates as well as your teacher—read what you have written. Ask them to point out your errors. No one becomes a good baseball player solely by studying the baseball rule book. We learn baseball by playing the game. We learn grammar by writing, by discovering our flaws as we go along, and by correcting them as we continue.

PERSISTENT PROBLEMS

In the following list, I have compiled problems in grammar and punctuation that trouble my students. (Punctuation is part of grammar in that it is one of the forces that holds sentences together and helps us arrange them.) It is not an exhaustive study. But it will help you overcome some common errors.

I hope something else will happen as you study this section: I want you to gain the confidence to use English with more variety. It's a shame, for example, that many people avoid the subjunctive mood of verbs altogether because they fear to use the subjunctive incorrectly. The subjunctive is uncommon in English, but now and then it adds elegance to language. You can get away with using the simple past tense for verbs, but using the various perfect tenses can add subtlety to your thought that makes your work more interesting.

Punctuation seems unimportant to most of my students—a matter of dots and squiggles on a page. Why bother with it? But conventional punctuation holds sentences together as mortar keeps a brick wall from tumbling down. Bad punctuation may confuse and irritate readers. In my recommendations I have followed the advice of the reference manual published by the University of Chicago Press, *The Chicago Manual of Style*. The looming authority of this celebrated work is so great it should be a reference book in every writer's library.

1. Make the Subject and Verb Agree in Number.

If the subject of a sentence is singular, it must use a singular verb; if the subject is plural, the verb must be plural. In nearly all verbs, except the irregular *to be* verbs and *to have* (*am, are, is; was, were; has, have, had*), the only variation between singular and plural forms is in the third-person singular of the present tense. We say, "I dance, you dance, we dance, they dance," but "she dances." The simple past of most verbs uses the same form for both singular and plural: "I danced; he danced; they danced." Helping verbs will vary like the present tense, but since the most common helping verbs are *to be* and *to have,* we don't need to learn many special forms. In this regard English is simpler than languages that do not use helping verbs. So we can be grateful for some simplicity in our complicated tongue.

We are most likely to make errors in subject-verb agreement when we insert a clause or phrase between a subject and a verb. The danger becomes acute when the phrase is a preposition with a plural object. That happens in sentences like this: "Each of the cars *were* fast." *Each,* the subject of the sentence, is singular. The prepositional phrase *of the cars* throws a writer off so that here we have the plural verb *were.* The sentence should read like this: "Each of the cars was fast." *Anybody, everybody, anyone, each, every, neither, nobody* and *someone* are all singular and require a singular verb.

> *Each* of the players *is* eligible until final exams.
>
> *Every* one of the coaches *chews* gum.
>
> *Nobody goes* there any more; it's too crowded.
>
> *Everybody* in the grandstand *is* applauding.
>
> *Each* of the choices *is* possible; *neither is* desirable.

Now and then a compound subject considered as a unit takes a singular verb:

> Cops and robbers *is* an old American children's game.

But don't assume that readers will see the unity you may see in a compound subject. You may write, "The gathering and classifying of data goes on relentlessly in all the sciences." In your mind *gathering* and *classifying* may be a single act, and you may use the singular verb *goes.* But many readers will assume that they are two acts, and you will confuse them by using a singular verb. Except in a few idiomatic expressions, use the plural verb with a compound subject.

Some collective nouns occupy a shadowy borderland. In American English we use a plural verb in the following sentences with singular subjects: "A number of movies produced last year were filled with violence and sex." "A majority of the team were unable to graduate."

2. When a Singular Noun Subject of a Sentence is Joined by *Or* or *Nor,* the Verb Should Be in the Singular.

> *Neither* economics *nor* history *is* an exact science.
>
> A *tub* or a *shower* is in every room.

3. When a Plural Noun in a Compound Subject is Joined by *Or* or *Nor* to a Singular Noun, the Verb Agrees with the Nearest Noun.

Neither the *singer nor* her *managers are* happy.

Neither her *managers nor* the *singer* is happy.

Try to revise sentences like these to eliminate the unpleasant awkwardness of the constructions: "The singer and her manager are unhappy."

4.   Use the Correct Verb Form after the Adverb *There*.

In a sentence beginning with *there,* the verb must agree with the subject, which usually comes immediately after the verb.

Don't say, "*There is* singing and laughter upstairs tonight." Say instead, "*There are* singing and laughter upstairs tonight."

5.   Use the Nominative Case for a Pronoun Subject of a Dependent Clause, Even if the Clause Itself Serves as an Object.

Don't say, "He was prepared for *whomever* might ask a question." Say, "He was prepared for *whoever* might ask a question." *Whoever* is the subject of the verb *might ask* and so must be in the nominative case.

Don't be confused by parenthetical clauses within dependent clauses. A parenthetical clause has no grammatical effect on the subject of a dependent clause of which it is a part. Therefore don't say, "The woman *whom* he believed was drunk was in a coma." *He believed* is a parenthetical clause. Say this: "The woman who he believed was drunk was in a coma." The pronoun *who* governs the verb was.

His aunt, *who* he said had known Virginia Woolf, kept a detailed diary.

Now complications enter. When you write a pronoun that is the subject of an infinitive, the pronoun is in the *objective* case.

She supposed *him to be* a friend. We imagined *her to be* wise and good.

The pronoun is in the objective case even if the infinitive is understood rather than written:

She supposed *him* a friend. She thought her *loyal.*

The subject of an infinitive acts as the agent of action the infinitive describes. Any subject of an infinitive always follows a transitive verb, one that takes a direct object. Infinitives themselves are nonfinite verbs; we sometimes call them *verbals.* A nonfinite verb cannot express past or present time by itself. To express time, a verbal must be joined to a finite verb: "He wanted to be famous." The past tense of the verb *wanted* adds time to the infinitive *to be,* which has no time of its own. We could as easily say "He wants to be famous" or "He will want to be famous." If the infinitive has a subject, the subject becomes part of an infinitive phrase and serves as the direct object of the preceding transitive verb.

> They told *us to be* careful.

6. Use the Objective Case for a Pronoun that Serves as a Direct Object, an Indirect Object, or the Object of a Preposition.

Do not use the objective case for a pronoun that serves as a subject. The confusion between subjective and objective case in pronouns is probably the most common single error in student writing and common speech.

Don't say, "Just between *you and I,* his poetry is terrible." Say this instead: "Just between *you and me,* I stop my ears when he reads." Don't say, "He laughed *at Clara and I.*" Say, "*He laughed at Clara and me.*" Don't say, "*Me and Wilma* spoke to them last night." Say, "*Wilma and I* spoke to them last night." Don't say, "*Her and me* decided to bicycle in France." Say, "She and I decided to bicycle in France." Don't say, "*Myself and Richard* invite you to the staff party." Say, "*Richard and I* invite you to the party."

7. Form the Possessive Case Correctly.

My students have more trouble with the possessive case than with any other mark of punctuation. About half of them cannot form the possessive according to the conventions of English. To form the possessive, you must use the apostrophe [']. To form the possessive of singular nouns, add *'s* at the end.

> Ann's job; Gertrude's voice; Doc's friendship; the hotel's buffet; Israel's troubles; the superintendent's office

Use *'s* even when the singular noun ends in *s.*

> Burriss's house; Erasmus's first book; Charles's pen

The rule is not observed in some traditional phrases:

> For goodness sake! In Jesus' name

Be sure to add the apostrophe *s* in words that end with *z* or *x.*

> Groucho Marx's films; Berlioz's music

To form the plural possessive use the simple apostrophe after words whose plurals end in *s:*

> the Joneses' street; the dogs' door

If the noun has an irregular plural that does not end in *s,* form the possessive by adding an apostrophe *s* just as you would if the noun were singular:

> children's literature; men's clothing; women's rights

8. Use the Correct Verb Tense.

Tense is the time of a verb. English has six tenses.

Present: I play.

Simple past: I played.

Simple future: I will play.

Present perfect: I have played.

Past perfect: I had played.

Future perfect: I will have played.

Each tense has a *progressive* form that expresses continuing, or progressive, action within the time noted in the tense:

Present progressive: I am playing.

Past progressive (imperfect): I was playing.

Future progressive: I will be playing.

Present perfect progressive: I have been playing.

Past perfect progressive: I had been playing.

Future perfect progressive: I have been playing.

The simple present tense can do several things. It reports habitual action:

Birds *migrate* every year.

The sun *rises* every morning.

Wars *are caused* by stupidity.

Habitual action extends to verbs that describe the action in literature because the written word is assumed to be always speaking:

David Copperfield himself *is* not as interesting as other characters in the book.

Socrates *teaches* that the way to wisdom begins with the command, "Know thyself."

The Constitution *links* the right to keep and bear arms to serving in the militia—what we call today the National Guard.

The *present progressive* tense is the most idiomatic way we have of speaking of something happening right now.

She is *coming* down the street.

They *are repaving* the highway between Boston and Lynn.

The *present progressive* can become a future tense by adding an adverb of future time:

She *is* coming *tomorrow*.

They are playing softball *next Sunday*.

Adding *do* or *does* shows emphasis. The *present emphatic* is used in negations.

I *do not* like snakes.

She *does not* like people who do not like snakes.

The present emphatic is used to affirm something that someone else has denied. For example, someone accuses you of disliking rock music, and, if you have any hearing left, you say, "I do like rock music."

The present tense may create confusion for writers who get carried away with the sense of action conveyed by the present. These writers often use the present tense to describe past action, especially when they write about history or an exciting story.

> Franklin Roosevelt is elected because he promises to do something about the Depression, and Hoover keeps saying that the Depression is almost over.

Narration in the present tense may be successful sometimes. Thomas Carlyle used it to great effect in his great book, *The French Revolution.* But in general avoid the present tense in writing about the past. Modern professional historians in Britain and America write in the past tense. The present sounds strained in telling English-speaking readers about the past, and since it violates a common convention, it is also confusing. The simple past is usually formed by adding *-ed* as a suffix to the present stem of the verb. "I play" becomes "I played." The past participle is made in the same way. "I have played." But English is complicated by having about three hundred irregular verbs. They are irregular because they form the past tense or the past participle in some way other than adding -ed. We say "I draw" but not "I drawed." We say "I drew" and "I have drawn." We say "I see" but not "I seed." We say "I see," "I saw," and "I have seen."

We usually learn irregular verbs as we learn to talk and hear others use them. In some regions of the country people diverge from standard English. In the farming community where I grew up, people said, "I seen him when he done it" and "He drawed me a plan for the barn, and I taken a lot of time to study it over." These were intelligent, sensible people. Similar people in other regions today may use verbs in nonstandard forms. When you are in doubt, consult a dictionary—the most valuable tool a writer has. Any good dictionary lists the various standard forms of irregular verbs.

The *simple future tense* is formed with *shall* and *will.* Strict grammarians used to insist that *shall* be used with the first person and *will* with the second and third persons. American writers generally ignore this distinction. We nearly always say, "He will be fifty on his next birthday" and "We will be happy to see you at the party." Today in American English *shall* seems to indicate an emphatic statement. "They shall not pass." "I shall be there." It is almost as if *shall* were always in italics in our minds.

We should give a few more words to the progressive form, showing action that continues. The *past progressive,* or *imperfect,* is the most common form. Use it to show action going on while something else is happening: "I *was traveling* west during June." The sentence means that while June was going by, I was traveling West. Here are other examples:

> He *was sleeping* when the robbery occurred.

While players on the losing team *were holding* their postgame prayer meeting in the locker room, the gamblers waited outside with the bribe money.

We call the *past progressive* the *imperfect* because the end of the action is not described. That is, the action of sleeping continued as long as the robbery occurred, and the action of holding the prayer meeting went on for an indefinite time. We are not told how long any of these actions continued. Think of the progressive as duration. The action continues for a while or it continued or will continue over a period of time. Don't use the progressive when the past will do.

9. Avoid Illogical Mixing of Verb Tenses.

The simple verb tenses are seldom difficult. We combine them logically. We would never think of saying, "I was there when you will come." We say, "I will come when you are there." We know that the present tense of *are* in the second clause is governed by the future tense of the verb *will come* in the first. Sometimes we stumble when we consider how to join the past tense with the present, but a little thought usually leads us aright. We mix past and present in the following sentences when someone in the past made a statement that continues to be true for all time.

Plato believed that the soul is immortal.

Thomas More thought that death is not the worst fate.

Normally the past tense in a first clause will demand a past tense in a second clause, and we usually join such clauses without difficulty:

He played baseball because he loved the game, not because he was paid a high salary.

Players for the Boston Red Sox thought he was crazy.

Problems with mixing tenses usually arise when the perfect tenses are used. The *present perfect* always conveys a sense of action that started in the past and continues to the present, where either the action itself or its effects continue. The present perfect tense is formed by using the present tense of the verb *to have* with the past participle of the main verb in the construction.

We *have worked* since yesterday afternoon.

The work started in the past and is still going on at the time the sentence describes. The present perfect tense can easily be used in combination with the present tense:

He *has been* a great baseball player, but he is retiring at the end of this season.

She *has been grinding* rust off the car all afternoon with the electric sander, and now she is tired.

The present perfect tense can be used with the future, since both tenses join at the time when the statement about future action is made.

> They *have been traveling* all night, and they will travel all day today and tomorrow.

The past perfect tense uses the past tense *had* of the verb *to have* with the past participle of the main verb in the construction. It always implies that an action ended before or just as another action began:

> They *had been waiting* an hour when the train arrived.

The waiting ended at the moment the train arrived; both actions took place in the past. The past perfect cannot be used before the present perfect. We cannot say, "Country music had been popular and has remained so." A reader wants to know this: "It had been popular before what?" The past perfect sets up the expectation of an end point, and if you do not have an end point, you must provide one or change the sentence:

> Country music *had been* popular before 1950, but in that year it attracted national attention.

Here the prepositional phrase *before 1950* provides the end point that the past perfect leads us to expect, and the later clauses go on from that point to make another statement. Sometimes we imply the end point, especially in oral English. We may speak of a friend who came to an early-morning history class in a tuxedo. Someone says, "Did you know that John came to class this morning in a tuxedo?" You ask why, and your friend says, "He *had been* at a party all night long." From the last sentence spoken by your friend, you *infer* an end point already mentioned in an earlier sentence. The implied thought is this: "John had been at a party all night long and came to class in the morning in his tuxedo." The end point of the action *had been* is his arrival in class. You also cannot properly use the past perfect with the present tense. You should not say, "He had to learn to walk before he learns to run."

You should not use the past perfect as a substitute for the simple past. That is, don't say, "Henry VIII *had been* born in 1491" unless you intend to follow that sentence with another related to it by the simple past. It is better to say, "Henry VIII *was* born in 1491." You may use the past perfect in a paragraph whose sentences lack a dependent clause only if the end point of the past perfect is clearly stated in another sentence:

> Henry VIII came to the throne in 1509. He *had not been meant* to be king. His older brother Arthur *had been heir* to the throne, but Arthur died. A persistent legend holds that young Henry *had been destined* to become a priest, but Arthur's death changed that destiny and the destiny of England as well.

Here we have several sentences in the past perfect, all moving toward the end point stated in the first sentence.

The past perfect tense is used too much, especially in the writing of history. Use the simple past unless the past perfect is clearly needed.

The future perfect tense describes a future act that must be concluded before or just as another future act begins.

> We *will have been* here a week before you arrive.

> The apples *will have been picked* before then.

As in all perfect tenses, the future perfect makes you think of the time when one action ends and another begins. The action in the future perfect tense must end before some future moment or just as some future action begins. Always recall that perfect tenses imply a time considered as the end point of an action, a time when the action of the sentence is complete from the point of view of the sentence. You may say, "I have been waiting for an hour," using the present tense. You may go on waiting for another hour, or you may now be ending your wait, but neither possibility is the concern of this sentence. This sentence is concerned with the action that has gone on for an hour, and that hour is complete by the time the sentence is written or spoken.

A special problem sometimes arises with infinitives in the perfect tense. Some years ago a submarine of the Soviet Union sank off the coast of Norway. Several American newspapers ran this line:

> "It must have been hellish to have been on that submarine," said Johan Joergen Holst, Norway's minister of defense.

The use of the perfect tense *to have been* is incorrect. The line should have been, "It must have been hellish to be on that submarine." *To be* is an infinitive; it takes the time of the finite verb that controls it. Therefore to write *must have been* presumes that the infinitive *to be* is controlled by the perfect tense of the main verb phrase.

10. Use the Subjunctive Form of the Verb in Dependent Clauses that Make a Statement Assumed to Be Contrary to Fact.

> I wish I *were* in the Caribbean.

I am not in the Caribbean; hence the subjunctive form *were*.

> If he *were* more tactful, he would have more friends.

He is not more tactful; so he does not have more friends. Here is the most common use of the subjunctive—the form of the verb that in French or German or Greek is much more common than in English. We say that verbs are in the *subjunctive* or the *indicative* mood. The *indicative* is used to represent simple statements of fact. The *subjunctive* carries with it always a mood of doubt or yearning or fear or command that in English lingers only in a few uses. Indeed it is used so seldom that the chief problem of the subjunctive is that insecure people afraid of being incorrect may use it inappropriately. The subjunctive is *not* used, for example, after every *if* in a sentence. Use the subjunctive only to make a statement clearly contrary to fact as in the examples above. Don't use it for factual statements that may involve some uncertainty about the past. You should say this, "If what she said *was* true, he was guilty." This is a simple indicative statement. You do not know whether she spoke the truth or not. You merely make the statement that if she did speak the truth, he was guilty. That is a fact. The indicative is used in factual statements. If you knew beyond any doubt that she was lying, you would say this: "If what she said *were* true, he was guilty." *Had* and *should* may express the subjunctive. "*Should* you win the Nobel Prize, I will help you spend the money." It is entirely uncertain that you will win the Nobel Prize. But if you do, I will help you spend the prize money. "*Had* the Germans not feared Russia so much in 1914, they might have beaten France quickly." The Germans did fear the Russians; they did not concentrate all their army in France; they not only did not win the war quickly; they did not win it at all. The subjunctive use of *had* introduces a condition clearly contrary to fact.

11. Use Commas According to Standard Practice.

The comma appears more than any other punctuation mark in English. It is important for you to use it according to standard practice to avoid confusing readers.

A. Use the comma with a coordinating conjunction to separate independent clauses in a sentence.

Independent clauses can usually stand alone as sentences. The coordinating conjunctions are *and, but, nor,* and *for,* and sometimes *yet* and *so.* The comma and the conjunction bind such clauses together.

> Dolphins have brains bigger than humans, but they spend all their time in the water, *and* they can't even play checkers.

> The star quarterback of Sourmash State University could not read simple English after four years of college, *nor* could he find a pro team willing to hire him.

Do not use the comma alone to hold independent clauses together. Do not use a comma like this:

> Intercollegiate football games used to be for the participants, now the fans demand that teams win at any cost, even if they must cheat.

The absence of the coordinating conjunction *but* after the comma confuses us. For a moment we think the participants are now the fans. We have to get to the end of the sentence to sort out its meaning. The fault here is called a *comma splice;* that is, the writer tries to splice the clauses together with a comma, but the comma cannot do the job. We should add the conjunction.

> Intercollegiate football games used to be for the participants, *but* now the fans demand that teams win at any cost, even if they must cheat.

You can use a semicolon [;] instead of the conjunction to separate independent clauses.

> Coach Dixie was outraged; his star quarterback quit football to study physics.

B. Use a comma after a long introductory clause or phrase that precedes the subject of an independent clause.

> Because the temperature on the highway was 115 degrees in the California desert, the air-conditioning in the diner nearly knocked me flat.

> Backed up against Antwerp, the Belgian army furiously counterattacked the Germans in September 1914.

> Having failed to win peace in Massachusetts by negotiation and compromise, the British decided to use force.

C. Use commas to set off parenthetical clauses and phrases that add descriptive material not essential to the principal assertion of the sentence.

Here is a parenthetical phrase set off with commas.

> He kept the fountain pen, *a gift from his father,* for the rest of his long life.

The phrase *a gift from his father* adds information to the sentence but is not essential to the main assertion of the sentence. The writer might choose to develop something from the detail that the fountain pen was a gift from a father to a son. But the main assertion of this sentence is that the *He* of the sentence kept the pen for the rest of his long life. The assertion would remain the same without the phrase; so the phrase is set off by commas. Here is a parenthetical (or nonrestrictive) clause set off by commas.

> Coach Dixie, *whose football teams had won six national championships,* had since childhood yearned to be a poet.

The information that Coach Dixie's teams had won six national championships is interesting, but it is not essential to the main statement of the sentence, which is that Coach Dixie had since childhood yearned to be a poet. Do not set off clauses and phrases that are indispensable to the main assertion. Here is an essential clause not set off by commas:

> He often dreamed *that he was reciting his poetry at halftime on the fifty yard line before 75,000 silent and admiring fans.*

The clause *that he was reciting his poetry at halftime on the fifty yard line before 75,000 silent and admiring fans* is essential to the meaning of the sentence. So it is not set off by commas. Without the clause, the sentence would not make the sense the writer intended. Be careful here. You can change the meaning of a sentence by setting off a clause or phrase with commas. Suppose you say this:

> Faculty members *who are slipshod and lazy* rob their students.

This sentence means that only faculty members who are slipshod and lazy rob their students. By not setting off the dependent clause with commas, you indicate that it is essential to the meaning of your sentence. You are writing about one kind of faculty member. But suppose you say this:

> Faculty members, who are slipshod and lazy, rob their students.

The commas tell us that you mean that all faculty members rob their students. You happen to add the information that faculty members are also slipshod and lazy, and so you deliver a double insult. You condemn the teaching profession for robbing students, and you announce that all members of that profession are slipshod and lazy.

Some writers set off all appositives with commas, but this habit may lead to confusion. Suppose you write this sentence:

> In his novel, *For Whom the Bell Tolls,* Ernest Hemingway made a tragedy of the Spanish Civil War.

The commas make the title parenthetical, something that could be left out without damaging the meaning of the sentence. They tell readers that the main assertion is this: "In his novel Ernest Hemingway made a tragedy of the Spanish Civil War." The sentence now implies that Hemingway wrote only one novel and that it was called *For Whom the Bell Tolls.* In fact he wrote many novels, and the writer should not set off the title of the book with commas.

D. Use the comma to set off adjectives that modify the same noun if the adjectives can be connected by the word *and*.

You may say this: "Johnson was the strong, silent type." You could also say, "Johnson was the strong and silent type." So to replace *and,* use a comma. But you would not use a comma to separate adjectives in this sentence: "The large old oak trees cast a deep shade on the lawn." You would not say, "The large and old and oak trees cast a deep shade on the lawn." Therefore, omit commas between the adjectives.

E. Use the comma to set off interjections or transitive adverbs at the beginning of a sentence.

Consequently, we thought Johnson was boring. Indeed, his mother thought Johnson was boring.

F. Use the comma to set off words or phrases in a series of three or more elements.

She wrote books, articles, and poems.

Lincoln's mighty words in the Gettysburg Address made the Civil War a struggle for government "of the people, by the people, and for the people."

G. Use a comma to set off direct quotations.

John Lyly said, "If one write never so well, he cannot please all, and write he never so ill, he shall please some."

H. Use a comma correctly with other punctuation.

A comma at the end of quoted material goes inside the quotation marks:

"Hating people is like burning down your own house to get rid of a rat," said Harry Emerson Fosdick.

But a comma goes outside parentheses or brackets at the end of the material so set off.

In hard times (the thought is from Euripides), friends show whether they are to be trusted or not.

She wrote me that she hated my "mispellings" [sic], but that my content was fairly good.

12. Use the Dash Circumspectly.

Many writers love the dash. (I am one of them.) It helps add seemingly spontaneous thoughts that break into our mind while we are writing a sentence. It provides a sense of a telegraphic style. It allows us to digress slightly or to signal readers that we want them to pay special attention to what follows. The first thing to do with a dash is make it correctly. On a typewriter or a computer, the dash is composed of two hyphens without a space between them, typed with no spaces between the last word before the dash and the first hyphen or between the last hyphen and the first word after the dash - - like this. If you use one hyphen - like this, you will confuse readers and upset the people who set your work into type. Some word-processing programs now make what printers call a one-M dash—a line longer than a hyphen that cannot be mistaken for anything but a dash.

Use the dash to set off an emphatic phrase:

Baseball players now charge for their autographs—up to $25.00 a signature!

You can also use the dash to set off an emphatic clause:

Longstreet surveyed the field at Gettysburg before Picket's Charge and wanted to withdraw, and events proved him right. But one man refused to listen—Robert E. Lee wanted to attack, and Lee was in command.

Dashes, like parentheses, sometimes set off slight digressions or definitions within a sentence. Dashes seem to be a little more emphatic than parentheses, though that depends on the writer.

Renaissance painting—assuming there was such a thing as the Renaissance—emphasized the human figure and a somewhat idealized human expression.

Sometimes for emphasis you may want to write a compound subject, follow it with a dash, and make a statement about that subject with a clause.

> Beethoven, Chopin, and Liszt—these are perhaps the greatest of the romantic composers.

It's not good to use dashes to set off more than one element in a sentence. Writers occasionally do so, but the effect is confusing. Be circumspect. You can often use a colon, parentheses, or a simple comma to set off elements that you might also set off with a dash. Too many dashes in a piece of prose always give me the uncomfortable feeling that the writer has a hypernervous condition and wants to emphasize everything. The effect is a little like being yelled at.

13. Use Standard American Forms for Quotations.

Use double quotation marks to set off direct quotations. If material you are quoting includes material in quotation marks, use single quotation marks (the apostrophe key) to set off those words within quotation marks in the original.

> Speaking of Sioux chief Sitting Bull, Evan S. Connell says, "A feminine element very often radiates from sexually powerful males and in the case of Sitting Bull this was so unmistakable that one journalist, fascinated by the oval face between long braids, spoke of his 'manhood and womanliness.' "[1]

English practice is the opposite of American practice; English publishers use apostrophes or single quotation marks where we use the double marks and the double marks where we use the single marks. Follow American practice. Commas go within closing quotation marks; semicolons and colons go outside.

> "You write in water," said Erasmus of work that had no result.
>
> "Hell will never be full until you be in it"; so said a Scottish proverbial insult.
>
> "Whom the gods love dies young": John F. Kennedy died when he was forty-six years old.

Do *not* put quotation marks around block quotations. Use indented blocks for quotations more than four or five lines long. In typed or computer-generated manuscripts, the blocks should be indented five spaces from the left margin. The indentation of a block of text is indication enough that you are quoting. If you add quotation marks, readers will assume you are beginning the quotation with a quotation from someone else.

The lines in the block quotation should be double-spaced. Within the block quotation, use quotation marks exactly as they appear in the quoted material. I have elsewhere in this book recommended that you not use block quotations whenever you can avoid them. It is usually better to paraphrase and to quote smaller sections of a text than one quotes in a block. But in books such as this one, block quotations are necessary, and everyone has to use them now and then. When you use them, study the examples in this book if you have questions about the right form.

Do not use quotation marks to set off slang, clichés, or other words that you wish to apologize for. Only inexperienced writers use these apologetic quotation marks. They seem to say, "I know this is a cliché or some other lazy language, but at least I have put it in quotation marks to let you know that I know I'm being lazy." When you are tempted to put quotation marks around a cliché, you know at once that you should think of some better expression. Obey your better impulse.

But do use quotation marks to indicate a usage by others that you do not share yourself.

> In the "People's Republic" of China, the people have no legal voice in their government.

Note: For decades the practice of writers in using quotations has been to make silent changes in capitalization when adapting a quotation from a source to their own texts. Here is a source.

> Persistent melancholy is one of the fundamental themes of Southern literature.

And here is the standard way of quoting that source:

> McDougal has called "persistent melancholy" a quality of Southern literature.

The *P* in the source is silently changed to *p* in the quotation to fit the sentence where the quotation is used. But of late a new typographical barbarism has been infecting publishers and writers with a foolish pedantry that would give us this version:

> McDougal has called "[p]ersistent melancholy" a quality of Southern literature. The pedant wants us to know that in the original the *p* in *persistent* was capitalized, but he in his almighty holiness and accuracy has let you know that he has altered the capital to make it lowercase. The result is ugliness on the page and simple nonsense. Use the standard practice of silent change from lowercase to capital or from capital to lowercase.

14. Use Ellipsis Marks Correctly.

My students have excessive trouble using ellipsis marks correctly. Ellipsis marks indicate that some words have been left out, usually out of a quotation. Make ellipsis marks by using the period key on your typewriter or computer. Put a space between the last word before the ellipsis and the first ellipsis dot; make the dot, space again, make the second dot, space again, make the third dot, space again, and resume the quotation. You should not make ellipsis marks without spaces between the marks like this (...). Ellipsis marks should always leave spaces . . . like this. Otherwise the rapid reader will stumble and will have to back up and reconsider what you have written. Here are a few sentences from Paul Fussell's book *The Great War and Modern Memory:*

> Recourse to the pastoral is an English mode of both fully gauging the calamities of the Great War and imaginatively protecting oneself against them. Pastoral reference, whether to literature or to actual rural localities and objects, is a way of

invoking a code to hint by antithesis at the indescribable; at the same time, it is a comfort in itself, like rum, a deep dugout, or a woolly vest.[2]

Here is part of a paper that quotes from this text, using ellipses to indicate some omitted words:

> Fussell argues that English troops in World War I used the pastoral tradition as an anodyne against the horrors they met in the trenches. He says, "Pastoral reference . . . is a way of invoking a code to hint by antithesis at the indescribable; at the same time, it is a comfort in itself."

The ellipsis marks show that words have been omitted between *reference* and *is,* and by checking the original, you can see what those words were. Notice that there is a space between *reference* and the first dot and a space after each of the dots, including the space between the last one and the word *is.* Notice, too, that there are no ellipsis marks after *itself,* although it is not the last word in Fussell's sentence. The quotation marks are sufficient to show readers that the writer has stopped quoting. Any reader assumes that Fussell's text goes on; no reader needs ellipsis marks to understand that you are not quoting everything Fussell says.

Neither do you need ellipsis marks at the beginning of a quotation, even if you are quoting only part of a sentence. The quotation marks tell readers that you are quoting, and they assume that you cannot quote all of your source. You don't need to create typographical monstrosities like this:

> Lincoln said that the Civil War was fought so that ". . . government of the people, by the people, and for the people . . ." might endure.

Remember always that the function of ellipsis marks is to show that you are leaving something out between your first quotation marks and your last. They certify your honesty, showing readers that you are not quoting something exactly as the author wrote it. The quotation marks themselves set off your quotation from what you choose not to quote in your source. Sometimes you may leave out a whole sentence, several whole sentences, or an entire paragraph from a long quotation. Then you must punctuate the last sentence before the ellipsis marks.

15. Use Colons to Set off Lists and Some Quotations.

> She wanted three things: a good job, respect, and loyal friends.

Note that the colon comes at the end of an independent clause. A colon should not break into an independent clause. You should not say this: "She wanted: a good job, respect, and loyal friends." You can see from the many examples in this book that colons frequently come at the end of text just before a block quotation. Colons can also join independent clauses when the second clause is meant to be a consequence or a clarification of the first:

> Jackson was furious: Someone had given him a monkey for Christmas, and he hated pets.

16. Observe the Rules for Parallelism.

Parallel grammatical forms can add power to your writing. The most simple parallelism is the series. "Churchill said, 'I have nothing to offer but *blood, toil, tears, and sweat.*'" But phrases and clauses can also make parallel forms. Parallel forms are joined by the coordinating conjunctions *and, but, or, for,* and *nor.* The words, phrases, and clauses joined by these conjunctions must be equal in form. In the example from Churchill above, the conjunction *and* helps join four nouns—*blood, toil, tears,* and *sweat.*

> I have heard the chimes at midnight and seen the sun at dawn.

> He liked neither beer nor wine.

The most common errors in parallelism are in a series. Here is a faulty parallelism:

> We came home, ate dinner, and we watched the All-Star game.

The correct form is this:

> We came home, ate dinner, and watched the All-Star game.

17. Use a Colon before a List or an Amplification of a Statement Made in an Independent Clause.

Sometimes you may wish to make a list after a statement.

> Coach Dixie valued three things: winning football games, drawing the largest salary in the Southeastern Conference, and drilling his players on the split infinitive.

Sometimes you may wish to amplify a statement.

> Coach Dixie lived by one principle: He never broke the rules if he thought he might be caught.

Avoiding Discrimination

Fair-minded writers are not mean-spirited in their prose. They do not insult minorities or demean women. Sometimes inexperienced writers use terms they do not recognize as insulting or degrading. Weed such language out of your writing.

WOMEN

One of the most persistent discriminations in language has been against women. For centuries ordinary English seemed to imply that only men were important. Now women demand equality not only in jobs and education and social life but also in language. They should have it. But the consequences to language have been confusing. We do not yet have a clear way out of some of these confusions, but with good will, we can try to solve some of the problems.

A persistent problem in sexist language is this: What do we do with the English custom of using *he, his,* or *him* when we need an indefinite singular pronoun that can indicate either a male or a female? In common English we have for years written this: "What do we want our reader to think about our writing? We want him to believe that we know what we are talking about." We know that "our reader" may include males or females or both. How do we express ourselves now?

With this example the solution is easy. We turn the singular into the plural: "What do we want our readers to think about us? We want them to believe that we know what we are talking about." I always try to use the plural forms in such constructions as this one so that I do not exclude women.

213

But sometimes we must use the singular.

> The thief entered the house by breaking a pane of glass in the backdoor, cutting himself in the process, and leaving a trail of blood through the kitchen to the bathroom where he washed up, leaving his blood all over one of my new white towels. The wound must not have been serious because he not only stole all my Dolly Parton records but came back for my life-sized painting of Elvis on black velvet.

Now what are we to do? If we have a simple statement we can use *he or she* or *him or her.* I have no problem writing or saying, "I have forgotten who borrowed my book. I would appreciate it if he or she would return it." But what do we do in the instance I have drawn here, requiring us to repeat the pronouns several times in a short space.

> The thief entered the house by breaking a pane of glass in the backdoor, cutting himself or herself in the process, and leaving a trail of blood through the kitchen to the bathroom where he or she washed up, leaving his or her blood all over one of my new white towels. The wound must not have been serious because he or she not only stole all my Dolly Parton records but came back for my life-sized painting of Elvis on black velvet.

The constant repetition of *he or she* seems clumsy to me.

Maybe we can solve the problem by extensive revision.

> The thief entered the house by breaking a pane of glass in the backdoor, incurring a wound that left a trail of blood through the house that was cleaned up with one of my new white towels. The wound must not have been serious because the thief not only stole all my Dolly Parton records but came back for my life-sized painting of Elvis on black velvet.

Or maybe the simplest solution is to assume that only a male thief would be interested in Dolly Parton records and a portrait of Elvis on black velvet.

I believe that the solution to the problem will be to use the pronouns *they, their,* or *them* as nonsexist substitutes for sexist pronouns. Purists will cringe at the thought, but what good would a purist be if he or she didn't cringe now and then? I hear educated people say things like this: "Anybody who works the night shift for twenty years will discover that their view of life changes in ways incomprehensible to their normal neighbors." This solution is not grammatically correct, and I must confess that I wince a little down inside when I hear it. But then I'm old, and I had a stern and loving seventh-grade English teacher in the tiny country school I attended in Tennessee. I can't shake old habits. But younger people don't mind *they* as a singular pronoun in such sentences, and it has the advantage of being efficient. *Anyone* who says English cannot change to accept uncomfortable usage does not know what *they* are talking about.

Even the ungrammatical use of *their* to refer to a single person is much better than *he/she* or, worse, the *s/he* that I see occasionally in memos. We should be able to read writing aloud, and I do not see how we can read *he/she* or the barbaric *s/he* in any sensible way. It also looks wretched on the page.

My own solution, used throughout this book, has been to revise away the problem. Most editors of books and magazines seem to have adopted this procedure. I sit and think and rewrite to use a plural instead of a singular indefinite pronoun, or as in the case of the infamous theft of the Dolly Parton records and the Elvis portrait I make extensive revisions. When I have to use a singular form, I vary the pronoun, using *he* sometimes and *she* sometimes. Many writers have adopted this use. (Some have suggested that men ought to use *he* and women *she* in their work.)

Many women writers such as Barbara Tuchman and Mina Shaughnessy have used the traditional *he* without feeling that they were betraying their sex. But both Tuchman the great historian and Shaughnessy the great teacher and student of writing died before the issue became as lively as it is today.

I find myself more and more comfortable using *he or she* or *her or him* in sentences where I do not have to repeat the phrase again and again. We will continue to wrestle with the issue for a time. If we sound clumsy or ungrammatical in our efforts to avoid sexist language, we offend traditionalists, of whom many survive. If we refuse to take note of social change and go on using *he* and *him* as if everyone on earth worthy of consideration were male, we offend the large and rapidly growing number of men and women who believe that clumsiness in language is a small price to pay for sexual equality. To my mind, at least, writers who multiply the use of the pronouns *he, his,* and *him* without appearing to think about the issue sound as if they have been snoring in a cave for the past quarter of a century.

Avoiding Sexist Words

All apart from the difficulties with pronouns, we can easily avoid some traditional offenses of sexist language. You don't have to say *policeman;* you can say *police officer.* You don't have to say *chairman;* you can say *chair.* We now call our *freshmen* "first-year students" or "first years," and the sky does not fall. Once we spoke of *man* or *mankind,* but we can just as easily use *humankind* for both words. We can say *the average person* rather than *the average man.* (Don't say *the average individual.*) *Waiters* and *waitresses* have become *servers.* And so it goes.

Some words should be abandoned. *Poetess* now seems degrading—although *actress* does not. Women should never be referred to as "the distaff side" or "the fair sex," and it is demeaning to call a wife "the better half" as if the notion that a woman can be superior to her husband is funny. The word *lady* now has a negative connotation, for many feel that it sets women apart and implies that they are worthwhile only if they act like delicate damsels in a nineteenth-century etiquette. *Ladies* have to be protected from ugly sights, vulgar language, bad smells, and undue physical exercise. Men must stand reverently in their presence, open car doors for them, and offer them seats on the bus or the train. *Women* can take care of themselves.

Above all, readers should not be addressed as though the only important people among them were men. Never identify women by telling who their husbands are unless that information has special importance to the matter at hand.

✳

If you write about a woman governor who gives all the state's business to her husband's bank, the relation between the two is worth mentioning. But a few years ago I received a notice about a conference on Thomas More where Mary Ellen Bork, president of the St. Thomas More Society of Washington, D.C., was to be one of the speakers. The circular identified her as the "wife of Judge Robert Bork." The conference was sponsored by a conservative religious group—perhaps reason for labeling Ms. Bork in a manner so offensive to feminists and to others often taken to be radical. I was offended by the circular myself. Ms. Bork happens to have a long and distinguished career of activity related to the study of Thomas More, and having met her, I find her gracious, energetic, and intelligent in her own right. It seems gratuitous indeed to identify her by reference to her husband—no matter how celebrated or notorious—he may have been. In a news story, that information might have been placed far down in the text, for it would interest some people curious to know if Ms. Bork was related to the judge. But it is demeaning as a primary identification.

Take care also with the proper titles of women. The term *Ms.* is now common, and I use it regularly to address correspondence to women. A few women object to the title and prefer the more traditional *Mrs.* if they are married and *Miss* if they are not. Courtesy requires that you call people what they want to be called, but though I might write to a woman as *Mrs.* or *Miss* if she prefers the title, I use *Ms.* regularly in speaking and writing in the third person.

AFRICAN AMERICANS

Blacks have probably suffered the worst abuses of language in our society. They have naturally rebelled. For many years the polite way to refer to blacks was as "colored people" or "people of color." We still have the National Association for the Advancement of Colored People. The word *Negro,* spelled with a capital *N,* was also used regularly for many decades, even in the 1960s during the civil rights movement. Dr. Martin Luther King, Jr., always spoke of "Negroes" and "the Negro."

At some point in the 1960s some blacks began to object to the word *Negro* because white Southerners often used the word, claiming that it demonstrated that they were not prejudiced because they did not use the other *N* word that was so vile. In fact, these same white Southerners kept right on resisting the integration of schools, libraries, transportation, and other public facilities in the South. Blacks found the use of *Negro* offensive, condescending, and hypocritical, and in the 1970s the word seemed to vanish almost overnight. If white people were named by their color, black people should be named by *their* color and not by some classification that recalled old prejudices. So *Negro* became *black.*

Recently another issue arose. Many people of color are not black but brown. Some people started using the hyphenated adjective *Afro-American.* But then Jesse Jackson, a black political leader, suggested that the term *African*

American be used in an effort to take the emphasis off color and put it on origin and to certify the American quality of people of color. The usage seems to
be catching on in the public discourse of institutions and in the popular press.

Yet a poll in *The New York Times* a few years ago showed that 70 percent
of Americans of African descent still prefer to be called *blacks* rather than
African Americans. I think the term *African American* is unlikely to endure
simply because it is such a mouthful. But we shall see. In the meantime I have
not known any blacks to be offended by the use of *black.* The issue is not resolved, and it will not be resolved for a long time. In the meantime blacks and
whites together must struggle with good will to overcome centuries of prejudice and its accompanying violence.

NATIVE AMERICANS

Much the same process of change has gone on among American Indians. To
many people they are now "Native Americans." Yet one of the most aggres-
sive organizations furthering their rights is the American Indian Movement.
My university happens to offer many special scholarships to American Indians, and those I have known refer to themselves unselfconsciously as "American Indians."

SEXUAL PREFERENCE

Sexual preference is another area where language is difficult. We seem to have
no choice in whether we are sexually drawn to members of the opposite sex or
to the same sex. It is cruel to use language that demeans people who are what
they are because of their genes. *Homosexual* is still, to most people, a neutral
term applying to both sexes, although to some it has pejorative connotations.
Increasingly the term *gay* is used for male homosexuals, although it can apply
to males and females. Usually people speak of "gays and lesbians," using "les-
bian" as the term for females.

POLITICAL CORRECTNESS

All these matters are difficult. They require a willingness to change and to remain open-minded about language. Academics are often attacked these days
for sins committed in the name of "political correctness," and some scathing
books have been written using anecdotal evidence to prove that American col-
leges and universities are being taken over by radical feminists and other threatening sorts. Usually when I hear or read such talk, I sense bigotry lurking just
beneath the surface. Something ugly in their tone reminds me of wealthy people in the last century discussing the servant problem over wine and caviar.

It is certainly true that any moment of great social change, especially change driven by a moral impulse, may lead to silliness. At an annual conference of writing teachers a few years ago, a woman told me with great indignation that a couple of years ago her university had denied her a Ph.D. until she changed every *he* in her dissertation to *he or she*. That seems excessive. Several years ago the *Modern Language Association* published an article of mine in one of its publications about teaching writing. In the article I used the term *straw man* for the common logical fallacy. I was firmly told by the editors that I could not use the term since the MLA had abolished all sexist language from its publications. My arguments for the traditional use of the term were in vain. I thought of withdrawing the article, but I finally let it go, saying what I felt, that the MLA seems to have a knack for being sillier than the rest of us in these times. (Notice that I have used *straw man* in this book. I doubt that anyone will be offended.) Every time the MLA meets, reporters have a field day in ridiculing it, and hardly anything positive ever appears about the organization in the popular press.

Well, so what! Righting injustice in any moral crusade has always called forth a few extremists who probably do more harm than good. But that's human nature. Occasional foolishness by this or that extremist does not invalidate the genuine need to reevaluate the way we use language. We're in this thing called life together. It is not just good manners to treat each other with dignity and respect. Our survival depends on it. Women are equal to men. They ought to be treated with complete equality, for to do otherwise is to demean men as well as women. We assume that old men can't learn new tricks—or new ways. The same truth holds for other groups within our society. When we demean them with language, we become less worthy human beings ourselves. The English-speaking world within which we write is democratic, and our language and the uses to which we put it should reflect the historic and worthy ideals that we profess.

How to Begin—and How
Not to Begin—an Essay

For most readers the beginning of your essay will kill it or make it live. Start in a dull and conventional way, and your reader will put it down—unless you happen to be writing about a sure cure for cancer or a formula for absolute certainty in betting on a horse race or the superbowl. For most of us, the beginning is all-important. Write a good one, and your reader will go on reading to see what you have to say. Write a bad one, and your reader will be your reader no longer.

No book can tell you all the ways to begin an essay. Your best bet is to study beginnings written by professional writers and to imitate them. Here are examples of common types. Note that all of them develop a point of tension at the beginning. Something is out of balance or unfinished or in some way portends conflict or opposition.

1. Begin by Telling a Story.

Even academic essayists often begin with an anecdote, a mini-drama that catches the reader's attention, and such beginnings are common in serious essays of all kinds. Here is an unusually striking example by writer Thomas Maeder.

> On October 30, 1995, Harry Eastlack arrived for a two-day symposium at the Wyndham Franklin Plaza Hotel, in Philadelphia. Forty-three families of people with fibrodysplasia ossificans progressiva, or FOP, were joining a high-powered assortment of orthopedic surgeons, molecular biologists, geneticists, and other doctors and scientists in hopes of making some sense of this puzzling disease.

219

Harry's sister and her husband volunteered to entertain the children afflicted with FOP and their siblings while their parents attended professional sessions and swapped experiences. Harry himself played no active role. He had died in 1973. Yet his silent presence revealed the tragedy and the challenge of FOP more eloquently than any chart, slide, or clinical description ever could.[1]

We read this paragraph with a sense of astonishment. Harry Eastlack attended a conference in 1995—but he had been dead since *1973*?? And we read on. The article tells of the strange and rare disease that killed Harry and the efforts to find a cure. He had left his body to the physicians who had treated him in hopes that research might save others from a malady that turns living human bodies to bones. We read the first paragraph, and we want to know what happened and what is happening.

Two cautions! Be sure the story truly introduces the essay that comes after it. Maeder's essay gives an account of the disease and tells of the suffering of other victims and of what medical research may do. The story fits this essay exactly.

Never represent a story as true when you have no evidence for the details. Don't make things up. For example, don't start a paper like this:

It was night in the royal palace in Greenwich, and a sleepy silence hung over the dark corridors and the rooms where servants lay snoring abed. Only Henry VIII was awake, and he walked the floor aimlessly before the great fire that blazed on the hearth in his room. He could not sleep because he could not purge his mind of the greatest problem of his reign: How could he have a son?

It's fine to imagine that Henry VIII had every reason for walking the floor at night, worrying about the succession to the throne of England. But no document gives any evidence that such a scene took place. If you are ever caught telling a lie when you write something you claim to be the truth, your reputation as a writer will be ruined forever.

2. Describe a Scene.

Akin to telling a story is a description that arouses curiosity. The reader wants to know, "What exactly is happening here?" "Why is this significant?" The scene must be interesting in itself. And it must point to the essay to follow. Here is another beginning of an essay from *Atlantic Monthly,* a serious magazine that cultivates a sprightly style in all its departments.

Every morning the Muslim call to prayer, an adenoidal chant whining from as many as five minarets in Ürgüp, our small town in central Turkey, incited roosters and posses of roaming dogs to join the chorus. This curious cacophony was my wake-up call, buried as I was in a windowless hollow sculpted from a cliff of soft rock. For a breath of dawn I would bolt from bed and around a stairwell to a balcony that looked out over a hillside pockmarked with cave dwellings and across a vast, dusty valley of undulating vineyards planted in tawny volcanic grit. There at eye level one hazy sunrise last September bobbed sixty, eventually a hundred, brilliantly colored hot-air balloons—gaudy bubbles drifting above the Cappadocian landscape of walnut orchards and erosion-sculpted rock.[2]

The descriptive style of Hatsy Shields, the author of this article, lures us on to see what else she has to say about Turkey.

3. Use a Provocative Quotation.

The quotation says something provocative, and we want to know what it means. The essay to follow explains it to us and reveals its significance. This is an especially good beginning for an academic essay because the quotation from an important historical figure or an important document pulls us into the middle of an issue quickly. A quotation also works as social commentary as in this opening paragraph by Doug Stewart to introduce an article in *Smithsonian* about the makeover of Times Square in New York City.

> "That Coke sign has its own phone number," Ed Hayman says. We're standing in Times Square at dusk like tourists, heads back, feet planted, watching a 42-foot animated Coca-Cola bottle go through its paces. High above the cab-filled junction of Broadway and Seventh Avenue, the bottle's giant cap slowly lifts up, a straw emerges and the bottle's contents seem to drain. Around it, an expanse of neon swirls and dances. The sign weighs 55 tons and incorporates 13,000 lightbulbs, 60 miles of fiber optics, miscellaneous robotic parts and a small weather station. And a phone. I ask Hayman, who works for New York's venerable Artkraft Strauss Sign Corporation, why anyone would want to call a billboard. "Mostly, we don't. It calls us." If a part of the sign overheats or gets stuck, he explains, a metallic computer voice will phone the signmaker's office and report, "I have Shut Down Sector Three," say, and give temperature readings and wind speeds, and also a sound check to boot. Artkraft, which built and maintains the sign, can't allow much downtime; for the privilege of having its name in lights here, Coca-Cola is paying more than a million dollars a year.[3]

Your quotation must be significant enough to build your essay upon. A bland quotation will not interest readers, and it may not draw them further into your work.

4. Begin with a Simple, Definite Statement.

Sometimes it's best to renounce all art and begin with a simple statement that provokes agreement or curiosity. Here is the first paragraph of an article in *American Heritage* by Bernard A. Weisberger on censorship for moral reasons.

> Once again the voice of the censor is heard in the land, and so are the contesting arguments of the civil libertarian, the artist, and the businessman who markets entertainment. It's an old fight with a new twist. The Supreme Court has struck down parts of a Communications Decency Act aimed at shielding young people from pornographic material on the Internet. Under threat of similar hostile legislation, the television industry has also been thrashing its way to a system of ratings (like those used by moviemakers) to guide parents in deciding what to let the children

watch. It's significant that while television has been coping with critics for some fifty years now, and movies for a hundred, it's the Internet that actually drew a federal censorship law.[4]

Notice that after the general beginning, this opening paragraph gives us some concrete details. A paragraph that stays general all the way through may be boring.

5. Ask a Question.

Occasionally a question makes a good beginning. The writer may answer it and proceed to the rest of the article. Or the writer may leave it there to be puzzled over until later in the essay. The question does not have to be the first sentence in the article, but it does have to come quickly.

> An African Eve is a seductive idea—dark-skinned, strongly built, the primeval woman, mother of us all. But did she actually exist? Was there actually an evolutionary Garden of Eden in Africa where we all originated more than 150,000 years ago?[5]

6. Use Contrast.

Many good essays begin with a statement of common belief or practice and quickly declare a contrary view. You set up a position or a situation that will be recognized by your readers, and you declare after a paragraph or two that you are going to take an opposite or at least a different view. Provocative argument essays often begin in this way. Here's Daniel Kadlec in *Time* in February 1998 when the United States was once again considering war with Iraq.

> Like presidential approval ratings, stock prices tend to inflate when the U.S. engages in armed conflict. Look no further than the tireless bull market that we enjoy today. It began in 1991 when the U.S. drove Saddam Hussein and his Iraqi army out of Kuwait. The first allied air raids came on January 17 of that year and sent the Dow Jones industrial average soaring 4.6% in a day. By mid-March the Dow had jumped 20%.
>
> Yes sir! The generals on Wall Street do love a war. There's nothing like the smell of smart bombs in the morning—as long as they're ours—to arouse feelings of invincibility. And what better frame of mind for dialing one's broker and cheerfully picking up another 100 shares of Boeing or Lockheed Martin? With Saddam the Sequel possibly only days away, I guess it's no shocker that the market has hit new highs for the first time in six months.
>
> Be warned, though, that a Saddam II, if it does happen, would be nothing like the original—at least not in the stock market.[6]

The rest of Kadlec's essay argues that any kind of failure by Americans in Iraq would send the market tumbling, and even success will not lead to the spectacular climb in stock prices that came after the Gulf War of 1991. Even success, Kadlec says, would only continue things as they are.

This kind of beginning presents an argument sharply and gets the opponent quickly into the statement of his or her own position.

BEGINNINGS TO AVOID

All hard-working teachers of writing have seen some beginnings so many times that the sight of one on the page is enough to induce an attack of terminal boredom. Here are some beginnings that make me reach for the snooze button. They betoken laziness, and if we see laziness at the start, we usually don't see the essay get better.

1. The Dictionary Definition.

Never begin an essay like this: "Webster's Dictionary defines crisis as 'a decisive or crucial time, stage, or event.'" Ugh!

Yes, the dictionary is an authority, and writers need authority. A dictionary definition contains an outline that an inexperienced writer may follow. Writing teachers see the tired old dictionary beginning hundreds of times—and groan every time. You can write a good essay about a definition only if different people use the same important word in different ways. If people did not use the word in different ways, the essay would be unnecessary. What does *socialism* mean? You can't satisfy demanding readers if you begin an essay on socialism by referring to a dictionary. Almost every important thinker who has used the word has used it in a special way. Socialism in Sweden is one thing; socialism in the former Soviet Union was something utterly different. A member of the British Labor party will use the word with an entirely different sense from that of an official of the American Medical Association. Your definition of an important word, derived from your own study, quoting from people who have used the word in the way you intended to use it, will make the substance of an excellent essay, but it will not be the bare-bones outline of a dictionary. It will be long enough to consider the important variations among the definitions of another.

2. A Vague and General Declaration about History.

The appeal to history is another old standby that makes teachers and other readers groan:

> Throughout recorded history sex has been important. Many people from earliest times to the present have talked and written and argued about sex. Stories about sex appear in the *Iliad* and the *Odyssey* and in the Bible, and Shakespeare wrote a lot about sex, too. Sex seems to be always with us. Therefore it is not surprising that sex education has become a controversial subject in America.

Another ugh! The good news about this kind of beginning is that the writer finally does get to the subject of the essay. Nearly every time I get the historical introduction, I mark a big *X* through it and point to the first paragraph afterward and say, "This is where your paper really starts." Unless the appeal to history is specific—telling a story from the past, for example—the comment that something has happened "throughout recorded history" or "from the beginning of history" is throat clearing. The writer is getting ready to say something. Far better to get right to the point.

3. The Justification of the Topic.

Many inexperienced writers begin essays with a kind of apology. Their first statement defends their choice of topic: "Why should we discuss the minor characters in Shakespeare's Macbeth?" "The difference between the theology of Luther's sermons and his formal theological treatises has often been considered by scholars of the Reformation." They follow these opening statements with a survey of previous scholarship, leaving themselves a tiny hole to crawl through, expressing humility all the time, while they beg us to let them try to make their own contribution.

This is the typical beginning of dissertations, and it is a major reason dissertations nearly always have to be revised for publication. Nobody will read them unless they begin with something more interesting than pleading. The implied comment in this sort of beginning seems to be something like this: "I know you think that nobody as young and inexperienced as I am can possibly have anything to say on this subject, but if you will just be patient and give me a break and don't hit me, I'll prove that I have a modest contribution to make."

You don't have to have the permission of previous scholars to make your point. If you think the minor characters in Macbeth are worth saying something about, get to work and prove your point. If you find Luther's theological treatises different from his sermons, show your readers what you mean. Don't unroll a long and tedious list of previous scholarship. You may use other scholarship along the way. Indeed you should if you are to have any authority. Refute it, modify it, or use it to confirm your case. But don't begin with an uninteresting summary of what others have done as if you had no right to consider a subject without starting with a recapitulation of the past. Real writers want to tell readers something. They don't apologize for daring to have an idea. Begin with something strong, something to catch your readers' eyes and make them continue.

4. The Blueprint Beginning.

I've already expressed my opinion of the blueprint beginning above in discussing Little Red Riding Hood. Avoid it. Imagine how startled you would be to find the following beginning of an article in *Sports Illustrated:*

> In this article I am going to tell you about the World Series. I shall tell you what teams played in it, provide some background about their records during the season, their victories and their defeats, managers and coaches, star players, and I shall recount tantrums by players over their contracts, their run-ins with drugs, their fights in barrooms, their abuse of their wives, their infidelities, and their adorable children, and I shall make some remarks about their ambitious parents. I shall include a summary of each of the games and will conclude with the results and at long last tell you who won.

You know—almost unconsciously—that this kind of beginning is deadly dull and that reading the story to follow will be like wading knee-deep in mud to get to the end. Don't use it.

5. The Man from Mars.

Variations on this beginning include the archaeologist from a future civilization or the person awakened from the dead of an earlier epoch to look on our own time. "If Thomas Edison were to come back from the dead, he would be astounded to see how far the motion picture has progressed since his primitive invention that set film turning through cameras." If Thomas Edison were to return from the dead, he would be on so many talk shows and would have so much to say that his impressions of film would be unimportant. These are tired old beginnings. If they once had verve, it withered long ago. Don't use them. Thousands of uninspired writers have worn them out.

Clichés

Study the following list, and avoid the expressions you find there. They have been worked to death. They may have had some power once, but it has long since turned to dust. On occasion, you may find some special reason to use one of the phrases; and when we are pressed, we are all likely to tumble into using some of them because they come so easily to mind. That is just what is wrong with them. Although no one will hang you or beat you for letting one creep into your prose, it's a good idea to change the cliché into simple English whenever you can. Instead of calling a marathon an "acid test," you can say that it is a test of stamina and character. That says more specifically what you might want to say than the cliché "acid test."

abreast of the times
absolute truth
acid test
across a wide [broad] spectrum
across the spectrum
add insult to injury
after all is said and done
against the current
agony of defeat
agree to disagree
all walks of life
a man [or woman] for all
   seasons
at this point in time

avoid like the plague

[the] ball's in his court
basic needs
basic truth
beat a hasty retreat
be that as it may
better half
better late than never
better part of valor
beyond a shadow of doubt
[the] birds and the bees
bite the dust
bitter end

227

❋

black as night
bloody but unbowed
blue as the sky
bolt from the blue
bottom line
bottom of my [her, his] heart
bottom of the barrel
bottom of the deck
brainchild
brave as a lion
bright as a new penny
bring down the house
bring home the bacon
broad array
broad daylight
brown as a nut
brutally frank
brutal murder
burn the midnight oil
bustling cities
by the same token

calm, cool, and collected
cat on a hot tin roof
chip off the old block
cloud nine
cold as ice
cold, hard facts
cold light of day
come to grips with
communicate effectively
consensus of opinion
conspicuous by his absence
cool as a cucumber
could have knocked me over
    with a feather
crack of dawn
crisis of confidence
critical juncture
crowning glory

crying on the inside
cut and dried

dead as a doornail
deaf as a post
deep as the ocean
deep, dark secret
diabolical skill
distaff side
doomed to
    disappointment
do or die
down and out
down but not out
down for the count
down the primrose path
dry as dust
dyed in the wool

each and every
[to] each his own
easy as falling off a log
every dog has its day
every tub on its own
    bottom

face the music
factor
facts of life
fatal flaw
few and far between
filthy lucre
first and foremost
fit as a fiddle
fleecy clouds
fond memories
fond recollections
fresh as a daisy
frozen north

get the lead out
gone but not forgotten
go over like a lead balloon
go over with a fine-tooth
   comb
grave danger
green with envy
gutless wonder

hail fellow well met
hale and hearty
hands-on
happy as a clam
happy as a lark
happy medium
hard row to hoe
head up [the committee]
heady mixture
hearts and minds
heave a sigh of relief
higher than a kite
highest priority
high spirits
hit me like a ton of bricks
hit the nail on the head
hopes dashed
hotter than hell [Hades]
hush fell over the crowd
hustle and bustle

imminent danger
implement
in a nutshell
in a very real sense
in essence
innocent as a newborn babe
in some cases
integral part
in terms of
in the final analysis

in this day and age
it goes without saying
it is incumbent upon
it is interesting to note
it stands to reason

ladder of success
larger than life
last but not least
last-ditch [anything]
last straw
learning experience
lick and a promise
light as a feather
like father, like son
little lady
live and learn
live from hand to mouth
live like a king
lying in her teeth

mad as a hatter
make a shambles of
man about town
meaningful experience
meaningful relationship
method in her madness
mind like a steel trap
miss is as good as a mile
mitigate against [not only a cliché
   but incorrect]
more sinned against than sinning
more than meets the eye
murmur of approval

neat as a pin
needle in a haystack
nip and tuck
nip in the bud
nose to the grindstone

no sooner said than done
nothing ventured, nothing gained
not too distant future
nuclear holocaust

off his rocker
off the beaten track
off the track
off the wall
once and for all
one hundred and ten percent
one rotten apple spoils the
    barrel
ongoing
only time will tell
on the fast track
on this planet
other side of the coin
out of the blue

painfully obvious
paint the town red
paramount importance
pass the buck
pave the way
pebble on the beach
pencil thin
pertinent facts
pick and choose
pivotal figure
plain as the nose on your face
plain Jane
pleased as punch
poor but happy
poor but honest
precondition
preplanning
pride and joy
primrose path
prioritize

proof is in the pudding
proud owner
proud possessor
put your best foot forward
put your foot in it

quick as a flash
quick as a wink
quick as lightning

raise [rear] its ugly head
rank and file
rather unique
raving lunatic
rude awakening

sadder but wiser
scarce as hens' teeth
sell like hot cakes
sharp as a razor
sharp as a tack
short and sweet
short end of the stick
shot in the arm
shoulder to the wheel
sigh of relief
silver platter
simple as salt
sink or swim
skeleton in the closet
skin of your teeth
slow but sure
smart as a whip
smelling like a rose
smooth sailing
sneaking suspicion
sober as a judge
soft place in my heart
sound as a dollar
spread like wildfire

*

stick out like a sore thumb
stock in trade
straight and narrow
straw that broke the camel's back
strike while the iron is hot
sunny south
supreme moment
sure winner

tangled skein
tangled web
tempest in a teapot
tender mercies
tested in the fire
thin as a rail
tip of the iceberg
tired but happy
to all intents and purposes
tough nut to crack
tried and true
truth is stranger than fiction
twinkling of an eye

two-edged sword
undercurrent of excitement
unstinted praise
up in arms

viable alternative
vicious circle [cycle]
vital role

walk a chalk line
walk a fine line
walking on air
walk the line
walk the straight and narrow
wet blanket
when all is said and done
when the going gets tough, the
    tough get going
white as snow
work like a dog
work like a horse
wreak havoc

Notes

CHAPTER 1

1. Roger Angell, "Remembering Mr. Shawn," *The New Yorker,* Dec. 28, 1992/Jan. 4, 1993, p. 136.

2. John Simon, *Paradigms Lost,* New York, Penguin Books, 1981, p. 18.

3. Simon, p. 45.

4. Dennis E. Baron, *Grammar and Good Taste,* New Haven, Conn., Yale University Press, 1982, p. 141.

5. Rosellen Brown, "His Late Espoused Saint," *New York Times Book Review,* July 11, 1993, p. 24.

6. E. D. Hirsch, Jr., *The Philosophy of Composition,* University of Chicago Press, 1977, pp. 60–61.

7. Giovanni Boccaccio, *The Decameron of Giovanni Boccaccio,* trans. Frances Winwar, New York, Modern Library, n.d., p. 16.

8. John M. Barry, *Rising Tide: The Great Mississippi Flood of 1927 and How It Changed America,* New York, Simon & Schuster, 1997, pp. 15–16.

CHAPTER 2

1. Barbara W. Tuchman, "In Search of History," *Practicing History,* New York, Knopf, 1981, p. 20.

2. Frances Trollope, *Domestic Manners of the Americans,* Donald Smalley (ed.), New York, Knopf, 1949, pp. 78–79.

3. David McCullough, *Truman,* New York, Simon & Schuster, 1992, p. 829.

4. William H. Honan, "Historians Warming to Games of 'What If'" *New York Times,* Jan. 7, 1998, p. A19.

CHAPTER 3

1. Michel de Montaigne, 3:1, *Oeuvres complètes,* Paris, Gallimard, 1962, p. 767.
2. Montaigne, 2:10, p. 389.
3. Bruce Handy, "It's All about Timing," *Time,* Jan. 12, 1998, p. 77.
4. John Ross, "Stamps—What an Idea!" *Smithsonian,* January 1998, p. 16.
5. Ross, p. 18.

CHAPTER 4

1. Gilbert Allardyce, "What Fascism Is Not: Thoughts on the Deflation of a Concept," *American Historical Review,* October 1990, pp. 1051–1079.
2. Milton Friedman, "There's No Justice in the War on Drugs," *New York Times,* Jan. 11, 1998, p. WK 19.
3. Barbara Tuchman, *Practicing History,* New York, Knopf, 1981, p. 23.

CHAPTER 5

1. Corby Kummer, "Real Olives," *The Atlantic,* June 1993, p. 116.
2. James Baldwin, "Notes of a Native Son," Boston, Beacon Press, 1955; *Modern American Prose,* New York, McGraw-Hill, 1993, p. 40.
3. Lorenzo Albacete, "The Poet and the Revolutionary," *The New Yorker,* Jan. 26, 1998, p. 36.
4. Loren Eiseley, "The Judgment of the Birds," *The Immense Journey,* New York, Random House, 1956; *Modern American Prose,* 3d ed., New York, McGraw-Hill, 1993, p. 155.
5. John McPhee, "The Swiss at War," *La Place de la Concorde, Swiss,* New York, Random House, 1956; *Modern American Prose,* 3d ed., p. 325.

CHAPTER 6

1. Robert A. Caro, *The Years of Lyndon Johnson: The Path to Power,* New York, Knopf, 1982, p. 413.
2. Jeffrey Kluger, "The Right Stuff, 36 Years Later," *Time,* Jan. 26, 1998, p. 58.
3. Richard Ellmann, *James Joyce,* new and revised ed., New York, Oxford University Press, 1982, p. 69.
4. Ellmann, p. 134.
5. Ellmann, p. 136.
6. Ginia Bellafante, "The Poetics of Style," *Time,* Feb. 2, 1998, p. 68.
7. Ellmann, p. 135.
8. Jon Krakauer, "On the Edge of Antarctica: Queen Maud Land," *National Geographic,* February 1998, p. 69.
9. *Pudd'nhead Wilson,* "Pudd'nhead Wilson's Calendar," Chapter 11.
10. Philip Caputo, *A Rumor of War,* New York, Holt, Rinehart & Winston, 1977, p. 163.
11. John M. Barry, *Rising Tide: The Great Mississippi Flood of 1927 and How It Changed America,* New York, Simon & Schuster, 1997, p. 182.

12. Barry, p. 381.

13. Susannah McCorkle, "Back to Bessie," *American Heritage,* November 1997, p. 56.

14. Barbara Holland, "Bang! Bang! You're Dead," *Smithsonian,* October 1997, p. 128.

15. Joan Jacobs Brumberg, *The Body Project: An Intimate History of American Girls,* New York, Random House, 1997, p. 143.

16. Barry, p. 262.

17. *Yale Companion to Jewish Writing and Thought in German Culture, 1096–1996,* Sander L. Gilman and Jack Zipes (eds.), New Haven, Conn., Yale University Press, 1997, p. 729.

18. Tom Miller, "Remember the Maine," *Smithsonian,* February 1998, p. 49.

19. Patricia Bosworth, *Anything Your Little Heart Desires,* New York, Simon & Schuster, 1997, p. 215.

20. Anthony Lane, "The Shipping News: 'Titanic' Raises the Stakes of the Spectacular," *The New Yorker,* Dec. 15, 1997, p. 159.

CHAPTER 7

1. "The Collective Behavior of Fads: The Characteristics, Effects, and Career of Streaking," *American Sociological Review,* August 1988, p. 572.

CHAPTER 8

1. Maureen Dowd, "The Price of His Pleasure," *New York Times: Week in Review,* Jan. 8, 1998, p. 15.

2. Sophronia Scott Gregory, "Diss' Is the Word of the Lord," *Time,* July 26, 1993, p. 61.

3. John Simon, *Paradigms Lost,* New York, Penguin Books, 1980, pp. 17–18.

4. Quoted in Dennis E. Baron, *Grammar and Good Taste,* New Haven, Conn., Yale University Press, 1982, p. 218.

5. H. L. Mencken, *The American Language,* one volume abridged edition, Raven I. McDavid, Jr. (ed.), New York, Knopf, 1979, pp. 133–135.

6. *Harper Dictionary of Contemporary Usage,* William Morris and Mary Morris (eds.), New York, Harper & Row, 1975, p. 312.

7. Jill Abramson, "Baby Boomers, and There the Likeness Ceases," *New York Times,* Feb. 16, 1998, p. A11.

CHAPTER 9

1. Jon Krakauer, "On the Edge of Antarctica: Queen Maud Land," *National Geographic,* February 1998, p. 47.

2. Philip Caputo, *A Rumor of War,* New York, Holt, Rinehart and Winston, 1977, p. 129.

3. Bertrand Russell, quoted in Ronald W. Clark, *Einstein: The Life and Times,* New York, World, 1971, p. 87.

4. Peter Gay, *Freud: A Life for Our Time,* New York, Norton, 1988, p. 353.

5. Joseph Conrad, *Lord Jim,* London, Everyman Library, 1992 (first published 1890), Chapter 9, pp. 101–102.

6. Donald Davidson, "What Metaphors Mean," *On Metaphor,* Sheldon Sacks (ed.), University of Chicago Press, 1979, p. 40.

7. Tom Clancy, "Know the Answers before Going to War," *New York Times,* Oct. 13, 1998, p. A29.

8. *The New Yorker,* Dec. 5, 1988, p. 132.

9. Deborah Solomon, "The Persistence of the Portraitist," *New York Times Sunday Magazine,* Feb. 1, 1998, p. 27.

10. "Block That Metaphor," *The New Yorker,* Dec. 26, 1988, p. 90.

11. Irving Howe, *World of Our Fathers,* New York, Simon & Schuster, Touchstone Books, 1976, p. 174.

12. Molly Ivins, *Molly Ivins Can't Say That, Can She?* New York, Random House, 1991, p. 107.

13. John Kenneth Galbraith, *Economics in Perspective,* Boston, Houghton Mifflin, 1987, p. 60.

14. *Elements of Literature,* Robert Scholes, Carl H. Klaus, Michael Shermon (eds.), New York, Oxford University Press, 1978, p. 41.

15. Mike Barnicle, "Be Happy! (It's a Trend)," *Boston Globe,* Feb. 10, 1998, p. B1.

16. Michael Kinsley, "The New Politics of Abortion," *Time,* July 17, 1989, p. 96.

CHAPTER 10

1. Walter Jackson Bate, *Samuel Johnson,* New York and London, Harcourt Brace Jovanovich, 1977, p. 395.

2. Nathaniel Tripp, *Father, Soldier, Son: Memoir of a Platoon Leader in Vietnam,* South Royalton, Vermont, Steerforth Press, 1996, p. 222.

3. Matt Ridley, *The Origins of Virtue: Human Instincts and the Evolution of Cooperation,* New York, Viking, 1996, p. 224.

4. Harry Berger, Jr., "The Early Scenes of 'Macbeth': Preface to a New Interpretation," *Making Trifles of Terrors: Redistributing Complicities in Shakespeare,* Stanford, Calif., Stanford University Press, 1997, pp. 72–73.

5. Martin Gilbert, *The Boys: The Story of 752 Young Concentration Camp Survivors,* New York, Henry Holt & Co., 1997, p. 209.

6. "Strollers," *Consumer Reports,* November 1988, p. 723.

7. David Remnick, "Postscript," *The New Yorker,* Nov. 17, 1997, p. 39.

8. Anne Matthews, *Bright College Years: Inside the American Campus Today,* New York, Simon & Schuster, 1997, p. 225.

9. Tamala M. Edwards, "Crazy Is As Crazy Does: Why the Unabomber Agreed to Trade a Guilty Plea for a Life Sentence," *Time,* Feb. 2, 1998, p. 66.

10. Robert Wright, "Politics Made Me Do It," *Time,* Feb. 2, 1998, p. 34.

11. Tripp, p. 142.

CHAPTER 11

1. Evan S. Connell, *Son of the Morning Star: Custer and the Little Bighorn,* San Francisco, North Point Press, 1984, p. 231.

2. Paul Fussell, *The Great War and Modern Memory,* New York, Oxford University Press, 1975, p. 235.

APPENDIX 2

1. Thomas Maeder, "A Few Hundred People Turned to Bone," *Atlantic Monthly*, February 1978, p. 81.

2. Hatsy Shields, "Inside Anatolia: Taking the Road Less Traveled in Turkey, Too, Makes All the Difference," *Atlantic Monthly*, February 1998, p. 38.

3. Doug Stewart, "Times Square Reborn," *Smithsonian*, February 1998, p. 36.

4. Bernard A. Weisberger, "Chasing Smut in Every Medium: Whenever a New Information Technology Has Been Born, There's Been Somebody on Hand to Try to Censor It," *American Heritage*, December 1997, p. 12.

5. Brian Fagan, "All about Eve," *Archaeology*, November/December 1992, p. 18.

6. Daniel Kadlec, "Wall Street Goes to War," *Time*, February 23, 1998, p. 48.

Index

✱